Turkey's Accession to the European Union

Turkey's accession to the European Union is undoubtedly one of the Union's most contested potential enlargements. The narrative that dominates the debate surrounding this issue primarily relates to problems such as a lack of respect for fundamental human rights in Turkey, the Kurdish question and the continuing stalemate concerning Northern Cyprus.

This book looks at these issues, but also proposes that a review of Turkey's experience with the EU in its numerous incarnations suggests that these concerns may mask a deeper disquiet. While there are several questions that Turkey must address, particularly in the area of human rights guarantees, the concerns which raise debates regarding Turkish membership are not issues that are unique to Turkey. Turkey's EU experience also raises fundamental questions about religion and the EU project that have greater implications than simply Turkish accession. Through the lens of the Turkish example, this book addresses these broader questions, such as the nature of European 'identity', Europe's Christian past, the limits of pluralism and the fundamental question of religion in the European public sphere.

This book will be of great interest to those engaged in research on European law and politics at undergraduate or postgraduate level. It is also aimed at academics with an interest in human rights and the European Union and with a regional interest in Turkey.

Edel Hughes is a Lecturer in Law at the University of Limerick, Ireland.

Routledge Research in EU Law

Turkey's Accession to the European Union

The politics of exclusion?

Edel Hughes

Routledge
Taylor & Francis Group

LONDON AND NEW YORK

First published 2011
by Routledge
2 Park Square, Milton Park, Abingdon, Oxon, OX14 4RN

Simultaneously published in the USA and Canada
by Routledge
711 Third Avenue, New York, NY 10017

*Routledge is an imprint of the Taylor & Francis Group,
an informa business*

First issued in paperback 2012

© 2011 Edel Hughes

Typeset in Garamond by Glyph International Ltd.

British Library Cataloguing in Publication Data
A catalogue record for this book is available from the British Library

Library of Congress Cataloging in Publication Data
Hughes, Edel.
  Turkey's accession to the European Union : the politics of exclusion/Edel
Hughes.
    p. cm.
  ISBN 978-0-415-57785-4 (hardback) – ISBN 978-0-203-84364-2 (ebook)
1. European Union–Turkey. I. Title.
  KJE5092.T9H84 2011
  341.242′209561–dc22   2010009673

ISBN13: 978-0-415-57785-4 (hbk)
ISBN13: 978-0-203-84364-2 (ebk)
ISBN13: 978-0-415-81350-1 (pbk)

Do mo mháthair, Nancy

Contents

Foreword

In unpacking the debate which has accompanied the accession of Turkey to the European Union, *Turkey's Accession to the European Union: The Politics of Exclusion?* critically examines the historical backdrop to the Turkish candidacy as well as the obstacles which have prevented the Turkish case from moving forward. What is revealed is, as the author argues, a 'compatibility crisis' which cannot adequately be explained without engaging in the debate (indeed struggle) over European identity (or as Delors once called it, the soul of Europe). In fact, it is only in the understanding of the larger debates and challenges on the question of European identity that we can fully grasp European anxiety toward the Turkish case.

The resurfacing of the current public debate on religion in Europe relates to the settlement of post-colonial migrants, the majority of which are Muslims. These communities exist outside the historical formation of church–state relations that have shaped European 'values' and are challenging the very underpinning of what comprises a 'liberal' democratic state. In particular, it is the role of Islam in a secular 'Christian' Europe and the possible inclusion of 70 million Muslims that provides the backdrop to the compatibility crisis. Is it possible to reform Turkey to fit into a European project which seeks to create a common Union identity?

The arguments raised by this book provide not only an understanding of Turkey's fraught path to accession but, importantly, speak to the existing challenges (and opportunities) of a multicultural Europe. Leaving aside the immediate demographic impact Turkish accession would bring to the EU, immigration statistics reveal that, with the exception of the United Kingdom, Muslims already account for the largest religious identity bloc within Europe. There are a number of issues to arise from this demographic fact. The European self-identification with a Christian cultural identity stands in contrast to the demographic realities immigrant populations bring. With few European converts, Islam remains the religious identity of immigrants, creating a space between the ostensibly 'secular', 'modern' and 'liberal' West and the 'otherness' of Islam.

That 'immigration and Islam are almost synonymous' within Europe, informs, as Casanova argues, the increasing 'secularization' of some European states.

This trend is set against the marked demographic shifts across Europe which, in turn, have brought diverse (and competing) religious (and associated political, social and cultural) interests to the territory occupied by the European Union (EU). For EU member states, the question of how to merge this diversity into the principles and ideals of member states must be addressed. The approach that has emerged thus far, detailed in Chapter 4 of this book, is an essentially illiberal (and largely unsustainable) secularism expressed in illiberal restrictions on religion in the public sphere; a religious pluralism grafted to traditional European norms and values.

How this reading of Europe informs the Turkish experience within the EU accession process is critical. After examining the stated obstacles to Turkish membership – Cyprus, the Kurdish question and the conflict in south-east Turkey as well as Turkey's human rights record – all of which have played a part in Turkey's accession case – the author concludes that, however valid these concerns may be, they 'may mask a deeper disquiet'; one that this book goes some way to unveil.

Kathleen Cavanaugh
ICHR, National University of Ireland
Galway

Acknowledgements

The research for this book began with a Ph.D., completed at the Irish Centre for Human Rights (ICHR), National University of Ireland, Galway, in 2009. To that end, my first and foremost words of thanks are for my thesis supervisor, Dr Kathleen Cavanaugh, for her expert guidance, support, encouragement and patience over the years I spent completing the study. I wish to thank my viva voce examiners, Professor Andrew Williams and Professor Joshua Castellino for their helpful advice and suggestions. My sincere thanks also to Professor William Schabas, Professor Ray Murphy and Dr Vinodh Jaichand, who made my time at the ICHR both stimulating and enjoyable.

My time spent at the ICHR was made all the more enjoyable due to the presence of a large group of Ph.D. researchers engaged in the same process. I am grateful to Danny Aguirre, Jérémie Gilbert, Anthony Cullen, Maeve Barry and Guinevere and Richard Barlow for their encouragement and friendship over the years. Particular words of gratitude are owed to Michael Kearney, David Keane and Shane Darcy for their support, advice, helpful comments and proofreading skills!

I would like to thank my family, in particular my mother, Nancy, to whom this book is dedicated, for support and encouragement during a long career in full-time education! Words of sincere gratitude are also owed to Ray Friel, Head of the School of Law at the University of Limerick and my colleagues at the School for their support and friendship since 2006.

I owe a debt of gratitude to Kerim Yildiz, who first provoked my interest in issues concerning human rights. I am also grateful to the staff of the Kurdish Human Rights Project, in particular for facilitating access to documents, which otherwise would have been difficult to find. My thanks also to Professor James O'Connell of the University of Bradford for access to his articles.

My final words of thanks are for Javier Santoyo. For your love, support, encouragement, good humour and endless patience over the last seven years, *muchas gracias, Capi*!

Table of cases

European Union documentation

'Commission Presents Its Recommendation on the Continuation of Turkey's Accession Negotiations', 1, Brussels, 29 November 2006, IP/06/1652

Communauté Économique Européenne Commission, 'Négociations avec la Turquie pour un Accord d'Association', 'Solution Actuellement Demandée par la Turquie', 1, Brussels, 3 February 1961, I/S/0713/61

Communauté Économique Européenne Commission, 'Note sure l'Association de la Turquie à la Communauté' 1, Brussels, 23 September 1959

Communication from the Commission to the European Parliament and the Council, 'Enlargement Strategy and Main Challenges 2007–2008' Brussels, 6 November 2007 COM(2007) 663 final

Conclusions of the Presidency, Madrid European Council, 15–16 December 1995

Conclusions of the Presidency, Luxembourg European Council, December 1997, EU Bulletin no. 12.97

Conclusions of the Presidency, Helsinki European Council, December 1999, EU Bulletin no. 12.99

Conclusions of the Presidency, Brussels European Council, December 2004 EU Bulletin no. 12.04

'Considerations d'Ordre Général sur L'Association de la Turquie à la CEE', Brussels, 1 October 1959, I-4275/59-F

Council of the European Union 'EU Annual Report on Human Rights 2007', Brussels, 18 October 2007, 13288/1/07REV 1

Decision No. 1/95 of the EC–Turkey Association Council of 22 December 1995 on Implementing the Final Phase of the Customs Union (96/142/EC)

Declaration on Cyprus adopted by the European Council at its meeting in Dublin, 26 June 1990, Bulletin of the European Communities, No. 6/1990

Declaration of the Zagreb Summit, 24 November 2000

'État de la procédure au sujet de la demande d'association de la Turquie à la Communauté Économique Européenne', 'Note Introductive', Brussels, 9 September 1959, R/644/59

EU–Turkey Negotiating Framework, 3 October 2005

European Commission 'Commission Opinion on Turkey's Request for Accession to the Community' SEC (89) 2290 final/2, 20 December 1989

Treaties

The Treaty of Peace Between the Allied and Associated Powers and Turkey, signed at Sèvres, 10 August 1920

Treaty of Peace with Turkey, signed at Lausanne, 24 July 1923

Treaty Establishing the European Coal and Steel Community', signed at Paris, 18 April 1951

Convention Establishing an Association Between the European Economic Community and Turkey, signed at Ankara, Turkey, 12 September 1963

Treaty on European Union, (The Maastricht Treaty) 7 February 1992, OJ C 224/1 (1992)

Treaty of Lisbon amending the Treaty on European Union and the Treaty establishing the European Community, signed at Lisbon, 13 December 2007, Official Journal of the European Union, 17 December 2007, 2007/C 306/01

Introduction

Turkish accession to the European Union (EU) has generated a great deal of anxiety and Turkey is, undoubtedly, the EU's most contested candidate. While the narrative that dominates the debate on Turkey and the EU is, ostensibly, related to a lack of fundamental human rights guarantees and continuing problems surrounding Cyprus, a review of the case suggests that these concerns may mask a deeper disquiet.

Since first applying for associate membership of the then European Economic Community (EEC) in 1959, Turkey has overcome numerous barriers to achieving membership and in 2004, it appeared that Turkish accession would finally become a reality when the European Council agreed to open accession negotiations. However, in November 2006, yet another considerable obstacle was placed in the path to membership when EU foreign ministers, acting on the recommendation of the European Commission, voted to suspend eight of the 35 chapters comprising Turkey's negotiations to join the EU.[1] To date, therefore, negotiations have been opened on 12 chapters (Science and Research, Enterprise and Industry, Statistics, Financial Control, Trans-European Networks, Consumer and Health Protection, Intellectual Property Law, Company Law, Information Society and Media, Free movement of Capital, Taxation, and Environment), one of which (Science and Research) was provisionally closed.[2] The Commission has also recently indicated that its suspension decision of 2006 remains in place.[3]

The pace of accession negotiations is inextricably linked to the reform process that accession conditionality has engendered in Turkey, a fact which has been stated categorically on a number of occasions.[4] Turkey's eventual membership is not a foregone conclusion, despite the length and extent of the accession process, as well as the degree of reforms instituted at the domestic level. While domestic reform has been an essential component of recent accessions to the Union, what has set Turkey apart from the ten countries that acceded in May 2004 and the accession of Romania and Bulgaria in January 2007, has been the time invested in the accession process. Turkey's relationship with the EU has after all been in existence since 1959; whereas it was only in 1993 that the European Council noted that 'the associated countries in Central and Eastern Europe that so desire shall become members of the European Union' and those countries went on to achieve full membership in 2004.[5] Similarly, the accession of Romania and Bulgaria ahead of Turkey surprised commentators, who pointed to their underdeveloped economies and very real problems regarding endemic corruption.[6] It had even been suggested that Turkey had made greater advancements than these countries in preparing for accession and, in particular, that its progress was 'far superior' to that of Romania.[7]

There are, of course, several questions which Turkey must address, particularly in the area of fundamental human rights protections. Having said this, the concerns which raise debates regarding Turkish membership are not issues that are unique to Turkey; a point rarely noted. In the post-September 2001 landscape, restrictions on freedom of expression, for example, can now be seen in numerous 'liberal' democratic states where the all-encompassing aim of fighting 'terrorism' is invoked to justify a plethora of constraints on individual freedoms that these same purportedly liberal democratic states have criticized in Turkey and elsewhere. Equally, other aspects of the concerns highlighted in respect of Turkey, such as issues related to minority rights protection, have not been secured in numerous European countries, including the two newest EU members, Romania and Bulgaria.

A 2008 report on the global human rights situation noted that in Romania, Roma and other minorities continued to be subjected to serious discrimination,[8] whereas in Bulgaria, '[d]iscrimination against minorities, particularly Roma, continued against a general backdrop of suspicion towards refugees, asylum-seekers and migrants'.[9] Nor is the intolerance of minorities a problem that is confined to the newest member states. In Italy, one of the founding members of the EU, the targeting of the Roma minority by state authorities[10] highlights the inherent double standards in EU human rights policy, whereby acceding states are subjected to more stringent assessment of their conformity with human rights obligations than current member states.[11] It also raises questions as to whether Turkey, as an accession state, is being treated differently to those that have recently acceded. If, as it is argued, Turkey was accepted as a potential member on the basis that it would provide a catalyst for political reform,[12] then it arguably follows that further reforms would more easily be effected with Turkey in the EU, rather than outside it, given that Turkey would have to comply with a host of EU legislation in the area of equality and non-discrimination. Whereas it can be argued that the carrot–stick approach to EU membership has provided the catalyst for reform in a number of key areas, it is also probable that without concomitant progress towards membership, reform fatigue is likely to set in.

1 Terms of enlargement

The legal basis for enlargement of the European Union is contained in Article 49 of the Treaty on European Union, which establishes that any European state that respects the principles of the Union as outlined in Article 6(1) of the Treaty can apply to become a member of the Union.[13] Current enlargement strategy towards the Western Balkans and Turkey emphasizes the 'fundamental issues of state-building, good governance, administrative and judicial reform, rule of law, reconciliation, compliance with [the] International Criminal Tribunal for the Former Yugoslavia (ICTY), and civil society development'.[14] The enlargement process undertaken by the EU, to date, has generally been seen as a positive development[15] and more specifically it has been noted that it has led to 'a far more interventionist and ongoing process of scrutiny of the human rights records of the applicant countries by the European Commission, than ever was the case before'.[16] The EU expansion process has also traditionally proceeded on the assumption that expansion of the Union is beneficial for both applicants and existing members, thereby ensuring its popularity even when applicant countries have had to implement extensive changes in order to comply with the conditions of entry. In 2004, when ten new countries joined the EU, it was suggested that the enlargement was an act of 'West European charity towards neighbors in the continent's East' but that the EU was also acting in its own self-interests.[17] Indeed the archival research conducted in the preparation of Chapter 1 of this study reveals that a similar attitude prevailed in Turkey–European Community relations during the negotiation of the Association Agreement in 1959, when the then EEC stated that an agreement formalizing relations with Turkey would be in the best interests of both Turkey and the European Community (EC).[18]

This sentiment has, however, largely been absent from the more recent debates surrounding Turkey's prospective membership and the discourse has been framed in such a way that there are no perceived benefits to the Union from having Turkey become a full member. In this regard, Shäuble, in advocating a 'privileged partnership' for Turkey that would be short of full membership, has suggested that the inclusion of Turkey would see Europe risk 'overstretching itself'.[19] While Shäuble's argument against including Turkey in the EU would appear to be based primarily on aspects of economic and political conditionality, suggesting Turkey is not 'ready' to join the EU, arguments have also been proffered which suggest a more deep-rooted, fundamental incompatibility between Turkey and the EU. Tibi, for example, foresees 'massive social and political conflicts' should Muslim migrants fail to integrate into Europe and suggests that the integration of Turkey with its 'great variety of Islamist political movements' in the EU would be fraught with difficulties.[20]

These concerns regarding Turkish membership are reflective of both categories of argument on which opposition to Turkey joining the EU is usually based. The first, demonstrated by Shäuble's concern regarding the ability of the EU to 'absorb' Turkey, questions the capacity of the EU to incorporate a country such as Turkey and reflects an anxiety regarding the survival of the achieved political order. The second argument, reflected in Tibi's fundamental concerns regarding the compatibility of Muslim Turkey with an ostensibly secular EU, is a value-based one.[21] Arguments concerning the capacity of the Union to 'absorb' a country the size and nature of Turkey are easily rebutted[22] and the accession of the arguably less economically developed countries of

Romania and Bulgaria in January 2007 has not resulted in the demise of the EU. Other reasons on which to base the exclusion of Turkey concern the historically strong involvement of the military in politics and the relatively poor and agricultural nature of the country.[23] That said, the value-based arguments are the most troublesome and suggest an unspoken cultural, or even specifically religious requirement that many EU commentators feel Turkey does not fulfil. Diez suggests that the value-based argument:

> presupposes that: (1) the predominance of different values is distributed on a geographical basis; (2) such value differences matter to communities, so they are worth preserving; and (3) the difference between Turkey and the present EU member states is sufficiently greater than that among member states, so it is justifiable to treat Turkey differently and to deny membership.[24]

2 Turkey in Europe: a compatibility crisis?

Justification for excluding Turkey from full membership of the EU is premised on a number of contentions.[25] Among them is the fact that, with a population of over 70 million, the country is simply too big. The President of France, Nicolas Sarkozy, has unambiguously called for EU enlargement to be suspended, noting that Europe must have borders; not all countries have a vocation to be in Europe.[26] Equally, Valéry Giscard d'Estaing, former French president and chairman of the presidency of the European Convention,[27] has stated his opposition to Turkey joining the EU in no uncertain terms, noting that Turkey has 'a different culture, a different approach, a different way of life ... its capital is not in Europe, 95 per cent of its population lives outside Europe, it is not a European country ... in my opinion it would be the end of the EU'.[28] Other arguments suggest that Turkey is not ready to join the Union, in spite of it having satisfied the conditions necessary to begin accession negotiations, which were formally opened in October 2005. Germany's Christian Democrats oppose Turkey joining the EU on the same basis as the other 27 member states, preferring instead to offer Turkey a 'privileged partnership' which would be short of full membership; a position also held by the European People's Party, the umbrella organization of Christian Democrats and centre-right parties from all EU member states.[29] Nor would it appear that Turkish membership will receive much support from the first full-time president of the European Council, Herman Van Rompuy, who, during a meeting held at the Belgian Parliament in 2004 stated, 'Turkey is not a part of Europe and will never be part of Europe. An expansion of the EU to include Turkey cannot be considered as just another expansion, as in the past. The universal values which are in force in Europe, and which are also fundamental values of Christianity, will lose vigour with the entry of a large Islamic country such as Turkey.'[30] It would appear that when it comes to Turkey's case for accession, many EU member states are suffering from 'enlargement fatigue'.[31]

The issue of Turkey's accession has taken place within a broader debate about European identity and culture. From the outset, it would appear that the European Union has attempted to promote the idea of a common Union identity. The introduction to the 'Fourth General Report on the Activities of the Community' in May 1961 described the European Commission as 'contributing to the establishment of a European idea which is penetrating more and more deeply into the consciousness of the public' and advocated an awareness of a 'Community spirit' in all aspects of the member states' activities.[32] More recently, the Treaty on European Union speaks of 'reinforcing the European identity'[33] but exactly what constitutes that identity is not defined, and may, in fact, be indefinable.[34] As Casanova has suggested:

> One wonders whether Turkey represents a threat to Western civilization or rather an unwelcome reminder of the barely submerged yet inexpressible and anxiety-ridden 'white' European Christian identity. The public debates in Europe over Turkey's admission have shown that Europe is actually the torn country, deeply divided over its cultural identity, unable to answer the question whether European identity, and therefore its external and internal boundaries, should be defined by the common heritage of Christianity and Western civilization or by its modern secular values of liberalism, universal human rights, political democracy and tolerant and inclusive multiculturalism.[35]

The difficulty inherent in the definition of a 'European' identity notwithstanding, it is a concept that has gained in importance in recent years. Whether this is due to economic factors, such as the completion of the Single Market and the imposition of a single currency across 15 countries and 320 million EU citizens, or political factors, such as the increased emphasis on democratization and awareness of the EU and its institutions, it is also likely that it is due, in large part, to the enlargement process. The question of identity becomes increasingly pertinent as both the composition of the Union and the list of potential members grows. However, it can be argued that current discussions reflecting fears of a diluted European identity fail to take cognizance of Europe's history. In this regard, a study by the Netherlands Scientific Council for Government Policy posits that:

> [g]eographical and cultural–historical approaches often used to define Europe take insufficient account of its dynamic and malleable nature. After all, Europe has a long history of fragmentation, conflict, and especially, shifting political borders that were all legitimised in various ways. What remains is not a fixed entity, but a dynamic social construct, an *imagined community* that can change according to circumstance and political leadership.[36]

The reasons proffered by Giscard d'Estaing, Sarkozy and Germany's Christian Democrats, among others, for keeping Turkey out of the EU suggest that there is something essentially 'un-European' about Turkey and, by extension, that there is some readily identifiable common 'European' identity discernable across EU member states to which Turkey does not conform. The possibility of a 'European identity' has, as Williams notes, existed for centuries:

> The possibility of a 'European identity' in the construction of a continental polity was not a phenomenon introduced by the Community. Its possibility, if not its existence, has been posited for centuries. Since at least Abbé de St. Pierre and Rousseau, it had formed the basic assumption from which strategies for peace within the continent, for co-operation and mutual advancement, for some kind of unity of purpose, had evolved.[37]

That the EU in its numerous incarnations has attempted to espouse the notion of an 'identity' is also clear. The preamble to the Treaty establishing the European Coal and Steel Community in 1951, for example, speaks of the countries concerned being '[r]esolved to substitute for age old rivalries the merging of their essential interests; to create, by establishing an economic community, the basis for a broader and deeper community among peoples long divided by bloody conflicts'.[38] The most recent EU treaty, the Treaty of Lisbon, notes that the European Union's aim 'is to promote peace, its values and the well-being of its peoples'.[39] There is also the suggestion, in pointing to a lack of common history between Turkey and Europe, that the countries of Europe share 'a great community of common descent':

> Turkey is, of course, the looming question that has brought this long-buried discourse of origins out of hiding. People who want to keep the Turks out have suddenly discovered that the roots of Europe lie in its Christian heritage. Those who share our continent, but do not share this Christian heritage, are seen as Europe's other.[40]

But if, as has been suggested '[t]he acknowledgement of differences – the reciprocal acknowledgement of the Other in his otherness – can also become a feature of a common identity',[41] coupled with Habermas's contention that '[w]hat forms the common core of a European identity is the character of the painful learning process it has gone through, as much as its results'[42] this arguably suggests that if we are to persist with the idea of a 'European' identity, then surely it should be an inclusive rather than exclusionary concept that would welcome the 'other', if it is to be viewed as such, brought about by Turkey's accession. Indeed, commentators such as Todorov and Bracher reject traditional definitions of European identity, which are primarily based on the Judeo-Christian and Greco-Roman heritages and instead propose a more 'pluralistic' conception of European identity that would also encompass other non-European heritages.[43]

Additionally, increasingly relevant in the debates on the composition of the 'social construct' that is Europe and the political construct that is the EU, is whether or not religion plays a role in this overtly secular entity. With the potential accession of Turkey, the EU is faced for the first time with the prospect of an almost exclusively Muslim population joining the ranks of the Union. While for some, this represents an opportunity for Europe and the EU to embrace a culture different to that of any European country, for others this difference has led to questions regarding the nature of the Union and Turkey's compatibility with it. Interestingly, this debate surfaces at a time of increasing global desecularization, and the fundamental tensions perceived between the purportedly democratic secular 'values' of the EU and those of Turkey contribute to questions regarding whether Europe is really as secular as most would maintain. As Menéndez has noted, Europeans have been forced to 'come to terms with the plurality of national conceptions of freedom of conscience and religion, and to consider whether such plurality is compatible with the strengthening of a common European identity'.[44]

This study will critically engage with the contentious questions that continue to separate Turkey from EU integration, and examine whether underpinning this process is an unstated obstacle, that may take the form of a 'religious' requirement, which many in Europe feel Turkey does not fulfil. In order to examine this question, a number of relevant considerations are probed in an attempt to establish whether something more than the stated obstacles continue to separate Turkey from membership. The central argument of the study is that while legitimate concerns persist with regard to Turkish membership, a hidden religious obstacle, rarely acknowledged in the public debates on the issue, also remains. In an effort to demonstrate this, the study examines the current impediments to membership and then asserts that the hidden obstacle can be gleaned from the manner in which both EU member states and the European Court of Human Rights alike have dealt with the manifestation of Islam in the public sphere. Their approach suggests that concerns regarding Islam and a potential retreat from secularism cannot but inform the debates surrounding Turkey's accession.

The first section, in Chapters 1–3, will examine the historical backdrop, obstacles and approach of the EU to Turkish accession. While an audit of the issues raised under the accession process will be undertaken, the focus will be on whether the EU's carrot–stick approach to human rights reform is effective in Turkey's case and if so, why do human rights concerns continue to be cited as a reason for the lack of progress in the accession process. Chapter 1 provides an analysis of the historical background of Turkey's pursuit of EU membership. Three aspects of Turkey's EU bid are examined: the secular underpinnings of the state, as firmly established by Atatürk at the beginning of the twentieth century; the formal path to accession thus far, beginning with negotiations for an association agreement which was eventually signed in 1963 and ending with the decision to open accession negotiations in October 2004; and the backdrop to the Kurdish question. While the issue of secularism in Turkey has been considered elsewhere,[45] Chapter 1 aims to place the particular form of Turkey's secularism within the context of its potential EU membership.

There has been little scholarly research conducted on Turkey–EU relations prior to the signing of the Association Agreement in 1963 as discussions of Turkey's current bid tend to begin after this point. Chapter 1 of this study fills this gap by tracing the development of Turkey's quest for recognition as an EU candidate country, drawing from research conducted at the historical archives of the European Union.[46] A review of these documents reveal the interesting and contentious nature of the discussions prior to the signing of the Association Agreement in 1963, but also the fact that the agreement was considered to be beneficial not only for Turkey, but also for the then European Economic Community. The similarities in Turkey–EU relations – then and now – also resonate, with Turkey contending that Greece, who was also in negotiations with the European Commission to conclude an agreement, was being treated more favourably. The Kurdish conflict lies central to understanding the human rights issues raised in Turkey. The European Commission has indicated that the resolution of this issue in a civil, non-military resolution is key to accession. There are numerous works detailing the background to the conflict in the south-east, as well as numerous reports of non-governmental organizations outlining the abuses of human rights perpetrated during the conflict. However, Chapter 1 endeavours to discuss the debates surrounding the Kurdish question specifically in relation to the impact that the issue has on the bid for EU membership.

Chapters 2 and 3 engage with the stated obstacles currently preventing Turkey from progressing on the path to membership and provide an analysis as to the efficacy of the EU approach to reform. The accession process has necessitated major reforms within Turkey's domestic legal system. Nowhere is this more evident than in provisions relating to the protection of fundamental rights. A series of nine harmonization packages have been introduced in order to satisfy accession criteria, as well as comprehensive amendments to the Civil and Penal Codes and the Constitution. These developments are examined in Chapter 2, which looks in detail at human rights considerations in the EU accession process. It provides an overview of how the European Commission has assessed Turkey's performance in the pivotal areas of human rights protection and looks in detail at issues related to freedom of expression in Turkey, given that the Progress Reports continue to point to freedom of expression as a specific area of concern.[47] As well as the particular problems highlighted regarding freedom of expression, the issue of minority rights protection has also been cited as a concern by EU actors. An overview of the prevailing minority rights protection in Turkey and assessment in light of European norms in the area is provided.

In addition to the human rights considerations, the other major obstacle ostensibly preventing Turkish progression towards membership is the Cyprus question. Chapter 3 provides an analysis of the protracted Cyprus 'conflict' and assesses the justifiability of the EU having placed the burden of moving towards a solution solely on Turkey's doorstep, a fact which is largely ignored by most commentators on the subject. A detailed assessment of international efforts at finding a resolution to the conflict, most significantly the Kofi Annan Plan, is provided as well as an appraisal of recent developments, including the exploratory talks which could eventually lead to the reunification of the island.

Unpacking and examining the issues which the EU has targeted in the accession process reveals that there is more to the question of Turkey's membership in the EU than the public narrative suggests. Against the backdrop of a broader 'European identity' debate, the final section of this study will, therefore, examine the impact of religion on EU–Turkish relations and suggest that the accession process highlights the increasing tension between legal pluralism[48] and illiberal secularism[49] within Europe. Chapter 4 turns to the question of religion and interrogates the argument that Europe's undeniably Christian heritage has consequence in contemporary developments within the EU. It is undoubtedly true that in influential works on early European integration, religion (i.e. Western Christianity) is posited as a crucial feature underlying conceptions of Europe and European identity.[50] With a few notable exceptions, there has been little scholarly attention to this question, yet it is an issue which is becoming more important within the EU, a point which was aptly illustrated by the fevered debates surrounding the inclusion of a reference to 'Christian values' in the preamble to the European Constitution.[51]

Turkey's potential accession, as noted above, appears to have reignited the debate surrounding the concept of Europe and European identity and culture, a debate mainly engaged in by those who would assert that Europe's much lauded 'common heritage' is one of the reasons as to why Turkey does not 'belong' in the EU. That the religion question is also a vital one is evidenced by a body of case law emanating from both domestic courts within EU member states and the European Court of Human Rights (ECtHR), which highlight Europe's unease at religious manifestation in the public sphere.[52] On examination of the pertinent ECtHR cases, this study suggests that the Court in its illiberal rulings can even be said to be sanctioning the actions of militant democracy.[53] Given that all EU member states are also members of the Council of Europe, the 'guardian of European values and principles',[54] and therefore subject to the jurisdiction of the ECtHR, it is not unrealistic to suggest that the reasoning of the Court in these pivotal cases is both reflective of and instructive to member states grappling with issues of religion in the public sphere at the domestic level. As evidenced in 2005, a Muslim country joining the EU is a fundamental concern among Europe's religious elite.[55] Notwithstanding the EU's activity in the area of racism and anti-discrimination, which legislates against discrimination on a number of grounds, including religion,[56] the case law of the ECtHR and domestic courts regarding the public manifestation of Islam suggest that the accession of a country of more than 70 million Muslims may also be a determining factor among the political elite.

Notes

1 See 'Commission Presents Its Recommendation on the Continuation of Turkey's Accession Negotiations', Brussels, 29 November 2006, IP/06/1652. The Commission

recommended that 'the Intergovernmental Conference on Accession with Turkey should not open negotiations on policy areas relevant to Turkey's restrictions as regards the Republic of Cyprus until the Commission confirms that Turkey has fulfilled its commitments'. The suspended chapters included those relating to free movement of goods; right of establishment and freedom to provide services; financial services; agriculture and rural development; fisheries; transport policy; Customs Union; and external relations.

2 See 2009 Progress Report, SEC(2009)1334, Brussels, 14 October 2009 5 and L. Phillips, 'Turkey Opens Environment Ch. in EU Accession Talks', EU Observer, 21 December 2009 (available at: http://euobserver.com/15/29187) (last accessed 27 December 2009).

3 2009 Progress Report, SEC(2009)1334, Brussels, 14 October 2009 5.

4 For example, the European Commission noted in its 'Enlargement Strategy 2007–2008' that '[t]he pace of negotiations depends on the results of the reforms in Turkey. Turkey's progress could gather momentum if it succeeds in meeting opening benchmarks.' The Commission also concluded that Turkey 'should fulfil the commitments related to full non-discriminatory implementation of the Additional Protocol to the Association Agreement' and until it did so, the eight chapters suspended in December 2006 would not be opened. See Communication from the Commission to the European Parliament and the Council, 'Enlargement Strategy and Main Challenges 2007–2008', Brussels, 6 November 2007 COM(2007) 663 final, 18.

5 Conclusions of the Presidency, Copenhagen European Council, June 1993, SN 180/93 para. 7(A)iii.

6 See, for example, R. Shepherd, 'Romania, Bulgaria, and the EU's Future', *Current History* (March, 2007),117–22, 117–18, noting that on acceding to the EU, Romania's gross domestic product (GDP) was 35 per cent of the European average and Bulgaria's was 32 per cent. Additionally, Romania was ranked number 88 on Transparency International's 2006 Corruption Perceptions Index, putting it in the same category as Sri Lanka and Panama. Bulgaria, at number 57, ranked alongside El Salvador and below Namibia but was marginally ahead of Poland, which acceded to the EU in 2004 and ranked number 62 on the index. Shepherd also makes the point that of the ten countries that joined the EU in 2004, four of them have experienced political upheavals which might well debar them from membership were they applying now. The Prime Minister of Hungary, Ferenc Gyurcsany, was recorded admitting that he had lied about the state of the economy for years; the Slovak elections in 2006 saw the rise of the populist leftist Prime Minister Robert Fico, who went into government with the far-right Slovak National Party and the Movement for a Democratic Slovakia, led by the authoritarian former Prime Minister Vladimir Meciar; the Polish government includes the homophobic League of Polish Families and the Self Defense Party, headed by Andrzej Lepper, who has publicly praised Adolf Hitler's early economic policies; and the Czech Republic was unable to form a meaningful government for a long period after the elections of June 2006.

7 See J. Parker 'West Meets East: A Discussion of European Union Enlargement and Human Rights', Tulsa J. Comp. & Int'l L., 11 (2004), 603–39, 639.

8 Amnesty International Report 2008, State of the World's Human Rights: Romania.

9 Amnesty International Report 2008, State of the World's Human Rights: Bulgaria.

10 See G. Lagana, 'Roma Face Fear and Loathing in Italy', *Guardian* 24 July 2008.

11 On this point, see generally A. Williams, *EU Human Rights Policies: A Study in Irony* (Oxford: Oxford University Press, 2004).

12 See F. Tarifa and B. Adams, 'Who's the Sick Man of Europe? A Wavering EU Should Let Turkey In', *Mediterranean Quarterly*, 18(1) (2007), 52–74, 55.

13 Treaty on European Union, 7 Feb. 7 1992, OJ C 224/1 (1992). Article 6(1) states that the Union is 'founded on the principles of liberty, democracy, respect for human rights, and fundamental freedoms, and the rule of law, principles which are common to the Member States'.

14 Communication from the Commission to the European Parliament and the Council, 'Enlargement Strategy and Main Challenges 2007–2008', Brussels, 6 November 2007 COM(2007) 663 final, 4.

15 The 'Enlargement Strategy' of 2007–2008 concluded that enlargement 'contributed to peace, democracy and stability throughout the continent and brought concrete benefits in terms of increased trade, investment and economic growth' resulting in the Union becoming more competitive and better able to respond to the challenges of globalization. Enlargement had also 'enhanced the EU's weight in the world' (*ibid.*, 16).

16 G. de Búrca, 'Beyond the Charter: How Enlargement has Enlarged the Human Rights Policy of the European Union', Fordham Int'l L. J., 27 (2004), 679–714, 700. However, the point that the enlargement process has exposed the double standards in relation to requirements for existing and potential member states remains a valid one.

17 J. Zielonka, 'Europe Moves Eastward: Challenges of EU Enlargement', J. Democracy, 15(1) (2004), 22–35, 22.

18 See below Chapter 1, Section 2.1.

19 W. Shäuble, 'Talking Turkey: Is Europe Ready for a Muslim Member?', *Foreign Affairs*, 83 (2004), 134–7, 135.

20 See B. Tibi, 'Europeanizing Islam or the Islamization of Europe: Political Democracy vs. Cultural Difference', in T. A. Byrnes and P. J. Katzenstein (eds), *Religion in an Expanding Europe* (New York: Cambridge University, 2006), 204–25, 205, 218.

21 See T. Diez, 'Expanding Europe: The Ethics of EC–Turkey Relations', *Ethics and International Affairs*, 21(4) (2007), 415–22, 416.

22 Albeit that Turkey presents issues of a somewhat unprecedented nature, its membership cannot be denied on the basis of sheer population size alone. The EU, after all, already contains Germany which, with a population of over 80 million, is greater in number than Turkey.

23 See F. Schimmelfennig, 'Entrapped Again: The Way to EU Membership Negotiations with Turkey', UCD Dublin European Institute Working Paper, 08–8, July 2008, 1–2.

24 Diez, 'Expanding Europe', 416.

25 Tarifa and Adams, 'Sick Man of Europe', 57, asserting that there are four main categories of arguments generally made against Turkish membership in the EU: 'First, there is the geographic argument that Turkey does not qualify for EU membership since only a small fraction of the country is physically located 'inside' Europe. Second, the case is often made that Turkey's membership would have a negative effect on an already suffering European economy as well as cause a massive migration problem. Third, many critics contend that European values

and Turkish culture and society are essentially incompatible. This argument can be found in debates on human rights, Islam, and the role of the military in Turkish governance. Finally, there is the issue of Greek–Cypriot–Turkish relations, which continually threatens to derail accession talks.'

26 Quoted in J. Casanova, 'The Long, Difficult, and Tortuous Journey of Turkey into Europe and the Dilemmas of European Civilization', *Constellations*, 13.2 (2006), 234–47, 234. Kirişi notes that Europe is divided as to whether or not Turkey is to be viewed as European or as the 'other': 'There is clearly a group of Europeans who do not define or see Turks and Turkey as the "others" of Europe. Traditionally for example the British, the Spanish, the Poles, and the Swedes have not adopted a particularly exclusionary discourse on Turkey. Yet, in countries such as Austria, Denmark, Holland, France, and Germany, the opposition to Turkish membership is pronounced, and in these countries Turks are indeed often framed as the "other" purely based on religion' ('Religion as an Argument in the Debate on Turkish EU Membership', in D. Jung and C. Raudvere (eds), *Religion, Politics and Turkey's EU Accession* (New York: Palgrave Macmillan, 2008), 19–41, 30–1.

27 The European Convention, or the Convention on the Future of Europe, was a body established by the European Council in December 2001 with the task of producing a draft constitution for the European Union that the Council would finalize and adopt. The Convention completed its work in July 2003 with a Draft Treaty establishing a Constitution for Europe. See generally, J. Shaw, P. Magnette, L. Hoffman and A. Vergés Bausili (eds), *The Convention on the Future of Europe*: *Working Towards an EU Constitution* (London: Federal Trust, 2003).

28 See 'Giscard Remarks cause Uproar in Ankara, and Brussels', *Turkish Daily News*, 11 November 2002. Tarifa and Adams make an interesting point in respect of Giscard d'Estaing's geographic argument against Turkish membership, asserting that if Turkey is not eligible for EU membership on geographic grounds, then that calls into question the membership of the Mediterranean island nations of Cyprus and Malta, as well as the French *départements d'outre-mer* of Guiana on the northern coast of South America, Martinique, the Guadeloupe archipelago in the Caribbean Sea, Reunion in the Indian Ocean; the islands of Saint Pierre and Miquelon off the eastern coast of Canada; the Spanish territory of the Canary islands in the Atlantic off the north-western coast of Africa; and the Netherland Antilles islands in the Caribbean which are all part of the EU and use the euro as their currency ('Sick Man of Europe', 59).

29 Casanova, 'Long, Difficult, and Tortuous', 235.

30 T. Barber, 'Van Rompuy against Turkey Membership', *Financial Times*, 19 November 2009.

31 See 'Beyond Enlargement Fatigue?: The Dutch Debate on Turkish Accession' (Report), European Stability Initiative, Berlin, Istanbul, Brussels, 24 April 2006.

32 EC Bull 5–1961, 12–14, cited in A. Williams *EU Human Rights Policies*: *A Study in Irony* (Oxford: Oxford University Press, 2004), 166. Williams also notes that '[t]he myth of identity between peoples (rather than states) provided the rhetorical connection that bound these elements inextricably to one project, that of the union of Europe. It also set a determined agenda designed to attract other European states ready to assume in "*tous les domaines*" the same responsibilities and obligations now accepted by the then current Members. The prospect of embracing an affinity with a past, which was only made coherent by a mythic

and undefined notion of what it was to be "of Europe", and a utopian future, was therefore held out to states who could qualify under those terms. The Project (linked rhetorically to all aspects of society and in particular culture) thus set its own definitional limits' (*ibid.*, 166–7).

33 Preamble to the Treaty on European Union – the 'Maastricht Treaty', signed on 7 February 1992, Maastricht, the Netherlands.

34 On the difficulty of defining a European identity, see J. A. Caporaso, 'The Possibilities of a European Identity', Brown J. World Aff., 12 (2005–6), 65–75, 66, noting that the question of European identity cannot be answered solely from a description of Europe's constituent units: 'Knowing who is a member of the EU or the larger European region does not tell us whether a European identity exists. Membership in a political association may both require some initial common affinity and produce a stronger feeling of "we-ness," but simple membership – even common problem solving – does not forge a distinct identity comparable to national identities.'

35 Casanova, 'Long, Difficult, and Tortuous', 241 (reference omitted).

36 Netherlands Scientific Council for Government Policy, *The European Union, Turkey and Islam* (Amsterdam: Amsterdam University Press, 2004), 35 (references omitted, emphasis in original).

37 Williams, *EU Human Rights*, 163.

38 'Treaty Establishing the European Coal and Steel Community', signed at Paris, 18 April 1951, preamble.

39 Treaty of Lisbon Amending the Treaty on European Union and the Treaty Establishing the European Community (2007/C 306/01), signed at Lisbon, 13 December 2007, Article 2(1).

40 U. Beck, 'Understanding the Real Europe', *Dissent*, 50(3) (2003), 32–9, 32.

41 J. Habermas and J. Derrida, 'February 15, or What Binds Europeans Together: A Plea for a Common Foreign Policy, Beginning in the Core of Europe', *Constellations*, 10(3) (2003), 291–7, 294.

42 J. Habermas, 'Why Europe Needs a Constitution', *New Left Review*, 11 (2001), 5–26, 21.

43 T. Todorov and N. Bracher, 'European Identity', *South Central Review*, 25(3) (2008), 3–15.

44 A. J. Menéndez, 'A Christian or a *Laïc* Europe? Christian Values and European Identity', *Ratio Juris*, 18(2) (2005), 179–205, 181.

45 For example, see N. Berkes, *The Development of Secularism in Turkey* (New York: Routledge, 2nd edn, 1998).

46 European University Institute Historical Archives of the European Union, Florence, Italy (available at: www.iue.it/ECArchives/EN/).

47 The 2007 Progress Report on Turkey's Accession to the EU noted that 'the prosecution and conviction for the expression of non-violent opinions under certain provisions of the Turkish Criminal Code are a cause of serious concern' (Turkey 2007 Progress Report, EN(COM(2007) 663), Brussels, 6 November 2007, 14). The most recent report of October 2009 noted some progress but pointed to a lack of legislative guarantees to protect freedom of expression in Turkey. See European Commission Turkey 2009 Progress Report, SEC(2009)1334, 18–19.

48 For the purposes of this study, the term 'legal pluralism' is employed to denote 'the presence in a social field of more than one legal order' (see J. Griffiths, 'What is Legal Pluralism?', *Journal of Legal Pluralism*, 24 (1986), 1–55, 1).

49 For the purposes of this study, the term 'illiberal secularism' is employed to denote the idea that 'liberal' countries are increasingly resorting to illiberal methods as a means of maintaining secularism. For example, Casanova suggests that the French legislation prohibiting the wearing of Muslim veils and other ostensibly religious symbols in public schools may be 'an extreme example of illiberal secularism' ('Immigration and the New Religious Pluralism: A EU/US Comparison', paper presented at the conference The New Religious Pluralism and Democracy, Georgetown University, April 21–22, 2005, 10).

50 See generally C. Dawson, *Understanding Europe* (New York: Sheed and Ward, 1953), D. de Rougement, *The Meaning of Europe* (London: Sidgwick & Jackson, 1963) and *The Idea of Europe* (New York: Macmillan, 1966).

51 For an excellent critical appraisal of the arguments for and against including the reference to 'Christian values' in the preamble to the European Constitution, see Menéndez, 'Christian'.

52 The phrase 'public sphere' is used throughout the study to denote 'the public expression of opinions of all actors of the "civil society", which includes interest groups such as trade unions or public interest groups, political associations and political parties' (S. Bredt, 'The European Social Contract and the European Public Sphere', *European Law Journal*, 12(1) (2006), 61–77, 63).

53 'Militant democracy' refers to the restricting of certain rights in order to uphold these same rights for the greater good; 'a form of constitutional democracy authorized to protect civil and political freedom by preemptively restricting the exercise of such freedoms' (P. Macklem, 'Militant Democracy, Legal Pluralism, and the Paradox of Self-Determination', Int'l J. Con. Law, 4(3) (2006), 488–516, 488).

54 'Turkey in Europe: More than a Promise?', Report of the Independent Commission on Turkey, September 2004, 12.

55 Casanova notes that in his first book published as Pope Benedict XVI, *L'Europa diBenedetto nella crisi delle culture* (Cantagalli Siena, 2005), the Pope questions Turkey's potential EU membership given its Muslim culture and lack of 'Christian roots' ('Long, Difficult, and Tortuous', 247, n. 23).

56 Article 13 of the Treaty of Amsterdam 1997 empowered the EU to take action dealing with discrimination on a number of grounds which had previously not been countenanced, including racial or ethnic origin, religion or belief, age, disability and sexual orientation. See 'Equality and Non-Discrimination in an Enlarged European Union', Green Paper on Equality and Non-Discrimination in an Enlarged EU, COM(2004) 379 final.

1 Weighing history
Turkey's path to accession

1 Introduction

Despite the fact that Turkey's geographical location renders it a natural bridge between East and West, since the early twentieth century, Turkey has arguably been more Western than Eastern in its domestic and international political outlook.[1] The attempts of successive administrations to secure Turkey's place within the EU merely reaffirm this position. The issues surrounding its current position as an EU 'candidate country' are various and complex. That said, Turkey's historical efforts to secure its current position as a modern democratic and secular republic ensures that with political and economic requirements fulfilled, there should, *in theory*, be no bar to achieving full Union membership.

Among the contentious matters surrounding Turkey's bid to join the EU are economic and fiscal performance; human rights protections, especially with regard to the large Kurdish minority, the occupation of northern Cyprus; and the harmonization of Turkey's domestic legislation with that of other EU countries. The nature of the state, in particular the Islamic revival of recent years and the continuing influence exerted by the army on matters of state, as well as problems with freedom of expression and minority rights, constitute two of the primary expressed areas of concern among EU commentators. This is reflected in the body of opinion which suggests that perhaps Turkey does not belong in the EU or, at the very least, that the EU cannot 'absorb' such an addition.[2] Current discussion of Turkey's EU aspirations tends to suggest that the process began with Turkey's application for associate membership of the European Economic Community in 1959 and the subsequent signing of the Association Agreement in 1963.[3] However, before engaging in an analysis of Turkey's current and potential path to membership, this chapter will first elaborate on the salient events in Turkish history that inform the current accession bid. Despite the strictly secular character of the modern Turkish Republic, its significance as a democratic state with a predominately Muslim population pinpricks the concept of European identity and sits rather uneasily as Turkey attempts to join the ranks of the European Union. This process, as will become evident, is unquestionably the European Union's most contentious enlargement and foresees no swift conclusion.

2 The establishment of modern Turkey: early secular beginnings[4]

The exclusion of religious sentiment from the legal and political domain is, especially in the current Western context, seen as a prerequisite for the effective functioning of a modern democracy. While it can be argued that Christian values have influenced the development of many European states, religion has theoretically had no role in the public sphere in modern Turkey since the reign of Mustafa Kemal (Atatürk).[5] In fact, Atatürk's radical programme of secularization is one that was aggressively pursued during the formative years of modern Turkey although, some commentators argue, not altogether successfully.[6] The European Union purports to be an emphatically secular entity, a fact that was reflected in the decision not to include any reference to 'God' in the preamble to the European Union Constitution (latterly 'Reform Treaty' or 'Treaty of Lisbon').[7] That said, the prospect of the inclusion of a predominantly Muslim state of more than 70 million inhabitants is seen as one of the biggest challenges the Union has yet to face and some Ankara commentators argue that the issue of religion is still a hidden obstacle.[8]

2.1 From Ottoman empire to Turkish republic

Six centuries of continuous Ottoman rule stand in marked contrast to what was to follow in twentieth-century Turkey. Whereas the Young Turks, who attained power through the constitutional movement in 1908, attempted to maintain the dynasty and manipulate its legacy in order to carry through reforms, their successor was to abolish the monarchy and establish a secular republic.[9] Atatürk's first dalliance with constitutional politics came as a result of the Allied (Britain, France, Italy, Greece) occupation of Istanbul on 16 March 1920, where the Allies arrested some 150 nationalists and deported them to Malta.[10] The parliament was suspended in protest. Atatürk called for the election of a new parliament, which would be seated in Ankara, the headquarters of the national movement. The new parliament, the Grand National Assembly, met in Ankara on 23 April 1920 and, in May of that year, appointed its own executive committee with Atatürk as its president. Widely considered to be the single most influential reformer in modern Turkish history,[11] Atatürk achieved his most renowned military victory against the Greeks in August 1921 on the Sakarya. The effects of the comprehensive victory were extensive; Atatürk, as commander of the nationalists, was quickly recognized as an important factor and in October of 1921 a new Franco–Turkish treaty was signed with the nationalists, considerably improving the conditions granted to the Turks in the 1920 Treaty of Sèvres.[12] By September 1922, control had been reasserted over Anatolia. In order to rid eastern Thrace of the Greeks, the Turkish forces had to cross the Dardanelles, still occupied by the Allied forces. Although the French and Italian forces withdrew, the British initially refused, until the signing of an armistice at Muydana on 11 October 1922. The Allied governments agreed to a restoration of Turkish sovereignty in Istanbul, the Straits and eastern Thrace, with the Greeks acceding to the armistice on 14 October 1922.[13]

Following such conclusive military success, Atatürk set about establishing his programme for political change. A peace conference was arranged for November 1922, culminating in the Treaty of Lausanne in July 1923. By the time the agreement was signed, Turkey, under Atatürk's direction, had achieved all of its demands, apart from the territorial claim over Mosul.[14] Before the opening of the conference, however, the British had invited the Sultan to send a delegation along with the nationalist delegation thus refusing to recognize the nationalist government as the sole representatives of the Turkish nation. This caused such consternation in the Grand National Assembly that it presented Atatürk with the pretext to abolish the Sultanate.[15] Parliament voted to abolish the Sultanate on 17 November 1922, ultimately paving the way for the Declaration of the Republic on 29 October 1923 – 'the first experiment in a republican form of government in the Islamic world'.[16]

2.2 Two concepts of state: secular and Islamic

The abolition of the Sultanate resurrected the secularist–Islamist debate within Turkey, one that remains to date. Although the elimination of the Sultanate did not cause major repercussions within Turkey, discussions on the question of the Caliphate were the source of a real battle.[17] Following the departure of the Caliph[18] the Assembly deposed him and elected a replacement. In particular the clergy looked to the new Caliph as the last opportunity, as they saw it, to create a veritable Islamic state.[19] On 1 April 1923 the Assembly dissolved itself for elections, following months of growth in support for the Caliphate among Assembly members. All nationalists in the Assembly were combined to form the new People's Party, with the Kemalist faction winning a slight majority in the elections. When the new National Assembly convened on 2 August 1923, it was clear that the form of government was to be either Islamic or secular.

Supporters of the Caliphate associated a republican government with atheism and communism and saw the Caliph as the natural head of state. However, in September 1923, Atatürk appointed a special committee of the People's Party to draft a republican constitution and together with the committee discussed the various forms of republican government possible for Turkey. Aware that the prevailing mood did not favour the acceptance of a new constitution, Atatürk discontinued the drafting process and declared that a republic could be proclaimed simply by adding to Article 1 of the Constitution of 1921 that 'Turkey is a people's state governed by a republican form of government'. On 29 October 1923 the Bill declaring a republic was introduced and, in spite of protests from some of the supporters of the Caliphate, it was adopted that same day.

Despite Atatürk's election as President of the Republic of Turkey under the amended Constitution, the secular–Islamic tensions were by no means over. The supporters of the Caliphate had succeeded in introducing an article in the amended Constitution stating '[t]he religion of the Turkish state is Islam' (Article 2) and, thus, the republic over which Atatürk presided was Islamic. The role and function of the Caliphate continued to be a divisive issue; its supporters wanted the Constitution amended further to clarify the position of the Caliphate, arguing that it was of greater importance than the Constitution, whereas Atatürk and his supporters began to question the need for, and significance of, the Caliphate, arguing that it was nothing more than an historical memory. Atatürk set about canvassing the unrealistic nature of the Caliphate and succeeded 'in arousing national feelings to a higher level than that of religious zeal'.[20] The Bill providing for the abolition of the Caliphate was passed in the Assembly on 3 March 1924.

2.3 Reinforcing secularism through reform

The resonance of the abolition of the Sultanate and subsequent demise of the Caliphate should not be underestimated. This triumph of secularism over Islamic sentiment provided the impetus for Atatürk to implement a whole range of reforms consolidating Turkey's position as a secular republic. The area of education, in particular, received a radical overhaul; Atatürk ordered the closure of all *madreses* and *kuttabs* (religious schools) and abolished religious orders, vesting all responsibilities for education in the Ministry of Education. The reforms did not end at education; Islamic law was replaced with European-style legal codes, Latin letters substituted for Arabic script and, most importantly, the Constitution was to be completely secularized.[21]

2.3.1 A populist approach

As early as July 1920, Atatürk announced to the Assembly that the general tendency of the Turkish nation was veering towards populism and popular government.[22] Atatürk's application of the principle, however, expanded its usual political and cultural implications to envelop economic and social ideas which, according to Lewis, found expression in several measures of the government.[23] The populist doctrine espoused by Atatürk and his supporters rejected class struggle and proposed populism as a union of classes, combined with the idea that Turkey also had the added problem of the struggle to align itself with 'Western' values.[24] This approach also served as an effective doctrine against the two dominant ideologies of the time – imperialism and communism.

It is suggested that Atatürk viewed the achievement of 'Western civilization' as the single most important factor in consolidating the accomplishment of Turkish independence. Advocating Westernization in the aftermath of the 'anti-Westernism' of the war years was difficult, but Atatürk was seen to have courage in his convictions. As Berkes notes:

> [Atatürk's] drive 'towards the West in spite of the West' by methods contrary to Western liberalism was merely the logical consequence of his

belief that the struggle for national liberation was one between advanced nations and nations that allowed themselves to be exploited by their insistence on their medievalism.[25]

One of the principal methods which Atatürk used to advocate Western ideology was in promoting the sciences, education and secularism, over traditional conservative beliefs. The 1926 Penal Code prohibited propaganda against the principles of secularism and outlawed religious functionaries from criticizing the laws and public authorities during the course of their work.[26] In 1939, the Law of Associations further cemented secularism by prohibiting the formation of religious societies and making it illegal for political parties to engage in religious activities or in the making of religious propaganda.[27]

2.3.2 *The civil code*

The abolition of the Caliphate, as well as the promulgation of numerous secular laws, did much in terms of harmonizing the Turkish legal system with that of Western European countries but there remained the question of drafting a new legal code, which would be suited to the evolved, independent and secular Turkey. The majority view tended towards the unification of all codes and legal provisions on the principles of the Western (civil) legal system. Following two years of debate, a new Civil Code, which was adapted from the Civil Code of Switzerland, was passed before the National Assembly on 17 February 1926.[28]

The passing of the new Code ensured the repeal of the religious *Şeriat* courts, with its rules declared null and void:

> Polygamy, repudiation – all the ancient bars to freedom and dignity of women – were abolished. In their place came civil marriage and divorce, with equal rights for both parties. Most shocking of all, to Muslim opinion, the marriage of a Muslim woman to a non-Muslim man became legally possible, and all adults were given the legal right to change their religion at will.[29]

The Code also governed issues such as commerce, maritime law, criminal law, civil and criminal procedure and created a new judiciary to administer the new laws but, importantly, excluded all provisions of the previous religious and customary legal systems.

2.3.3 *Societal and educational reforms*

Although the primary events in the secularizing process were undoubtedly the abolition of the Caliphate and the overhaul of the legal system, the reforms also extended to the area of 'mores and informal cultural institutions'.[30] Measures were introduced relating to head coverings, for example, and teachers and

students were prohibited from wearing veils, as were the families of government employees while attending public functions. More drastic was the move
to abolish the use of Arabic script. Following years of argument on the
subject, a Committee was appointed in 1928 to draw up a draft alphabet and
report on a new grammar to accompany the script. When the Committee
recommended that ten years be taken for the transition, with the two systems
operating in tandem, Atatürk quickly sought to discredit this idea. On
3 November 1928 a law was passed which prohibited the use of the Arabic
script in public affairs after 1 December 1928.[31]

Public education, as noted earlier, underwent a thorough secularization
process. This was secured in 1928 when the Ministry of Education moved to
eliminate religious instruction from the school curriculum as well as the
teaching of Arabic and Persian and in 1933 a law 'specifying the organization
and functions of the Ministry of Education confirmed secular education and
abolished earlier provisions concerning religious teaching in schools'.[32]

2.3.4 The Constitution of the Republic of Turkey

The republican Constitution, eventually adopted by the Grand National
Assembly in April 1924,[33] avowed the legislative authority of the Assembly
and vested the judicial function in independent courts, while affirming the
sovereignty of the Turkish people. The new 'regime' in Turkey was to be
founded 'upon fundamental reforms, such as the separation of Church and State,
of which the constitution is but a necessary expression'.[34] In the years since the
republican Constitution was first adopted, it has been subject to change and
revision on numerous occasions. In 1928, for example, the provision of the
Constitution declaring that Islam was the state religion was dropped. It has
also undergone more radical changes; in fact since the first modern Constitution
in 1921, there have been three subsequent texts, in 1924, 1961 and 1982, as
well as many amendments. Through subsequent incarnations, the Constitution
has bestowed many rights and freedoms typically associated with modern
democracies and affirmed the democratic secular nature of the state.[35] Some of
the more important amendments are set forth in the following paragraphs.

Following the military coup of 1960, the ruling junta, the National Unity
Committee, appointed a group of lawyers to draft a new Constitution that
'would both act as a legal obstacle to future political abuses and institutional-
ize the military's involvement in politics'.[36] The Commission, chaired by
Professor Sıddık Sami Onar produced a draft which, for various reasons, was
'received with a great deal of doubt and disappointment' and led to the
National Unity Committee convening a Constituent Assembly to prepare the
new Constitution.[37] The Constitution eventually adopted implemented a
series of changes, including the creation of a bicameral parliament, a National
Security Council composed of the armed forces chiefs, whose job was to assist
the cabinet deciding matters of national security, and a range of liberal reforms.
It established a Constitutional Court, legalized trade unions and granted

independence to television and radio stations and universities, in addition to providing for freedom of conscience, political belief, assembly, and press as well as the right to form political parties. However, despite the progressive Constitution of 1961, a series of problems – economic instability, successive weak coalition governments, the invasion of Cyprus in 1974 and the escalation of political violence – affected the country and resulted in the military, again, taking control of the government in 1980.[38] The new junta, the National Security Council (NSC), overturned the government on 12 September 1980 and went on to rule the country for the next three years and was the 'most repressive of Turkey's praetorian governments'.[39] The first steps taken by the NSC were to declare martial law throughout the country, dissolve parliament, ban all political parties and arrest thousands of suspected criminals and political offenders. The progress made in the Constitution of 1961 was soon eroded as the ruling junta forbade trade unions engaging in political activity, took control of universities, radio and television stations and strictly limited freedom of the press.[40] The 1961 Constitution was replaced in 1982 with a much less liberal document that created a unicameral parliament and granted wide-ranging powers to the president and immunity from the scrutiny of other branches of government.[41] When the new Constitution was accepted in November 1982, the leader of the NSC, General Kenan Evren, became president and this was followed by elections to select civilian politicians.[42]

The Constitution of 1982 clearly entrenches the reforms secured by Atatürk and stipulates the indivisible democratic and secular nature of the state. Although amendments have been made to the Constitution since then, this fundamental principle regarding the nature of the state remains. When sweeping amendments were made to the 1982 Constitution in 2001, no amendments were made to Part I ('General Principles'), thereby ensuring no changes to the vision of the Republic.[43] Article 2, in particular, is often quoted by those who rebuff the permissibility of the seemingly strong Islamic sentiments expressed by the current administration.[44] It states:

> The Republic of Turkey is a democratic, secular and social state governed by the rule of law; bearing in mind the concepts of public peace, national solidarity and justice; respecting human rights; loyal to the nationalism of Atatürk, and based on the fundamental tenets set forth in the Preamble.

The Preamble to the Constitution, which Article 2 incorporates, is forthright on the issue of the secular democratic nature of the State and states in part that:

> no protection shall be accorded to an activity contrary to Turkish national interests, the principle of the indivisibility of the existence of Turkey with its state and territory, Turkish historical and moral values or the nationalism, principles, reforms and modernism of Atatürk and that, as

required by the principle of secularism, there shall be no interference whatsoever by sacred religious feelings in state affairs and politics; the acknowledgment that it is the birthright of every Turkish citizen to lead an honourable life and to develop his or her material and spiritual assets under the aegis of national culture, civilization and the rule of law, through the exercise of the fundamental rights and freedoms set forth in this Constitution in conformity with the requirements of equality and social justice ...

The Constitution of Turkey is similar to many other modern constitutions yet Turkey is one of only 11 states with a predominately Muslim population which prescribe secularism in their Constitutions.[45] It contains a section on fundamental rights[46] and a relatively progressive section on economic and social rights and duties.[47] Analysis of both the document and Turkish history led one commentator to conclude that the principles of constitutionalism underlying the republic consist in part of statism and authoritarianism; military involvement in government, the economy and society; Atatürk's principle of populism; and legalism,[48] all of which are not necessarily associated with modern democratic republics. The fervent nationalism[49] that seems to permeate the Constitution is also reflected in the Penal Code and Turkey has recently come under the spotlight for prosecuting writers for insulting Turkey or 'Turkishness'.[50] These and other issues regarding the nature of the state are kept under close scrutiny by the European Commission as Turkey progresses on the path to EU membership.[51]

3 EU–Turkey formalized agreements

Turkey's wish to align itself with Western European institutions and values has been evident since the reforms instigated by Atatürk and outlined above. This commitment has been affirmed by Turkey's decisions to join the Council of Europe in 1949, the North Atlantic Treaty Organization (NATO) in 1955 and the Organization for Security and Cooperation in Europe (OSCE) in 1975. Despite these robust alliances with Western institutions, obtaining membership of the EU is proving to be a complex and difficult undertaking.[52]

Turkey's current position of 'candidate country' is not unique and is also occupied by Croatia and the Former Yugoslav Republic of Macedonia. That said, what has set it apart in its path to accession is the length of its accession bid – a process which has spanned some five decades. This is in contrast to the European Union's Stabilization and Association Process for the countries of the Western Balkans, which has only been in place since 2000.[53] Thus, the contention that 'Turkey, as a model of a pluralistic, secular and a modern state, hopes to be the "beacon of light" for the eastern republics to follow'[54] proved premature, with ten Eastern and Central European countries joining the EU on 1 May 2004 and Turkey (possibly) to follow at some future, yet unknown, date.

Turkey signalled its intention to become part of the EU when it first applied for associate membership of the European Economic Community (EEC) in 1959. The first major milestone occurred in 1963 when Turkey signed the Association Agreement with the European Economic Community. A considerable pause would follow until the next significant formal agreement between the then European Community and Turkey was signed, in the form of the 1995 Customs Union. The Customs Union allowed Turkey preferential access to the European single market and provided for substantial adjustment funds. Subsequently, in October 2004 the European Commission recommended that Turkey had sufficiently fulfilled the criteria necessary to open accession negotiations, which commenced on 3 October 2005.

3.1 The 1963 Association Agreement

The Convention Establishing an Association Between the European Economic Community and Turkey ('Association Agreement' or 'Agreement') was signed on 12 September 1963 in Ankara. This was a result of lengthy negotiations resulting from Turkey's application for associate membership in 1959 and dealt with issues related to trade and the promotion of economic cooperation between Turkey and the European Community. As such, the agreement constitutes the cornerstone upon which EU–Turkey relations are built and aspects of it, such as the Association Council, are still fully functioning. The intention of the agreement was 'to establish closer bonds between the Turkish people and the peoples united in the European Economic Community' and 'to ensure the constant improvement in the standards of living in Turkey and in the European Economic Community by accelerated economic progress and by harmonious development of trade exchanges, as well as to reduce the discrepancy between the economy of Turkey and that of the Member States of the Community'.[55] Concerns related to the Turkish economy in fact proved to be one of the main reasons for delaying the negotiation of an association agreement and indeed remains, ostensibly, one of the causes for unease in the current negotiations for full EU membership.[56] In a memo to the Director-General of the European Council in March 1959 the Commission noted that an association agreement, should Turkey request it, would not be an easy matter. The note concluded:

> Aussi, la conclusion d'un accord bilatéral d'association avec la Turquie – en supposant que ce pays en fasse la demande – ne serait pas chose facile. Un pareil accord apporterais peu à la Communauté, du moins sur le plan économique, tout en lui faisant prendre en charge les difficultés financiers d'un pays dont l'économie n'est pas aisément intégrable au Marché Commun. Il semble donc préférable de traiter le cas de la Turquie dans un cadre plus large, et de contenter, dans l'immédiat, d'aborder le seul problème de la contribution éventuelle de la Communauté à la stabilisation économique de la Turquie.[57]

[As such, the conclusion of a bilateral Association Agreement with Turkey, assuming that Turkey requests such an agreement, would not be an easy matter. Such an agreement would bring little to the Community, at least on the economic front, given the difficulties in integrating such an economy into the Common Market. It would therefore be preferable to look at the bigger picture in Turkey's case and to content ourselves, for the moment, with addressing the problem of the eventual contribution to the stabilisation of Turkey's economy by the Community.]

The Turkish government officially requested an association agreement with the EEC by virtue of two memos submitted to the President of the EEC on 31 July 1959 and the President of the Council of Ministers on 1 August 1959.[58] In its meeting of 11 September 1959 the Council of Ministers granted Turkey's request and authorized the Commission to proceed with exploratory talks.[59] The Commission noted the strong links that already existed between Turkey and the Community and, in expressing a sentiment that appears to have long dissipated from EU–Turkey negotiations, recalled that an association agreement would be in the interests of both Turkey and the Community:

Ils se bornent à rappeler les liens étroits qui existent déjà entre le Six et la Turquie, et concluent que l'Association de celle-ci à la Communauté serait particulièrement intéressante pour l'une et l'autre partie.[60]

[It is worth recalling the strong links that already exist between Turkey and the Six, and concluding that an association of this kind would be particularly interesting for both parties.]

In its consideration of the form that an association agreement with Turkey would take, the Commission outlined that such an association should take the form of a Customs Union ('union douanière') given that the objective of Turkey was the earliest possible integration with the Common Market: 'L'association de la Turquie à la CEE devra revêtir le caractère d'une union douanière, étant donné que l'objectif final de la Turquie est de réaliser le plus tôt possible son adhesion complète au Marché Commun' ['The Association of Turkey with the European Economic Community should take the form of a Customs Union, given that Turkey's objective is the earliest possible integration with the Common Market']. [61] Even at this early stage in Turkey–EEC relations, there were concerns among the Turkish delegates that Turkey was being treated differently to other applicant states.[62] In February 1961, the Turkish representatives requested that they be afforded the same association conditions as those of Greece and also that they be given further financial assistance. The Commission noted:

Conformément à son souci d'égalité de traitement avec la Grèce, la Turquie a revendiqué tout récemment un régime d'association très proche de celui qui serait accordé à la Grèce. Cependant, traitant des problèmes particuliers, elle a demandé une assistance financière beaucoup plus importante, quoique de nature différente, tout en se réservent sur le domain des mécanismes propres à l'union douanière toute liberté en ce qui concerne la suppression des restrictions quantitatives.[63]

[Relating to its concerns regarding equal treatment with Greece, Turkey has recently called for an Association regime similar to that already accorded to Greece. Nevertheless, in response to its own particular problems, Turkey has requested a more substantial financial assistance package and in respect of a Customs Union, freedom concerning the suppression of quantitative restrictions.]

Despite Turkey's request, the Commission concluded that to grant Turkey an association agreement similar to that envisaged for Greece would not be prudent given Turkey's relatively unstable economic and political situation.[64] It was also felt that agreeing to Turkey's demands to have the same agreement as Greece would set a dangerous precedent – 'danger de précédent de l'Accord avec la Grèce, qu'il deviendrait de plus en plus difficile de refuser aux candidats ultérieurs à l'Association'.[65]

Negotiations on the form and content of the Association Agreement continued until 1963 when it was signed and it was intended to be a precursor to a Customs Union, for which it made provision. It was also seen as the basis upon which Turkey would ultimately obtain full EEC membership. Article 2 confirmed its purpose as promoting 'the continuous and balanced strengthening of the commercial and economic relations among the Parties, taking into full account the need to ensure the accelerated development of the economy of Turkey and the raising of the employment level and of the standard of living of the Turkish people'.[66] Article 2(2) proposed that a Customs Union be provided in order to achieve these aims but envisaged that it be implemented in three stages: a preparatory phase during which Turkey would strengthen its economy with the assistance of the Community; a transitional phase in which Turkey would harmonise its economic policies with those of the EEC and during which the progressive establishment of a Customs Union would be assured; and a final phase which would be based on the Customs Union and entail strengthening the coordination of economic policies of the Parties.[67] An Association Council which would ensure the application and development of the system was established under Article 6 of the agreement. The time frame within which the process was set to operate was fixed at five years for the preparatory phase and no more than 12 years for the transitional phase with the final phase constituting the Customs Union itself.

The agreement also referred to issues such as establishing 'gradually' the free movement of workers between Turkey and EEC countries (Article 12) and eliminating the restrictions on the freedom of establishment (Article 13) and on the free performance of services (Article 14). The most crucial part of the agreement, in terms of the proposed development of Turkey's economy, was in its Financial Protocol. In the protocol, Turkey was granted permission to request loans of up to US$175 million from the European Investment Bank 'for financing investment projects which contribute to increasing the productivity of the Turkish economy' and which would contribute to the implementation of the aims of the Convention (Articles 1 and 2). The Financial Protocol was supplemented by further protocols in 1970 and 1977.[68] The Additional Protocol signed between the EC and Turkey in 1970 was particularly important as it gave 'substantial form' to the association and resulted in the EC dropping tariffs and quotas on the majority of industrial goods and granting many agricultural concessions.[69] Chapter I of the Additional Protocol set out the provisions for putting the Customs Union in place and Turkey was encouraged to harmonize its laws in respect of customs matters with those of the member states of the Community.[70]

An economic downturn in Turkey during the 1970s undermined progress towards cooperation,[71] a setback which was compounded by political instability in Turkey during the early 1980s. The military coup of 1980 led to a suspension in relations between the European Community and Turkey and a blocking of the fourth financial protocol. Relations were, however, 'gradually normalised after the restoration of a civilian government in 1983'.[72]

3.2 *Turkey's request for EC membership*

In April 1987, almost 30 years after Turkey first expressed an interest in joining the European Community, a formal application for full accession to the EC was lodged. The Commission's consideration of Turkey's request clearly concluded, however, that it was not an opportune time for further enlargement. The Commission intended to carry out an assessment of the results achieved by the third enlargement of 1 January 1986, which facilitated the accession of Spain and Portugal. Only when this was concluded would it countenance adding further members, and for that reason alone, 'it would be unwise, with regard both to the candidate countries and to the Member States, to envisage the Community becoming involved in new accession negotiations before 1993 at the earliest, except in exceptional circumstances'.[73] The Commission was careful not to rule out Turkey as a potential candidate country; in what is undoubtedly an allusion to an eventual Customs Union, the Opinion notes that the refusal to open negotiations at that stage should be accompanied by proposals 'which would not mean that our partners must abandon their aim of accession and would offer them the possibility of entering into a new stage along the road of a closer association between their country and the Community'.[74]

Unsurprisingly, some of the Commission's fears regarding Turkey in its 1989 Opinion are similar to those that remain prevalent among many member states. For example, the Commission pointed to the geographical area and population of Turkey and the fact that its 'general level of development' was substantially lower than the European average. Although the Commission felt that there had been improvements in economic infrastructure, there continued to be structural disparities, macro-economic imbalances, high levels of industrial protectionism, and a low level of social protection.[75] Economic problems aside, the Commission also remarked on the political situation in Turkey and was critical, in particular, of the continuing dispute with Cyprus. While it noted that there had been developments in the 'human rights situation and in respect for the identity of minorities', it had not yet reached the level required in a democracy.[76] The Opinion concluded with a commitment to completing the Customs Union; resuming financial cooperation, including releasing the resources of the fourth financial protocol which had been blocked following the freeze on Turkey–Community relations after the 1980 military coup; promoting industrial and technological cooperation; and strengthening political and cultural links between the Community and Turkey. It is evident from the language of the Opinion that the relations between Turkey and the European Community were very much seen as a work in progress; the last sentence, for example, speaks of the 'will of the two partners to build their future in common'. Although the EC was not denying Turkey full membership indefinitely, the Opinion delayed the prospect of membership for the foreseeable future. Steps were nonetheless taken to strengthen Turkey–Community relations and, in June 1990, the Commission issued the 'Matutes Package', designed to contribute to the progression of Turkey's economy and allow it to form closer ties with the EC. It offered Turkey the chance to reactivate the Association Agreement through the completion of the Customs Union and the strengthening of political and cultural links.[77] Although a Greek veto prevented the implementation of the 'Matutes Package', 'it formed the main basis for the EU' [*sic*] subsequent relations with Turkey'.[78]

3.3 The Customs Union

The Customs Union between the EC and Turkey, which was provided for in the signing of the Association Agreement in 1963, was eventually finalized by the Community and the Association Council in March 1995 and came into effect on 1 January 1996. The agreement was the EC's first significant Customs Union with a third state and was concerned entirely with the free movement of goods and related issues though other areas such as free movement of persons or services remained covered by existing agreements. The purpose of the agreement was to continue the promotion of the flow of commerce and within a year of the agreement the EU became the main supplier of Turkey's imports whereas Turkey's combined exports and imports grew to US$74 billion.[79]

A substantial part of the agreement addressed the harmonization of Turkey's laws with those of other EC member states. Turkey was obliged 'to adopt legislation, to reach agreements, and to apply Treaty articles equivalent to provisions adopted by the EC' as well as implement identical customs legislation and commercial policy as other member states.[80] The agreement foresaw the complete abolition of tariffs and quotas between the signatories as well as the implementation of a common trade policy. A total of US$2.5 billion was allocated by the EC to help the Turkish economy deal with the implications of the Customs Union, assisting some 7,000 Turkish businesses which faced competition from cheaper European products due to the removal of customs barriers.[81]

The Customs Union, although an economic document, can be assessed as a political agreement to a large extent. Its signing was considered to be a major breakthrough in the pursuit of full EU membership and to a large extent constitutes the most important step in EU–Turkey relations aside from the actual initiation of accession negotiations. At the very least it purported to represent 'an important qualitative step, in political and economic terms', in relations between Turkey and the EU,[82] although it has been criticized for merely increasing Turkey's dependence on the Union without actually increasing its equality within it.[83] A more critical reading of the Customs Union suggests that the EU, having developed its trade links with Turkey and to a certain extent engendered Turkey's reliance upon it as its largest trading partner, has little to gain from an immediate accession. It has also been asserted that the principal expected benefits of the agreement – an increased flow of foreign direct investment, easier access to EU and third-country markets, and further deepening of integration with the Union – have not been delivered.[84]

3.4 *The Luxembourg decision*

The formation of the Customs Union in 1995 would have, understandably, led to hopes that the next step in Turkey's path to EU membership would be the opening of accession talks. However, concerns regarding human rights protections led the European Parliament to slow its cooperation with Turkey in September 1996[85] and at the European Council meeting in Luxembourg in December 1997 the decision was taken to launch accession negotiations with 11 of the 12 applicant countries excluding Turkey. The decision was interpreted by Turkish officials as placing its membership application beneath that of the newer Eastern European applicants. The dejection resulting from this decision is evidenced in Nachmani's observation that:

> [t]he December 1997 EU Luxembourg decision to bypass Ankara and to invite eleven applicant countries to negotiate membership was bitterly perceived in Turkey, as if the Europeans were pushing a strategically significant and loyal colleague away from the West. Ankara regarded the resolution as an unjust, unfair, discriminatory step. Implicitly it put on Turkey the entire onus for the Greco–Cypriot–Kurdish and other minorities' conflicts with Turkey. It was for Turkey to accept her contenders' solutions and not the other way round, hence the pushing of Ankara to the end of the queue. Others were preferred to Turkey, including some who are less advanced, including the Cypriot Greeks. Inviting the

Republic of Cyprus while not solving first the Island's ethnic–political problems, and simultaneously excluding the Turkish Cypriots from the negotiations was particularly galling for Turkey, a clear expression of just how little regard or respect Europe had for her.[86]

Turkey's disappointment with the Luxembourg decision was clear despite the fact that the European Council had endeavoured to frame its decision in terms of confirming Turkey's eligibility to join the EU at some future date, rather than as an exclusion from the accession process altogether. Although the Council did not feel that 'the political and economic conditions allowing accession negotiations to be envisaged' were satisfied in Turkey's case, the decision set out a strategy which would 'prepare Turkey for accession by bringing it closer to the European Union in every field'.[87] The strategy would include development of the Ankara Agreement; intensification of the Customs Union; implementation of financial cooperation; harmonization of Turkey's laws and adoption of the *acquis*; and possible participation in the EU's research and development framework programme.[88] Notwithstanding this seeming attempt to appease Turkish concerns, the decision sent a salutary reminder to Turkey that in order to be considered for full membership, it would also have to fulfil its commitments. The Council noted that strengthening Turkey's links with the EU also depended on:

> that country's pursuit of the political and economic reforms on which it has embarked, including the alignment of human rights standards and practices on those in force in the European Union; respect for and protection of minorities; the establishment of satisfactory and stable relations between Greece and Turkey; the settlement of disputes, in particular by legal process, including the International Court of Justice; and support for negotiations under the aegis of the UN on a political settlement in Cyprus on the basis of the relevant UN Security Council Resolutions.[89]

The decision of the European Council to again reject Turkey's membership bid was not entirely unexpected.[90] Although the EU's refusal to include Turkey with the other 11 states caused little rancour outside of that country, Hugg notes that the conclusions of the Luxembourg summit represented an 'insensitive treatment of the Turkish application'[91] and, from the Turkish point of view, clearly damaged relations between the two parties. Following the decision, the Ankara administration stated that it was suspending dialogue with Europe and no longer wished to discuss issues such as relations with Greece, the situation in Cyprus or human rights.[92] On 4 March 1998 the Commission adopted a 'European Strategy for Turkey' which added substance to the Customs Union and extended it to other sectors and in September 1998 discussions took place between the Commission and the Turkish authorities indicating Turkey's willingness to re-engage with the accession process.[93]

3.5 The Helsinki rapprochement and subsequent developments

A unanimous decision of the European Council meeting in Helsinki in December 1999 to recognize Turkey as a candidate country for EU accession meant that Turkey had finally reached the concluding stages that would lead to full membership. The Council welcomed the positive developments that had taken place in Turkey and its commitment to further reform and harmonization in order to meet the Copenhagen criteria[94] and declared that Turkey was 'a candidate State destined to join the Union on the basis of the same criteria as applied to the other candidate States'.[95] Like other candidate states, the Helsinki decision confirmed that Turkey would benefit from a pre-accession strategy which would stimulate and support its reforms, including 'enhanced political dialogue, with emphasis on progressing towards fulfilling the political criteria for accession with particular reference to the issue of human rights'.[96]

The Council made a number of recommendations with regard to Turkey's preparations for acceding to the Union. In particular it requested that an Accession Partnership be established which would give guidance on the 'priorities on which accession preparations must concentrate in the light of the political and economic criteria and the obligations of a Member State' and that a national programme for the adoption of the *acquis* be formed. In addition, the Commission was asked to establish a single framework for coordinating all sources of EU financial assistance as well as to set forth a process by which Turkey's implementation of the *acquis* would be analysed. The Summit also established the possibility for Turkey's participation in Community programmes and agencies.

The importance of the 1999 conclusions of the Helsinki Council should not be underestimated; coming at a time when expectations in Turkey regarding the EU process were low,[97] the decision was considered to have produced 'a new dynamism and development in EU–Turkey relations with regard to the prospects of membership'.[98] The impetus provided by the decision also revived the Association Council which had been established under the terms of the Ankara Agreement. The EU–Turkey Association Council reconvened in Luxembourg in April 2000 for the first time in three years and adopted decisions on the establishment of subcommittees to monitor progress with the priorities of Accession Partnership and harmonization of legislation and opened negotiations aimed at the liberalization of services and mutual opening of procurement markets between the EU and Turkey.[99]

As a result of the Helsinki decision, the EU Council of Ministers adopted its Decision on the principles, priorities, intermediate objectives and conditions contained in the Accession Partnership with the Republic of Turkey ('Accession Partnership' or 'Partnership') in March 2001 identifying short- and medium-term priorities and objectives in Turkey's progression towards fulfilling the political criteria for accession, with implementation of its provisions to be monitored by Association Agreement bodies who would report regularly to the Commission.[100] The purpose of the Partnership was proffered as establishing the priority areas for further work by Turkey as identified in the European Commission's Regular Report of 2000 as well as setting out the financial means available to assist Turkey implement those priorities and conditions.[101]

Among the issues considered to be short-term priorities for Turkey's progress with respect to enhanced political dialogue and political criteria were a comprehensive settlement of the Cyprus problem; the strengthening of freedom of expression and association guarantees and the strengthening of legal provisions against torture.[102] Short-term expectations also included the implementation of a number of provisions relating to, *inter alia*, economic criteria, employment and social affairs and justice and home affairs. The expectations for Turkey's progress in the medium term were outlined by the Council under the same themes but related to issues which were perceived as being more difficult to implement. That said, the Council stipulated that, where possible, work on implementing the medium-term priorities should also begin in 2001. Medium-term political criteria included the resolution of outstanding border disputes; the development of conditions for the enjoyment of freedom of thought, conscience and religion; and the ratification of the International Covenant on Civil and Political Rights (ICCPR) and the International Covenant on Economic, Social and Cultural Rights (ICESCR). Further areas to be considered medium-term priorities were a review of the Turkish Constitution; the abolition of the death penalty; improvement of detention conditions in prisons; alignment of the constitutional role of the NSC as an advisory body to the government; the lifting of the state of emergency in the provinces in which it remained in the south-east; and the guarantee of cultural diversity and cultural rights for all citizens. [103]

Inherent in the Accession Partnership with Turkey is the principle of conditionality. The Partnership provided for substantial funding for Turkey but only on condition that it respect its commitments under the Association Agreement, satisfy the Copenhagen criteria and meet the specific priorities enunciated in the Partnership.[104] On the basis of the Accession Partnership, Turkey was also expected to formulate a national programme for the adoption of the *acquis*, which was published in 2001 and is more than 500 pages in length.

The programme includes chapters on political criteria, economic criteria, capacity to undertake membership obligations, administrative capacity and global financial assessment of the reforms.[105] In the programme provisions on 'political criteria' the Turkish government undertook to 'closely monitor progress in the areas of human rights, democracy and the rule of law, regularly evaluate the work underway for harmonization with the EU *acquis* and ... take all necessary measures to speed up ongoing work'.[106] The commitments outlined in the programme reflect the areas of concern highlighted in the Accession Partnership and include a pledge to improve guarantees related to freedom of thought and expression, association and peaceful assembly; further develop civil society; eliminate the practice of torture and overhaul practices and procedures related to pre-trial detention.[107] Other notable commitments in the programme relate to strengthening opportunities to redress the consequences of human rights violations; provide training for law enforcement personnel and civil servants on human rights issues; improve the functioning and effectiveness of the judiciary including the state security courts and abolish the death penalty.[108] The programme also concerned issues such as the alleviation of regional disparities and the promotion of cultural life and individual freedoms; the prohibition discrimination by, *inter alia*, adopting the United Nations Convention on the Elimination of All Forms of Racial Discrimination.[109] It also proposed to review the Constitution in light of the European Convention on Human Rights (ECHR) and undertake necessary amendments to other legislation; implement legislation to ratify the ICCPR and ICESCR; eliminate unfavourable conditions in prisons; and lift the state of emergency in the four provinces of the south-east in which it remained.[110]

It is clear from the programme for the adoption of the *acquis* that Turkey would have to implement a host of changes in order to achieve harmonization with the laws of EU member states. The comprehensive list outlined above relates only to political criteria; on the economic front a series of reforms in relation to liberalizing the economy, reducing inflation, restructuring the economy and implementing structural reforms were proposed.[111] Additionally the programme charts a wealth of provisions relating to Turkey's capacity to undertake membership obligations, which includes issues such as the free movement of goods, persons, services and capital, company law, competition and state aid, taxation, social policy and employment, as well as a host of other concerns.

3.6 The opening of accession negotiations

The pre-accession strategy employed by the EU in Turkey's case cannot but seem rigorous on an objective assessment and was not without its critics. Arikan, for example, claims that the EU–Turkey Association framework was used as a basis for a 'containment policy rather than as a basis for preparing Turkey for EU membership,'[112] whereas criticism of the most significant EU–Turkey development prior to accession, the signing of the Customs Union in 1995, has been widespread.[113] Despite this, the conclusion of the European Commission in October 2004, which attested that Turkey had sufficiently fulfilled the criteria necessary to begin accession negotiations, represented a triumph of the 'carrot and stick' approach adopted by the EU in relation to Turkey's membership aspirations.

The European Council endorsed the decision of the Commission in Brussels in December 2004 and committed itself to opening negotiations with Turkey 'without delay'. The Council welcomed the progress that had been made by Turkey in its reform process and expressed its 'confidence that Turkey will sustain that process of reform'.[114] As has always been the case in Turkey's long path to EU accession, there were a number of conditions which first had to be met. Turkey's progress in ensuring 'the irreversibility of the political reform process' would continue to be monitored and, alluding to the continuing Cyprus issue and concomitant fractious Turkey–Greece relations, the Council underlined the need for 'unequivocal commitment to good neighbourly relations'. The Council commended the improvement in Turkey's relations with its neighbours but noted that 'unresolved disputes having repercussions on the accession process should if necessary be brought to the International Court of Justice for settlement'. Furthermore, some six specified pieces of legislation (on Associations, a new Penal Code, establishment of Intermediate Courts of Appeal, a new Code of Criminal Procedure, legislation on the establishment of the Judicial Police and on the Execution of Punishments) would have to be promulgated in Turkey before accession talks could commence.[115]

Formal accession talks with Turkey were opened on 3 October 2005 in Luxembourg, where a negotiating framework was presented outlining the principles governing the negotiations, the substance of the negotiations and negotiating procedures.[116] Even with the opening of accession negotiations, Turkey's membership of the EU is nevertheless not guaranteed; the pace negotiations will take is to depend on 'Turkey's progress in meeting the requirements for membership' with the Commission keeping Turkey's performance under regular review.[117] That accession is not guaranteed is revealed in paragraph 2, which declares that although the shared objective of the negotiations is accession, 'negotiations are an open-ended process, the outcome of which cannot be guaranteed beforehand'. The capacity of the EU to 'include' Turkey is not even assured but rather shall be monitored by the Commission throughout negotiations[118] while Turkey is expected to continue its process of reform and:

> to work towards further improvement in the respect of the principles of liberty, democracy, the rule of law and respect for human rights and fundamental freedoms, including relevant European case law; to consolidate and broaden legislation and implementation measures specifically in relation to the zero tolerance policy in the fight against torture and ill-treatment and the implementation of provisions relating to freedom of expression, freedom of religion, women's rights, ILO standards including trade union rights, and minority rights.[119]

The framework also provides for the suspension of negotiations should Turkey seriously and persistently breach 'the principles of liberty, democracy, respect for human rights and fundamental freedoms and the rule of law on which the Union is founded'.[120] The responsibility for advancement of the negotiations is firmly vested in Turkey and will be measured by its progress in preparing for accession. This progress will be measured against the requirements of the Copenhagen criteria; Turkey's unequivocal commitment to good neighbourly relations; Turkey's support for the efforts to bring about a solution to the Cyprus problem; and the fulfilment of obligations under the Association Agreement.[121] Turkey is also obliged to align progressively its policies towards third countries with those of the EU and its member states and to engage with the Union in an intensive political and civil society dialogue.[122]

The principles governing the accession negotiations elaborate further on Turkey's responsibilities in order to achieve full membership. In terms of the 'substance of the negotiations'[123] outlined in the framework, this refers to Turkey's acceptance of the rights and obligations attached to the Union mainly through the adoption of the *acquis* and 'legislative alignment', i.e. harmonization of its laws with those of EU member states. The financial aspects of Turkey's accession are to be provided for in a financial framework but 'as Turkey's accession could have substantial financial consequences, the negotiations can only be concluded after the establishment of the Financial Framework for the period from 2014 together with possible consequential financial reforms'.[124] Thus, the earliest date that Turkey can achieve full membership of the Union is set at 2014.

Having outlined the historical basis of the Turkey–EU process, the following section moves to discuss the historical backdrop to one of the key factors in this process – the Kurdish minority in Turkey.

4 The Kurdish question in Turkey

The use of political violence in south-east Turkey has a long and tortuous history. The most recent phase began with the formation of the Kurdistan Workers' Party (PKK) in the late 1970s and has, of late, resurfaced following the ending of the PKK ceasefire in mid-2004. While the conflict in the south-east has received relatively little international attention, it has featured in the EU's considerations of Turkey's accession. Since the commencement of the accession process, a resolution to the Kurdish 'problem' has widely been conceived as an unofficial precondition for membership.[125] The impact of the conflict on Turkey's membership aspirations is therefore not insignificant and merits some review.

4.1 Turkish Kurds in the early twentieth century

4.1.1 Unstable peace: from the Treaty of Sèvres[126]
to the Treaty of Lausanne[127]

While the origin of the Kurdish people is uncertain, it is generally held that they have retained their distinctive identity for at least two thousand years.[128] The most modern phase in the history of the Kurds of Turkey can be said to begin in 1918 with the defeat of the Ottoman Empire.[129] At the Paris Peace Conference of 1919, there was general agreement that Turkey's minorities should be 'assured an undoubted security of life and an absolutely unmolested opportunity of autonomous development'.[130] According to McDowall however, the Kurds were unprepared to demonstrate their nationalist aspirations:

> The Kurdish people were ill-prepared to face the challenge of the postwar settlement and the new nationalism ... Internally the Kurds were

weakened by the traditional structures under which most of them continued to live. Tribal loyalty remained far stronger for village or pastoralist
Kurds than new ideas about a Kurdish nation. Aghas were a good deal
more concerned with holding or increasing their position locally than
with uniting with old adversaries in neighbouring valleys, or with those
urban Kurds more capable of negotiating with the outside world.[131]

Despite the evident tribalism, a number of the Kurdish intelligentsia
attempted to establish political groups that would advocate Kurdish independence or autonomy.[132] Of these, Kurdistan Taali Djemiyeti (Society for the
Recovery of Kurdistan) is viewed as the most important, as its leadership and
support were drawn from eminent Kurdish immigrants in Istanbul.[133]
Divisions quickly appeared within the Society between the autonomists, who
wanted to remain allied to the Turks, and the 'independentists', who felt that
they should be striving for complete self-determination. Aware that any independent state promised to the Armenians by the Allies would come at the
expense of the Kurds, a group led by General Sharif Pasha, a former Ottoman
diplomat, cooperated with the Armenians and presented a joint memoran-
dum to the Paris Peace Conference in 1919.[134] With the close of the Peace
Conference and the ensuing Treaty of Sèvres, the Kurds were brought 'closer
to statehood than ever before or since'.[135]

Those parts of the Treaty of Sèvres pertaining to Kurdish statehood
were unambiguous in the proposals for a Kurdish state and affirmed that
a commission of Allied appointees would draft 'a scheme of local autonomy
for the predominantly Kurdish areas lying east of the Euphrates, south of
the southern boundary of Armenia as it may be hereafter determined, and
north of the frontier of Turkey with Syria and Mesopotamia'.[136] Article 64 of
the treaty seemingly rubber-stamped the idea of an independent Kurdish
state:

> If within one year of the coming into force of the present Treaty the
> Kurdish peoples within the areas defined in Article 62 shall address
> themselves to the Council of the League of Nations in such a manner as to
> show that a majority of the population of these areas desires independence
> from Turkey, and if the Council then considers that these peoples are
> capable of such independence and recommends that it should be granted
> to them, Turkey hereby agrees to execute such a recommendation, and to
> renounce all rights and title over these areas.
>
> The detailed provisions for such renunciation will form the subject
> of a separate agreement between the Principal Allied Powers and
> Turkey.
>
> If and when such renunciation takes place, no objection will be raised
> by the Principal Allied Powers to the voluntary adhesion to such an inde-
> pendent Kurdish State of the Kurds inhabiting that part of Kurdistan
> which has hitherto been included in the Mosul vilayet.

The guarantees provided by the treaty were to remain strictly illusory in nature, as a lack of political will ensured that the provisions of the treaty relating to the Kurds remained unenforced. It has been suggested that 'Britain was the only one of the powers with more than a passing interest in seeing Kurdistan on the map'.[137] In any case, events in Turkey quickly overcame what little impetus was provided by the treaty. Atatürk's revolt in Anatolia was supported by a significant number of Kurds, who indicated their 'identity with the other Muslims of Anatolia and their fears of falling within an Armenian, and therefore Christian, state'.[138] With Atatürk's defeat of the Greeks in 1922 and the elimination of practically all of the remaining Christians in Anatolia, the Allies were forced to renegotiate the settlement of 1920.[139]

A new peace conference was arranged for November 1922, culminating in the Treaty of Lausanne in July 1923. Under Atatürk's direction, when the agreement was signed, Turkey had achieved all of its demands, apart from the territorial claim over Mosul.[140] The treaty, unlike its predecessor at Sèvres, contained no provisions relating to Kurdish autonomy or the possibility of a Kurdish State and, in fact, contained no references to the Kurds whatsoever. The dispute between Britain and Turkey over Mosul was referred by Great Britain to the Council of the League of Nations for settlement.

The Kurds sought to demonstrate their anger at the loss of Kurdistan and the move to incorporate Mosul into either Iraq or Turkey 'by way of an independence movement led by Sheikh Mahmud, which ultimately was suppressed by aerial bombardment of the British Royal Air Force'.[141] The only reference to the rights of Kurds came in the decision of the Commission of Enquiry, established under the auspices of the Council of the League of Nations, to inquire into whether or not Mosul should be part of Iraq or Turkey. The Commission, siding with Great Britain in deeming that the *vilayet* should become part of Iraq, attached two conditions, one of which stated that:

> regard must be paid to the desires expressed by the Kurds that officials of Kurdish race should be appointed for the administration of their country, the dispensation of justice and teaching in the schools, and that Kurdish should be the official language of all these services.[142]

The Council of the League of Nations, following the request for an advisory opinion from the Permanent Court of International Justice,[143] adopted the proposals set out in the report of the Commission of Enquiry in December 1925 and invited the British Government to:

> lay before the Council administrative measures which will be taken with a view to securing for the Kurdish populations mentioned in the report of the Commission of Enquiry the guarantees regarding local administration recommended by the Commission in its final conclusions.[144]

It took Turkey less than a year to accept the decision of the Council of the League of Nations and to settle the issue of borders. The Angora Treaty between Great Britain, Iraq and Turkey established cross-border control of Kurdish activity by stipulating that Asian States would refrain from corresponding in an official or political manner with chiefs, sheikhs or other tribal members who were nationals of the other state and in the territory of the other state and not permit in the frontier zone any organization for propaganda or meeting directed against either state.[145]

4.2 'Turkification' and Kurdish rebellion

Atatürk, having previously stressed the unity of Turks and Kurds and even the idea that the Kurdish region would regain some sort of special status, appeared to have revised his position by January 1923, stating:

> Those in our national borders are only a Kurdish majority in limited places. Over time, by losing their population concentration, they have settled with Turkish elements in such a way that if we try to draw a border on behalf of the Kurds we have to finish with Turkishness and Turkey, for example in the regions of Erzerum, Erzinjan, Sivas and Kharput – and do not forget the Kurdish tribes on the Konya desert. This is why instead of considering Kurdishness in isolation, some local autonomies will be established in accordance with our Constitution. Therefore, whichever provinces are predominantly Kurd will administer themselves autonomously. But, apart from that, we have to describe the people of Turkey together. If we do not describe them thus, we can expect problems particular to themselves ... it cannot be correct to try to draw another border [between Kurds and Turks]. We must make a new programme.[146]

While there is no evidence of a willingness to grant any sort of political power to the Kurds in this statement, there is still a certain amount of recognition of a distinct Kurdish identity. McDowall notes that a major shift was to take place during the following four weeks, '[w]hen Kemal's speech to the Izmir Economic Congress (17 February 1923) was published, all reference to the Kurds had been excised'.[147] Among the reasons for this change in policy was the fact that the social and political traditions of Kurdistan presented an obstacle to Atatürk's idea of a modern state built on the European model. Additionally, the disruptions in Kurdistan in 1922 and the estrangement of some Kurdish chiefs, as well as the fear that the resolution of the territorial battle over Mosul, in which the Kurds of southern Kurdistan gained a certain degree of autonomy, were a threat to the country's borders.[148]

The programme of 'Turkification' was aggressively pursued by Atatürk from 1923 onwards. In the elections for the new Grand National Assembly in the summer of 1923, it was felt in the Kurdish areas that the new candidates fielded and returned had 'been nominated by the government rather than elected by the people',[149] thereby exiling Kurdish dissent. Gradually, senior administrative appointments in Kurdistan were all filled by Turks and any references to Kurdistan were deleted from official documents, and Kurdish place names were replaced by Turkish ones. By 1924 the use of Kurdish in an official capacity was banned, effectively depriving people in Kurdish areas of education. The abolition of the Caliphate in 1924:

> cut the last ideological tie Kurds felt with Turks. The closure of the religious schools, the *madrasas* and *kuttabs*, removed the last remaining source of education for most Kurds. By stripping Turkey of its religious institutions, Mustafa Kemal now made enemies of the very Kurds who had helped Turkey survive the years of the trial, 1919–22. These were the religiously-minded, the shaykhs and the old Hamidiya aghas who had genuinely believed in the defence of the caliphate.[150]

In addition to the import of the abolition of the Caliphate, the subsequent 'turkification' and secularization of the education system meant that education was only provided in the Turkish language, which in turn required the abolition of any foundation or institution espousing a separate Kurdish identity. Kurdish associations, schools, religious groupings and publications were prohibited.

These radical changes to the fabric of Kurdish society coupled with 'the threat to Kurdish identity, and the threat to the traditional order of *aghas* and *shaikhs* (through the destruction of the Sultanate and Caliphate) served to unify many Kurds of different viewpoints'.[151] For the first time a Kurdish movement included not only the politically astute members of the Kurdish intellectual elite, but also *aghas* and *shaikhs*, who, in turn, mobilized large numbers of the Kurdish population. It is estimated that from 1924–1938, no less than seventeen Kurdish uprisings took place.[152]

In the aftermath of the failed rebellion in 1925, the area of the south-east was subjected to an 'extensive pacification programme',[153] during which it is estimated that between 40,000 and 250,000 peasants died, and hundreds of villages were destroyed.[154] This programme of 'pacification' continued until the end of 1927 and included mass deportations with the intention of stripping the area of its Kurdish population. Martial law was declared in the south-east in February 1925.[155]

4.3 Kurds in the post-Atatürk Turkey: an end to rebellion?

Following the successive defeats of Kurdish uprisings, a period of relative calm ensued for nearly thirty years. The measures engaged by the Turkish authorities during the rebellions – massacres, deportations, and militarization – understandably had a marginalizing effect on the Kurdish population, compelling them to a submissive silence.[156] The extent of the forced deportations is evidenced in McDowall's estimate that more than one million Kurds (including *aghas* and *sheihks*) had been forcibly displaced between 1925 and 1938.[157] In the aftermath of the Second World War, both Turks and Kurds voted overwhelmingly for the Democratic Party; thus the rule of Atatürk's Republican People's Party finally came to an end in 1950 in the first free general election. The election of the Democratic Party, which had been founded by Adnan Menderes and Celal Bayar,[158] coupled with the creation of new parliamentary parties, 'were undoubtedly a considerable move forwards for Turkey as a whole and even for Kurdistan, which was the Party's main stronghold'.[159] Votes from the Kurds were rewarded with a relaxation in the police and military repression in the south-east. Exiled *sheihks*, landlords and *aghas* were allowed to return home and recover their goods and lands in return for their parliamentary support. Many were elected to Parliament and some became Ministers, while infrastructure, schools and social facilities were improved in the region.[160] The new Kurdish elite 'espoused a new philosophy called *doğuculuk* ('Eastism') which advocated economic development in the neglected east'.[161] Kendal notes that the first group of 'Eastists' were based in Diyarbakır and published a daily newspaper in Turkish, in which they criticized the underdevelopment and lack of infrastructure in the east of the country. In 1959, however, the paper's publishers and those classed as 'Kurdists' (approximately 50 leaders of the movement), were arrested and imprisoned.[162]

It is worth noting that Turkey's position as a strategic ally of the United States had its origins in the Marshall Plan of 1948.[163] Under the direction of Menderes, Turkey amassed a sizable foreign debt and by 1957 was on the verge of bankruptcy. In exchange for aid from the Americans:

> Turkey sent thousands of Turkish soldiers (including many Kurds) to fight in Korea, joined NATO on February 18, 1952, turned itself into the advance post of imperialism below the southern flank of the USSR and, on February 26, 1954, authorized the US to set up bases and listening posts throughout the country, Kurdistan included.[164]

The economic instability in addition to the deep resentment within the army regarding its loss of power over the political life of the country culminated in a military coup in 1960.

4.3.1 *The military coup of 1960 and repercussions*

On 27 May 1960, Turkey was to undergo a military *coup d'état*. The catalyst for the insurgency stemmed from a belief in the army that the old revolutionary ideas of Kemalism had been abandoned, resulting in the country being governed for a year and a half by a 'Committee of the National Front made up of the main participants of the coup'.[165] Following elections in 1961, the Committee allowed a civilian government to take over once more.

The introduction of a new Constitution followed the elections and, according to McDowall, had the effect of improving the situation of the Kurdish community, although not before thousands had been deported by the military.[166] The new Constitution 'allowed freedom of expression, of the press and of association. Kurds were able to express their dissent through Turkish structures, organizations, publications and so forth, writing in Turkish and even in Kurdish concerning the history, folklore and economic problems of the "East", even though the authors risked imprisonment for their views'.[167] Conditions further improved for the Kurds with the formation of a new cabinet in 1962. Azizoglu, leader of the New Turkey Party and a Kurd from Diyarbakır, was appointed Minister of Health.[168] Although he was eventually accused of 'regionalism' and Kurdish nationalism, and forced to tender his resignation, during his tenure Azizoglu had 'more hospitals and dispensaries built in Kurdistan than all previous governments put together'.[169] Additionally, by 1963 the right to strike and form collective agreements had been recognized as being protected under the new Constitution although a ban on forming any regionalist associations which might divide the nation was maintained.

Kendal refers to 'Eastism', as 'a transitory period in the rebirth of the Kurdish national movement'.[170] This 'rebirth' was also influenced, in no small part, by the events taking place in Iraqi Kurdistan. The November 1960 armed Kurdish uprising, led by Mustafa Barzani, undoubtedly had a huge effect on the subsequent radicalization of Kurdish nationalists in Turkey; an outcome which the military had feared from the outset of the uprising in Iraq. General Gursel, leader of the junta, issued a pre-emptive warning to any Kurds of Turkey who might be tempted to imitate their neighbouring rebels in 1960: '[i]f the mountain Turks do not keep quiet, the army will not hesitate to bomb their towns and villages into the ground. There will be such a bloodbath that they and their country will be washed away.'[171] In 1965 a covert party called the Kurdistan Democratic Party (PKDT) was established in solidarity with Barzani's nationalist movement. Its supporters tended to be traditionalists, much like Barzani's supporters in Iraq, whereas, unlike the Turkish Workers' Party,[172] who were 'leftists', the PKDT were 'explicitly separatist'.[173]

Throughout the 1960s both Kurdish and leftist parties became increasingly vocal and amassed large numbers of supporters. In response, the government accelerated its campaign to eliminate subversive activity. This led to many of the Kurdish–Turkish journals that had begun publication in the mid-1960s being banned in 1967, and their editors arrested.[174] As the repression of the Demirel government increased from 1967 onwards, 'with the use of special commando groups to patrol Kurdistan and intimidate the population and ransack the homes of suspects, Kurdish students and militants (apparently close to the Turkish Workers' Party) called for mass demonstrations, which took place on 3 August 1967 … the first expression of Kurdish anger for 30 years'.[175] These demonstrations were encouraged by the publication in April 1967 of an anonymous article in the Turkish magazine *Ötüken* stating that the Kurds were a backward people devoid of history and culture, who wanted to carve Turkey into pieces.[176] Despite calls from Kurds to punish the author and ban the magazine for its violation of Section 12 of the Turkish Constitution, which proclaimed the equality of all citizens, no action was taken.

The demonstrations, which attracted up to 25,000 people in some cities, were violently suppressed by the Turkish authorities. In response to the oppression, an Organization of Revolutionary Kurdish Youth (DDKO) established the Eastern Revolutionary Cultural Centres in 1969, with the aim of promoting civil liberties and raising awareness of the social deprivation in the east of the country. With an increase in leftist groups in Kurdistan, confrontations with right-wing groups, often backed by the police, also increased, as did the number of political murders.[177] The popular Turkish Workers' Party became the first legal party to recognize the plight of the Kurds at its Fourth Congress in October 1970 when it tabled a motion on the Kurdish question. This resolution led to the party being banned.[178]

4.3.2 Formation of the Partiya Karkerên Kurdistan

By the end of the 1960s it was illegal to use the Kurdish language and a 1967 decree declared it 'illegal and forbidden to introduce to, or distribute in, the country, materials in the Kurdish language of foreign origin in any form published, recorded, taped or material in similar form', thereby prohibiting the promotion of the language in any guise.[179] In March 1971, the government was again overthrown by the military. Thousands were arrested, with widespread reports of murder and torture, particularly in the east, where there had been claims of an impending Kurdish uprising. Oppression of the Kurdish population was to continue 'erratically' throughout the 1970s.[180]

The most significant event in the history of modern Kurdish nationalism occurred in 1974 with the formation of the Partiya Karkerên Kurdistan (Kurdistan Workers' Party: PKK). At this time Abdullah Öcalan was working in the Ankara Higher Education Union and it was through this work that he was provided 'with the foundations of an ideological, political and strategic outlook'.[181] In 1974 he met with other militant Kurdish nationalists to draw up a plan for the formation of a distinctly Kurdish leftist organization, unaffiliated with Turkish leftist groups, all of which, it was felt, had ignored the Kurds' specific needs.[182] This was the first step in the formation of a liberation movement, known initially as Ulusal Kurtuluş Ordusu (National Liberation Army). Öcalan was elected as its leader. Initially the group was an ideological one, with a revolutionary youth wing formed with the aim of attracting Kurdish youths and intellectuals. During the period between 1978 and 1980 the party reorganized itself and refined its politics, to allow the group to become a 'political force'.[183] The organization would, in time, evolve into a political party – the PKK, which was officially formed on 27 November 1978, declaring itself the 'new organization of the proletariat of Kurdistan'.[184]

The formation of the PKK came just before what Yildiz has characterized as '[t]he most devastating period of recent history for the Turkish Kurds'.[185] Following yet another military *coup d'état* in 1980, martial rule was imposed in south-east Turkey. The limited concessions granted the Kurds under the 1961 Constitution were annulled with the new 1982 Constitution. The leader of the junta, General Evren, enforced the ban on the Kurdish language even more strictly than before, and ordered the raiding of villages and homes in the south-east and had tens of thousands of Kurds arrested. The situation was deemed so grave that, at this time, almost two-thirds of the Turkish army was deployed in the south-east.[186] By 1984 the PKK had declared a war of national liberation against the Turkish state. Intense conflict ensued during the period 1984–99, when an estimated US$120 billion was spent on military containment of the conflict alone and more than 40,000 people were killed.[187]

5 Summary

The preceding sections have addressed the historical background to Turkey's EU application, in particular the historical formation of the Turkish state, the logistics of Turkey's formal accession process thus far and the Kurdish question. The major milestones have been the signing of the Association Agreement in 1963, which constituted Turkey's first major agreement with the EEC, the agreement of the Customs Union in 1995 and the decision to begin accession negotiations in 2004.

Since the commencement of negotiations, Turkey's ambition of achieving full membership suffered a further setback in November 2006, when the European Commission recommended that eight of the 35 chapters in Turkey–EU negotiations for membership be suspended, ostensibly due to Turkey's failure to meet the requirements to normalize trade relations with the Republic of Cyprus. The Commission outlined that:

> Turkey has not fully implemented the Additional Protocol to the Ankara Agreement, and that restrictions to the free movement of goods, including restrictions on means of transport, remain in force ... The Commission recommends that the Intergovernmental Conference on Accession with Turkey should not open negotiations on chapters covering policy areas relevant to Turkey's restrictions as regards the Republic of Cyprus until the Commission confirms that Turkey has fulfilled its commitments.[188]

Despite Turkey's stated concerns that the Cyprus dispute is being used as a smokescreen for more fundamental objections to its place within the Union,[189] it nevertheless remains a fact that accession negotiations cannot progress until the issue is resolved (or at the very least until Turkey extends the provisions of the Customs Union to the Republic of Cyprus). In the intervening period, however, (and in response to the Commission's Reports detailing a slowdown in the reform process in Turkey), the Turkish government presented its

Programme for Alignment with the EU *Acquis* 2007–2013 on 17 April 2007. The programme, which contains the necessary legislative preparations to be completed within the period between 2007 and 2013 on the 35 chapters that constitute the basis of the accession negotiations, was prepared in consultation with 'all the Turkish public insitutions [*sic*] involved in the accession process, and also includes the contributions of non-governmental organisations'.[190] The document is intended to constitute 'a comprehensive roadmap which will serve as a guide for realising the reforms which [Turkish] people need in their daily lives, as well as a to-do-list for [Turkey's] legislative efforts towards alignment with the EU acquis leading up to 2013'.[191]

With regard to Kurdish–State relations, until recently the response of the Turkish authorities to the conflict in the south-east of the country was a purely military one. There have been widespread allegations of human rights abuses perpetrated by both sides to the conflict[192] and a reluctance on the part of successive Turkish administrations to engage with the underlying causes of the conflict. However, with the pro-EU reform process under way in Turkey and a peaceful resolution to the conflict in the south-east posited as an important factor in the accession process, the time would appear ripe for a renewal of peace negotiations. In a speech given in Diyarbakır in August 2005, Prime Minister Erdoğan became the first Turkish prime minister to acknowledge publicly that Turkey had a 'Kurdish problem', noting that Turkey had made grave mistakes in the past and resolved to solve the problem through democracy.[193] As well as Turkish interests in a negotiated settlement to the conflict, EU interests in securing a peaceful settlement to the conflict in the south-east are numerous. Tocci suggests:

> As such, EU actors have had a long-standing interest in Turkey's democracy and human rights, its internal stability and its foreign policy orientation, i.e. all issues which have been influenced by the Kurdish question. The EU's specific concern with Turkey's Kurds has also been fed by the Kurdish Diaspora in Europe, which since the 1990s has activated itself to put the Kurdish question on the European agenda. Fears of rising Kurdish and Turkish immigration further magnified EU interests in a peaceful stabilization of the Kurdish question. Finally and most recently, EU interests have resurfaced with the resumption of PKK violence in Turkey, the war in Iraq, the demography and status of the oil-rich city of Kirkuk, and the role of the Iraqi Kurds in the survival or dissolution of the country.[194]

It has even been suggested that the EU is in fact 'politically and morally obliged to facilitate a just and peaceful resolution of the Kurdish issue'.[195] The area of conflict resolution is one which features strongly as an objective of the EU's foreign policy, and it is therefore axiomatic that the EU would wish to see a peaceful resolution to the conflict in the south-east.[196]

While it is undoubtedly true that the EU has a large part to play in pushing Turkey towards resolving the conflict in the south-east, it is also true that the Union is not as robust in its approach to the issue as it was at the initial stages of Turkey's membership bid. Whereas resolution of the conflict was seen as an imperative in 1998,[197] it has been posited that a review of more recent EU literature tends to 'skirt around the Kurdish issue', and there has been 'a tendency to tone down references to the Kurds'.[198] Indeed the recent escalation in the conflict in the south-east and ensuing cross-border operations in Northern Iraq conducted by the Turkish military met with a relatively muted response from the EU.[199] Although progress reports of the European Commission continue to call for an overall improvement in Turkey's human rights protections, it may, nonetheless, be unrealistic to suggest that even Turkey's EU aspirations would be enough to provide an immediate solution to the protracted conflict in the south-east. Despite recent pronouncements of the current administration to deal with the Kurdish problem and the launching of a 'Kurdish initiative' in 2009, a lasting resolution to the conflict remains elusive.[200] This reality was highlighted in December 2009 when Turkey's Constitutional Court voted to ban the main Kurdish political party, the Democratic Society Party (DTP), dispelling hopes of a democratic solution in the near future.[201] Nonetheless, the decision to open formal accession negotiations with Turkey in December 2004 suggests that the EU is satisfied that Turkey's treatment of the Kurds meets the protection of human rights and minority standards enunciated in the Copenhagen criteria of 1993.[202]

Having set out the process by which Turkey has reached its current position as an EU 'candidate country', the next chapter turns to the question of fundamental human rights protections in Turkey and the impact that the carrot–stick approach employed by the EU in relation to this question has had on both the implementation of reforms in Turkey and the accession process thus far. This approach is one that has been engaged by the EU in previous accessions but, it is asserted, in Turkey's case, a lack of concomitant progress on the road to membership may result in a stalling of the domestic reforms ostensibly required to achieve accession.

Notes

1 See, for example, B. Stedman, 'The Republic of Turkey', Va. L. Reg. N.S., 13 (1927–8), 725–41, 738, noting that Turkey 'has ceased to regulate its life by the next world, but has come down to earth by adopting the European mentality and abrogating that of Asia'.

2 See, for example, W. Schäuble, 'Talking Turkey: Is Europe Ready for a Muslim Member?', Foreign Aff., 83 (2004), 134–7, 136, asserting that the Europeans are guilty of having ignored, for too long, a debate about the ultimate limits of EU extension and about the meaning of European identity.

3 See, for example, D. A. Kanarek, 'Turkey and the European Union: The Path to Accession', Colum. J. Eur. L., 9 (2003), 457–74.

4 A modified version of this section appears as E. Hughes, 'The Secularism Debate and Turkey's Quest for European Union Membership', *Religion and Human Rights*, 3 (2008), 15–32.

5 Atatürk was born Mustafa Paşa in 1881 and, in accordance with Turkish custom of the time was given the second name of 'Kemal' by his teacher at military school. The Turkish Grand National Assembly presented him with the name 'Atatürk', meaning 'father of the Turks' on 24 November 1934. For the purposes of clarity, he will be referred to as 'Atatürk' throughout this study.

6 See S. Zubaida, 'Trajectories of Political Islam: Egypt, Iran and Turkey', in D. Marquand and R. L. Nettler (eds), *Religion and Democracy* (Oxford: Blackwell Publishers, 2000), 60–79, 71, claiming that the '"secular" Turkish Republic is imbued and obsessed with religion'. See also İ Turan 'Religion and Political Culture in Turkey', in R. Tapper (ed.), *Islam in Modern Turkey: Religion, Politics and Literature in a Secular State* (London and New York: I.B. Tauris & Co. Ltd, 1991), 31–55, 52 concluding that religion in Turkey is also 'an underlying dimension of membership in a political community, it has a moderate role on the achievement of political legitimacy, it is one of the bases of political ideology, and finally, it is a source of values which affect political goal-setting and behaviour in society'.

7 See R. Dehousse, 'The Unmaking of a Constitution: Lessons From the European Referenda', Constellations, 13(2) (2006), 151–64 and I. Black 'Doubting North Wins Battle to Leave God Out of It', *Guardian*, 29 May 2003.

8 See J. Pettifer, *The Turkish Labyrinth: Atatürk and the New Islam* (London: Penguin Books, 1998), 165 noting that in 1989, Jacques Delors, then EC president, stated that 'Europe was a product of Christianity, of Roman law and of Greek humanism'.

9 F. Ahmad, *The Making of Modern Turkey* (London and New York: Routledge, 1993), 15.

10 *Ibid.*, 49.

11 Landau notes that '[w]hat is most impressive about Atatürk as reformer is the totality of his approach, his drive to institute change in practically all areas of life, from the roots up. His step-by-step implementation of these objectives testifies to a sense of realism and excellent timing: for him reforms were the art of the possible' (see J. M. Landau 'Introduction: Atatürk's Achievement: Some Considerations', in J. M. Landau (ed.), *Atatürk and the Modernization of Turkey* (Colorado, CO: Westview Press, 1984), xi.

12 B. Lewis, *The Emergence of Modern Turkey* (Oxford: Oxford University Press, 2nd edn, 1975), 253–4.

13 *Ibid.*, 254.

14 J. Allain, *International Law in the Middle East: Closer to Power than Justice* (Surrey, UK: Ashgate Publishing Ltd, 2004), 19.

15 Ahmad, *Making of Modern Turkey*, 51.

16 N. Berkes, *The Development of Secularism in Turkey* (New York: Routledge, 2nd edn, 1998), 443.

17 See *ibid.*, 451–60.

18 The last Padişah of the Ottoman Dynasty had been deposed as Sultan but he remained the Caliph. On 17 November 1922, he 'placed himself under the British protection as the Caliph of all Muslims of the world' and left Turkey. See Berkes, *Development of Secularism*, 451.

19 *Ibid.*, 452.

20 *Ibid.*, 460.

21 See P. J. Magnarella, 'The Legal, Political and Cultural Structures of Human Rights Protections and Abuses in Turkey', D.C.L. J. Int'l L. & Prac., 3 (1994), 439–68, 442.

22   Lewis, *Emergence of Modern Turkey*, 256.
23   *Ibid.*, 465.
24   Berkes, *Development of Secularism*, 462.
25   *Ibid.*, 464.
26   The provision prohibiting propaganda against secularism was contained in Article 163 of the Code. See *ibid.*, 466.
27   *Ibid.*
28   Lewis, *Emergence of Modern Turkey*, 272. See also V. Versan, 'The Kemalist Reform of Turkish Law and Its Impact', in Laundau, *Atatürk*, 247–51.
29   Lewis, *Emergence of Modern Turkey*, 273. Attesting to the progressive nature of the code, Stedman notes that '[t]he new code is practically a translation of the Swiss Civil Code, which the Grand National Assembly adopted because it was the most modern and most democratic of any European code and had been successfully applied to the three separate racial groups in Switzerland, the purest democracy in the world. The liberality of its provisions is evidenced by the fact that it even allows a Moslem to change his faith or marry a person of a different religion' ('Republic of Turkey', 729).
30   Berkes, *Development of Secularism*, 473.
31   *Ibid.*, 476.
32   *Ibid.*, 477.
33   The 1924 Constitution amended the Constitution of 1921 to confirm that the form of government of Turkey was a republican one.
34   E. Mead Earle, 'The New Constitution of Turkey', *Political Science Quarterly*, 40(1) (1924), 73–100, 74.
35   The principle of secularism was enshrined in the Constitution on 5 February 1937.
36   Magnarella, Legal, Political and Cultural Structures'.
37   E. Özbudun and Ö. F. Gençkaya *Democratization and the Politics of Constitution-Making in Turkey* (Budapest: Central European University Press, 2009), 14.
38   Magnarella, 'Legal, Political and Cultural Structures', 443.
39   *Ibid.*, 445.
40   *Ibid.*
41   For example, Article 105 of the new Constitution stated: 'No appeal shall be made to any legal authority, including the Constitutional Court, against the decisions and orders signed by the President of the Republic on his own initiative'; and Article 125 stated: 'The acts of the President of the Republic in his own competence and the decisions of the Supreme Military Council are outside the scope of judicial review' (*ibid.*, 445–6).
42   *Ibid.*, 446.
43   The most extensive amendments came in October 2001when Law No. 4709 of 13 October 2001 introduced amendments to the Preamble and 34 provisions of the Constitution of 1982. See E. Örücü, 'The Turkish Constitution Revamped?', *European Public Law*, 8(2) (2002), 201–18, 201–2, noting that the amendments could be regarded as a radical departure from the 1982 Constitution, a partial return to the more progressive Constitution of 1961, an attempt to further integrate into Europe but also as 'paying lip service to the demands of the European Union'.
44   See for example I. Traynor, 'Turkish General Warns Levels of Islamism "Alarming"', *Irish Times*, 27 September 2006, noting that General Ilker Basbug, then chief of land forces, warned the Erdoğan government that the danger of Islamism in

the country was reaching 'alarming' levels. General Basbug is quoted as having stated that the 'Turkish armed forces have always taken sides and will continue to do so in protecting the national state, the unitary state and the secular state'.

45 The other 10 countries are Burkina Faso, Chad, Guinea, Mali, Niger, Senegal, Azerbaijan, Kyrgyzstan, Tajikistan and Turkmenistan. See T. Stahnke and R. C. Blitt, 'The Religion–State Relationship and the Right to Freedom of Religion or Belief: A Comparative Textual Analysis of the Constitutions of Predominantly Muslim Countries', Geo. J. Int'l L., 36 (2005), 947–1078, 955.

46 Part II Chapter II of the Constitution is entitled 'Rights and Duties of the Individual' and contains provisions relating to the right to life, the prohibition of forced labour, the prohibition of torture and personal liberty and security. Other rights and freedoms typically guaranteed in constitutions such as freedom of assembly, expression and religion are also included in this section.

47 Part II Chapter III includes provisions on the protection of the family, education rights, land ownership, labour rights, health services and housing. Article 65 (as amended on 17 October 2001) states: 'The State shall fulfil its duties as laid down in the Constitution in the social and economic fields within the capacity of its financial resources, taking into consideration the priorities appropriate with the aims of these duties.'

48 Magnarella, 'Legal, Political and Cultural Structures', 447–9.

49 Although it can be argued that all constitutions are by their very nature fervently nationalist, the Turkish Constitution is particularly so. For example, the Preamble (as amended on 17 October 2001) refers to Atatürk, the founder of the Republic as an 'immortal leader' and an 'unrivalled hero'. The Preamble recognizes 'Turkish historical and moral values or the nationalism, principles, reforms and modernism of Atatürk' as well as the fact that 'all Turkish citizens are united in national honour and pride, in national joy and grief, in their rights and duties regarding national existence, in blessings and in burdens'.

50 High-profile cases include those of Orhan Pamuk and Hrant Dink, see below Chapter 2, Section 2.

51 See below Chapter 2, Section 1.

52 Paragraph 13 of the EU–Turkey Negotiating Framework provides that 2014 is the earliest date in which the financial aspects of Turkey's accession can be concluded and therefore the earliest date that Turkey can become a full member. Accession negotiations are 'open-ended' and thus there is no guarantee that Turkey will ever accede to the Union.

53 See 'The Declaration of the Zagreb Summit', 24 November 2000.

54 T. Ataöv 'Turkey, the CIS and Eastern Europe', in C. Balkir and A. M. Williams (eds), *Turkey and Europe* (London and New York: Pinter Publishers Ltd, 1993), 191–219, 193.

55 Preamble to the Convention Establishing an Association Between the European Economic Community and Turkey, signed at Ankara, Turkey 12 September 1963. The Agreement entered into force on 1 December 1964.

56 This study deals with the legal and political aspects of Turkey's membership bid to the neglect of the economic aspects. There is, however, a wealth of literature on the subject. See, for example, Z. Y. Herschlag, *The Contemporary Turkish Economy* (London: Routledge, 1988); I. Saǎba, 'Central–Local Fiscal Relations in Turkey: A Technical Analysis of Fiscal Equalization', *Turkish Studies*, 2(2) (2001), 121–42;

'Implementing the Economic Criteria of EU Membership: How Difficult is it for Turkey?', in A. Çarkoğlu and B. Rubin (eds), *Turkey and the European Union: Domestic Politics, Economic Integration and International Dynamics* (London: Frank Cass, 2003), 219–45; A. M. Lejour, R. A. de Mooij and C. H. Capel, 'Assessing the Economic Implications of Turkish Accession to the EU' (2004) CPB Netherlands Bureau for Economic Policy Analysis, no. 56; N. B. Gültekin and K. Yilmaz, 'The Turkish Economy Before the EU Accession Talks', in M. Lake (ed.), *The EU and Turkey: A Glittering Prize or a Millstone?* (London: Federal Trust, 2005), 61–79 and J. T. McCarthy, 'Turkey's Financial Sector: A Practitioner's View of a Work in Progress', in Lake, *EU and Turkey*, 79–87; A Hadjit and E. Moxon-Browne, 'Foreign Direct Investment in Turkey: The Implications of EU Accession', *Turkish Studies*, 6(3) (2005), 321–40; I. Isik and D. Uysal, 'The Sources of Productivity Growth in Turkish Banks by Ownership: The Initial Responses of Public, Private, and Foreign Banks to Liberalization', *Turkish Studies*, 7(3) (2006), 365–403; M. Ugur, 'The Economic Dimension of Turkey's EU Membership: A Stock-Taking Exercise at the Start of Accession Negotiations', in J. S. Joseph (ed.), *Turkey and the European Union: Internal Dynamics and External Challenges* (New York: Palgrave Macmillan, 2006), 16–42.

57 Note à Monsieur le Dr. Seeliger, Brussels, 6 March 1959, Direction 3–IC1, 6. (Author's translation.)

58 See 'État de la procédure au sujet de la demande d'association de la Turquie à la Communauté Économique Européenne', 'Note Introductive', Brussels, 9 September 1959, R/644/59.

59 The exploratory talks took place over two phases, from 28–30 September 1959 and from 2–4 December 1959. See 'Note sur l'Ouverture de Négociations avec la Turquie pour la Conclusion d'un Accord d'Association', European Economic Commission, Brussels, 4 March 1960, S/01026 rév.

60 Communauté Economique Européenne Commission, 'Note sure L'Association de la Turquie à la Communauté' 1, Brussels, 23 September 1959. European Economic Commission: 'Note on the Association of Turkey with the Community'. (Author's translation.)

61 'Considerations d'Ordre Géneral sur L'Association de la Turquie à la CEE', Brussels, 1 October 1959, I-4275/59–F. 'General Considerations on the Association of Turkey with the European Economic Community. (Author's translation.)

62 Members of the Turkish delegation felt that Greece, who was also in negotiations with the Commission, was being treated more favourably.

63 Communauté Economique Européenne Commission, 'Négociations avec la Turquie pour un Accord D'Association', 'Solution Actuellement Demandé par la Turquie', 1, Brussels, 3 February 1961, I/S/0713/61. Commission of the European Economic Community, 'Negotiations with Turkey on an Association Agreement', 'Present Solution Requested by Turkey'. (Author's translation.)

64 'En résumé, on pourrait conclure que l'extension à la Turquie d'un accord d'association de type grec ... serait réalisée dans des conditions économiques et politiques instables, dont l'éventuelle évolution défavorable pourrait mettre en jeu la réalisation des objectifs même de l'Accord ...', Communauté Economique Européenne Commission, 'Négociations avec la Turquie pour un Accord D'Association', 'Solution Actuellement Demandé par la Turquie', 2, Brussels,

3 February 1961, I/S/0713/61. Commission of the European Economic Community, 'Negotiations with Turkey on an Association Agreement', 'Present Solution Requested by Turkey', stating: 'In brief, we can conclude that the extension to Turkey of an Association Agreement of the same type as that of Greece would be to do so in an unstable political and economic situation which could potentially jeopardize the objectives of the Agreement' (author's translation).

65 *Ibid.*, noting 'the danger of setting a precedent with the agreement with Greece; that it would become more and more difficult to refuse candidates outside of the Association' (author's translation).

66 'Association Agreement, Unofficial Translation of the French Text', ILM, 3 (1964), 65–80, 66.

67 *Ibid.*, 66–7, Articles 2–5.

68 See European Commission Regular Report on Turkey's Progress Towards EU Accession 1998, 5.

69 See S. Peers 'Living in Sin: Legal Integration Under the EC–Turkey Customs Union', EJIL, 7 (1996), 411–30, 412.

70 Additional Protocol and Financial Protocol signed on 23 November 1970, annexed to the Agreement establishing the Association between the European Economic Community and Turkey and on Measures to be Taken for their Entry into Force, unofficial translation, Articles 6 and 48.

71 See P. R. Hugg, 'Turkey in Europe: Reconsidering the Luxembourg Exclusion', Fordham Int'l L. J., 23 (2000), 606–706, 646.

72 European Commission Regular Report on Turkey's Progress Towards EU Accession 1998, 5. The position held by the military in Turkey is one which is kept under review by the European Commission in its annual progress reports. The most recent report of 2008 concluded that 'no progress has been made in ensuring full civilian supervisory functions over the military and parliamentary oversight of defence expenditure. Senior members of the armed forces have made statements on issues going beyond their remit' (European Commission Turkey 2008 Progress Report, SEC(2008) 2699 final, Brussels, 5 November 2008, 9). This sentiment was repeated in the report of 2009, which stated that '[t]he armed forces have continued to exercise undue political influence via formal and informal mechanisms. Senior members of the armed forces have expressed on a large number of occasions their views on domestic and foreign policy issues going beyond their remit, including on Cyprus, ethnicity, the South-East, secularism, political parties and other non-military matters' (2009 Progress Report, SEC(2009)1334, Brussels, 14 October 2009 10). There has not been the suggestion, however, that the position of the military in Turkish society is an obstacle to Turkey achieving full membership. The current AKP-led government has successfully kept the military out of politics despite deep-rooted discontent within the military at an Islamist party in government. See generally Ö. Taspinar, 'The Old Turks' Revolt: When Radical Secularism Endangers Democracy', *Foreign Affairs*, 86(6) (2007), 114–30.

73 European Commission 'Commission Opinion on Turkey's Request for Accession to the Community' SEC (89) 2290 final/2, 20 December 1989, para. 4.

74 *Ibid.*, para. 5.

75 *Ibid.*, para. 8.1.

76 *Ibid.*, para. 9.

77 See H. Arikan, *Turkey and the EU: An Awkward Candidate for EU Membership?* (Surrey, UK: Ashgate Publishing Ltd, 2nd edn, 2006), 72–3, asserting that the 'Matutes Package': 'provided the main base for the EU to implement its containment policy for Turkey ... Obviously, the instruments of the Package were not only far beyond being sufficient to prepare Turkey for the EU membership, but also lacked a degree of clarity, certainty and evenhandedness as far as Turkey's membership is concerned.'

78 *Ibid.*, 73.

79 Hugg, 'Turkey in Europe', 622. A detailed analysis of the provisions of the Customs Union is beyond the scope of this study. For an excellent appraisal of the agreement, see Peers, 'Living in Sin', 411–30.

80 *Ibid.*, 414.

81 See A. Nachmani, *Turkey: Facing a New Millennium Coping with Intertwined Conflicts* (Manchester: Manchester University Press, 2003), 66, asserting that the Customs Union agreement was 'Turkey's highest achievement'.

82 Preamble to Decision No. 1/95 of the EC–Turkey Association Council of 22 December 1995 on Implementing the Final Phase of the Customs Union (96/142/EC).

83 See S. Ülgen and Y. Zahariadis, 'The Future of Turkish Trade Relations: Deepening vs Widening', Centre for European Policy Studies EU–Turkey Working Papers No. 5, August 2004, which concludes that the EU must undertake a significant effort to alleviate the concerns of the Turkish side with regard to certain aspects of the Customs Union.

84 Eder, 'Implementing the Economic Criteria of EU Membership: How Difficult is it for Turkey?', in A. Çarkoğlu and B. Rubin (eds), *Turkey and the European Union: Domestic Politics, Economic Integration and International Dynamics* (London: Frank Cass, 2003), 219–45, 228.

85 The Parliamentary Assembly of the Council of Europe (PACE) imposed human rights monitoring on Turkey in 1996 which continued until 2004. See 'Council of Europe Parliamentarians Vote to End Monitoring of Turkey', PACE Press Release, 22 June 2004 noting that Turkey 'had clearly demonstrated its commitment and ability to fulfil its statutory obligations as a member state of the Council of Europe'.

86 Nachmani, *Turkey*, 56.

87 See Conclusions of the Presidency, Luxembourg European Council December 1997, EU Bulletin no. 12.97, para. 31.

88 *Ibid.*, para. 32.

89 *Ibid.*, para. 35.

90 Some commentators had favoured offering Turkey a 'privileged partnership' with the EU rather than the possibility of full membership. See for example Schäuble, 'Talking Turkey', 134–7.

91 Hugg, 'Turkey in Europe', 650.

92 European Commission Regular Report on Turkey's Progress Towards EU Accession 1998, 7.

93 *Ibid.*, 7–8.

94 The genesis and development of the 'Copenhagen criteria' are discussed at length in Chapter 2 Section 3 of this study.

95 Conclusions of the Presidency, Helsinki European Council December 1999, EU Bulletin no. 12.99, para. 12.

96 *Ibid.*

97 EC–Turkey relations were seen as being particularly poor in 1999. The controversy surrounding the capture of PKK leader Abdullah Öcalan and the EU's statement that it expected Turkey 'to resolve its problems by political means with full respect for human rights, the rule of law in a democratic society and in full accordance with Turkey's commitments as a member of the Council of Europe' as well as allowing independent observers access to Öcalan's trial provoked outrage among the Turkish government. The Ministry of Foreign Affairs noted that any 'intention of the EU to send observers to the hearings is tantamount to accepting and encouraging the efforts to intervene in and influence the independent judiciary'. The then Turkish Prime Minister, Bülent Ecevit, asserted that Turkey could not discuss political matters with the EU as long as it refused its candidacy. See European Commission Regular Report on Turkey's Progress Towards EU Accession 1999, A (b) (unpaginated document) and S. Kinzer 'Europe's Tie to Turkey Takes a Turn for Chillier', *New York Times*, 16 March 1999, 7.

98 Arikan, *Turkey and the EU*, 76.

99 *Ibid.*, 77.

100 European Council Decision of 8 March 2001 on the principles, priorities, intermediate objectives and conditions contained in the Accession Partnership with the Republic of Turkey (2001/235/EC), Article 2.

101 Turkey: 2000 Accession Partnership, Annex to European Council Decision of 8 March 2001 on the principles, priorities, intermediate objectives and conditions contained in the Accession Partnership with the Republic of Turkey (2001/235/ EC), para. 2.

102 Other aspects identified as short-term priorities were the alignment of legal procedures in pre-trial detention with that of the ECHR; strengthening provisions for legal redress against all human rights violations; the provision of human rights training for law enforcement officials; improvement in the functioning and efficiency of the judiciary; the maintenance of the moratorium on the death penalty; and the development of a comprehensive approach to the problems in the southeast, including the removal of the prohibition on broadcasting in minority languages (*ibid.*, para. 4.1).

103 *Ibid.*, para. 4.2.

104 *Ibid.*, para. 6.

105 Turkish National Programme for the Adoption on the *Acquis*, 2001 (available at: http://ec.europa.eu/enlargement/pdf/turkey/npaa_full_en.pdf) (last accessed, 15 January 2010).

106 *Ibid.*, ch. 2.1.

107 *Ibid.*, ch. 2.1.1–2.1.4.

108 *Ibid.*, ch. 2.1.5–2.1.8.

109 *Ibid.*, ch. 2.1.9–2.1.11.

110 *Ibid.*, ch. 2.1.12–2.1.16.

111 *Ibid.*, ch. 3.

112 Arikan, *Turkey and the EU*, 81.

113 See for example N. Bülent Gültekin and K. Yilmaz, 'The Turkish Economy Before the EU Accession Talks', in Lake, *EU and Turkey*, 68, claiming that the impact of the Customs Union on the Turkish economy did not fulfil its potential. See also Peers, 'Living in Sin', 430, concluding that the Customs Union is incomplete.

114 Conclusions of the Presidency, Brussels European Council December 2004 EU Bulletin no. 12.04.
115 *Ibid.*
116 EC–Turkey Negotiating Framework, 3 October 2005.
117 *Ibid.*, para. 1.
118 *Ibid.*, para. 3.
119 *Ibid.*, para. 4.
120 *Ibid.*, para. 5.
121 *Ibid.*, para. 6.
122 *Ibid.*, paras 7–8.
123 Paragraph 18 of the Negotiating framework provides that the substance of negotiations will be conducted in an Intergovernmental Conference with the participation of all Member States and the Candidate State. The policy areas to be discussed are broken down into 35 areas, as outlined in the Annex to the Negotiating Framework.
124 EC–Turkey Negotiating Framework, 3 October 2005, para. 13.
125 For example, in the 1998 report on Turkey's accession progress, the European Commission noted the imperative of finding a 'civil, non-military' solution to the conflict in the south-east. See European Commission 'Regular Report on Turkey's Progress Towards Accession', (1998), 53.
126 The Treaty of Peace Between the Allied and Associated Powers and Turkey Signed at Sèvres, August 10, 1920 (hereafter Treaty of Sèvres).
127 Treaty of Peace with Turkey Signed at Lausanne, 24 July 1923 (hereafter Treaty of Lausanne).
128 D. McDowall, *The Kurds: A Nation Denied* (London: Minority Rights Publications, 1992), 11.
129 For a definitive account of the Kurds of historical Kurdistan, see D. McDowall, *A Modern History of the Kurds* (London: IB Tauris & Co. Ltd, 3rd edn, 2004).
130 Point Twelve of Woodrow Wilson's Fourteen Point Plan for World Peace, presented at the Paris Peace Conference, repr. as app. in M. Macmillan, *Paris 1919: Six Months That Changed the World* (New York: Random House, 2001).
131 McDowall, *The Kurds*, 32.
132 For a historical analysis of Kurdish nationalism in Turkey, see P. J. White, *Primitive Rebels or Revolutionary Modernizers?: The Kurdish National Movement in Turkey* (London: Zed Books Ltd, 2000).
133 McDowall, *The Kurds*, 32.
134 *Ibid.*, 33.
135 *Ibid.*
136 Article 62, Treaty of Sèvres.
137 Macmillan, *Paris 1919*, 446.
138 McDowall, *The Kurds*, 35.
139 One commentator attests to the fragility of the treaty, stating that it was signed by the Allies and Damad Ferid, representing the sultan's government 'in a showroom at the Sèvres porcelain factory on the outskirts of Paris: not a thing of beauty, but as easily smashed' (Macmillan, *Paris 1919*, 448).
140 See J. Allain, *International Law in the Middle East: Closer to Power than Justice* (Surrey, UK: Ashgate Publishing Ltd, 2004), 19.
141 *Ibid.*, 19 (reference omitted).

142 Question of the Frontier between Turkey and Iraq: Report to the Council by the Commission instituted by the Council Resolution of September 30th, 1924, Documents distributed to Council and State Members, League of Nations, C.400, M. 147, 20 August 1925, at 88 (repr. in Allain, *International Law*, 20).

143 The request for an advisory opinion from the Court concerned the character of the Council's decision-making power under Article 3(2) of the Treaty of Lausanne. Advisory Opinion, PCIJ Reports, Series B, No. 12, 21, November 1925.

144 Question of the Frontier between Turkey and Iraq: Decision of the Council, 16 December 1925, League of Nations, Official Journal, February 1926, Item 1651, at 191–2 (repr. in Allain, *International Law*, 21).

145 *Ibid.*, 22.

146 Statement made in reply to a journalist, Emin, in Izmit, (repr. in McDowall, *A Modern History*, 190).

147 *Ibid.*, 191.

148 *Ibid.*

149 *Ibid.*

150 *Ibid.*, 192.

151 McDowall, *The Kurds*, 36.

152 K. Kemal and G. Winrow, *The Kurdish Question and Turkey: An Example of Transstate Ethnic Conflict* (London: Frank Cass, 1997), 101. The most significant of these uprisings, the Sheikh Said rebellion, occurred in 1925. For a comprehensive account of Kurdish resistance in the twentieth century, see A. Kahraman *Uprising, Suppression, Retribution: The Kurdish Struggle in Turkey in the Twentieth Century* (London: Parvana, 2007).

153 White, *Primitive Rebels*, 76.

154 McDowall, *The Kurds*, 37.

155 *Ibid.*

156 See Kendal, 'Kurdistan in Turkey', in G. Chaliand (ed.), *A People Without a Country: The Kurds and Kurdistan*, M. Pallis (trs.) (London: Zed Books Ltd, 2nd edn, 1993), 38–45, 62. Kendal refers to this period as the 'quiet years'.

157 McDowall, *The Kurds*, 38.

158 Bayar had been a Prime Minister and finance spokesman under Atatürk.

159 Kendal, 'Kurdistan in Turkey', 38, 63.

160 *Ibid.*

161 McDowall, *The Kurds*, 39.

162 Kendal, 'Kurdistan in Turkey', 65.

163 *Ibid.*, 63–4.

164 *Ibid.*, 64.

165 *Ibid.*, 38, 65.

166 Kendal notes that the coup had not been welcomed by the Kurdish population as they feared a return to the Kemalist-style militarism. In describing the harsh tactics engaged in, he outlines that '[o]ne of the Committee's very first measures had been to intern 485 Kurdish intellectuals and notables in a military camp established at Sivas, where they were held for four months. Fifty-five of them, those the authorities deemed most influential amongst the Kurdish population, were exiled to the western cities of Turkey for two years ... Another of the Committee's earliest decrees set out to ensure "the Turkicization of the names of Kurdish villages and towns." It also decided to set up "religious boarding schools" in Kurdistan, where Kurdish children, separated from their own milieu

at a very young age, could be "Turkicized"... Half a dozen radio stations were set up in Kurdistan to broadcast in Turkish, in the hope that this would deter the population from listening to the Kurdish language broadcasts from neighboring countries' ('Kurdistan in Turkey', 65).

167 McDowall, *The Kurds*, 39.
168 Kendal, 'Kurdistan in Turkey', 66.
169 *Ibid.*
170 *Ibid.*, 67.
171 *Ibid.*, 65. Kurds were generally referred to as 'mountain Turks' by Turkish officials in an attempt to deny that they were ethnically distinct from Turks. Successive Turkish administrations have been reluctant to engage in a minority rights discourse; see below Chapter 2, Section 3.
172 The Turkish Workers' Party had been founded in 1961 by trade unionists.
173 McDowall, *The Kurds*, 40.
174 *Ibid.*
175 *Ibid.*
176 White, *Primitive Rebels*, 132.
177 McDowall, *The Kurds*, 41.
178 Kendal, 'Kurdistan in Turkey', 70.
179 Official Gazette, no. 12577 of 14 February 1967 (repr. in McDowall, *A Modern History*, 410).
180 McDowall, *The Kurds*, 43–50. Kendal examines the subjugation of the Kurds as falling within the categories of cultural, political and physical oppression (see 'Kurdistan in Turkey', 72–9).
181 White, *Primitive Rebels*, 134.
182 *Ibid.*, 135
183 *Ibid.*
184 C. More, *Les Kurdes Aujourd'hui: Mouvement National et Partis Politiques* (Paris: Éditions L'Harmattan, 1984), 188 (repr. in White, *Primitive Rebels*, 136).
185 K. Yildiz, *The Kurds in Turkey: EU Accession and Human Rights* (London: Pluto Press, 2005), 16.
186 Allain, *International Law*, 31
187 Taspinar, 'The Old Turks', 122.
188 'Commission Presents Its Recommendation on the Continuation of Turkey's Accession Negotiations', 1, Brussels, 29 November 2006, IP/06/1652. The eight chapters affected by the decision were Chapter 1, on free movement of goods; Chapter 3, on the right of establishment and freedom to provide services; Chapter 9, on financial services; Chapter 11, on agriculture and rural development; Chapter 13, on fisheries; Chapter 14, on transport policy; Chapter 29, on the Customs Union; and Chapter 30, on external relations.
189 See K. Bennhold, 'Turkey Assails EU's Decision to Partially Suspend Entry Talks', *International Herald Tribune*, 12 December 2006, quoting the Turkish Prime Minister's chief foreign policy adviser, Egeman Bağiş, as stating '[s]ome countries in the EU unfortunately want to keep it as a Christian club ... [s]ome countries are using Cyprus – and Cyprus is happy to be used'.
190 'Update on European Union Relations', Turkish Treasury, 18 April 2007 (available at: www.treasury.gov.tr/iro_files/Newsletter/2007/idi-20070418.pdf) (last accessed 15 January 2010).
191 *Ibid.*

192 There is an abundance of literature dealing with alleged human rights abuses during the conflict. Some of the more pertinent non-governmental reports include: Amnesty International, 'Turkey: A Policy of Denial', AI Index: EUR 44/24/95, February 1995; 'Turkey: Forced Displacement of Ethnic Kurds from Southeastern Turkey', A Human Rights Watch Short Report (1994) 6(12); Lawyers Committee for Human Rights 'Obstacles to Reform – Exceptional Courts, Police Impunity and Persecution of Human Rights Defenders in Turkey' (Report) (Lawyers Committee for Human Rights Canada 1999), 60–6; Amnesty International 'Turkey: The Duty to Supervise, Investigate and Prosecute' AI Index: EUR 44/24/99, April 1999; 'No Security Without Human Rights', Amnesty International; AI Index: EUR 44/084/1996, 1 October 1996, as well as numerous reports of the Kurdish Human Rights Project.

193 See N. Birch, 'Turkey Looks for Peace with Kurds', *Guardian*, 13 August 2005.

194 N. Tocci, *The EU and Conflict Resolution: Promoting Peace in the Backyard* (London: Routledge, 2007), 53.

195 Yildiz, *The Kurds*, 134.

196 See generally N. Tocci *The EU and Conflict Resolution: Promoting Peace in the Backyard* (London: Routledge, 2007). Apart from EU interests in securing a resolution to the conflict, it has also been suggested that it would serve as a stabilizing factor in the broader Middle East region. Gunter contends that '[a]s the Arab–Israeli dispute slowly winds down, the Kurdish problem will bid to replace it as the leading factor of instability in the geostrategically important Middle East. Furthermore, since the Kurds sit on a great deal of the Middle East's oil and possibly even water resources, the Kurdish issue will become even more momentous in the twenty-first century' (see M. M. Gunter, 'The Kurdish Problem in International Politics', in J. S. Joseph (ed.), *Turkey and the European Union: Internal Dynamics and External Challenges* (New York: Palgrave Macmillan, 2006), 96–122, 96). See also A. B. Çelik and B. Rumelili, 'Necessary But Not Sufficient: The Role of the EU in Resolving Turkey's Kurdish Question and the Greek–Turkish Conflicts', *European Foreign Affairs Review*, 11 (2006), 203–22, 212, asserting that '[t]hrough Turkey's involvement in the European integration process, the Turkish state started treating its Kurdish question as a democratization issue if not an unpronounced minority representation issue'.

197 As noted above, the 1998 report on Turkey's accession progress, the European Commission outlined the imperative of finding a 'civil, non-military' solution to the conflict in the south-east. See European Commission 'Regular Report on Turkey's Progress Towards Accession' (1998), 53.

198 Yildiz, *The Kurds*, 137–8. Yildiz and Muller are critical of the approach adopted by Europe in relation to the Kurds, asserting that Europe has failed to issue any real condemnation of Turkey's policies towards the Kurds, despite the high incidence of human rights abuses perpetrated during the conflict: 'This stems to a significant extent from European conceptions of the Turkish regime as a benign Western ally, a NATO member and a prospective EU partner. The Kurds in Turkey are seen in Europe through Ankara's eyes, frequently portrayed in the press and elsewhere as violent terrorists engaged in an illegal separatist campaign ... The Iraqi Kurds, on the other hand, have been portrayed far more sympathetically as their interests have been aligned with those of the West in their opposition to the Ba'athist regime' (K. Yildiz and M. Muller, *The European Union and Turkish Accession: Human Rights and the Kurds* (London: Pluto Press, 2008), 171).

199 The Portuguese Presidency of the EU relayed its concern to Ankara by calling on the Turkish authorities to 'exercise restraint, to respect the territorial integrity of Iraq and refrain from taking any military action that could undermine regional peace and stability' ('EU Calls on Turkey to Halt Strikes in Northern Iraq', *Guardian*, 17 December 2007).

200 See E. Uslu, 'AKP Prepares a Comprehensive Plan to Address the Kurdish Question', *Eurasia Daily Monitor*, 6(142) (24 July 2009).

201 See R. Tait, 'Turkey Bans Main Kurdish Party over Alleged Terror Links', *Guardian* 12 December 2009.

202 On this point, Yildiz and Muller have contended that allowing Turkey to begin negotiations 'without significant progress towards resolving the Kurdish issue has serious implications for the future security of Turkey's Kurdish population. Forging ahead with accession before the situation of the Kurds is adequately addressed attaches unwarranted legitimacy to Turkey's treatment of them, and suggests that the issue is of secondary importance and requires no particular sustained or comprehensive attempts at resolution ... In deciding that Turkey has fulfilled the Copenhagen Criteria, then, the EU has manifestly failed to fulfil its responsibilities towards the Kurds' (*European Union*, 181). For discussion of Turkey's compliance with the Copenhagen criteria and analysis of the European Commission's reports on the issue, see below Chapter 2, Section 1.

2 A rights-based approach?

1 Introduction

There are a number of stated reforms which are required for Turkey's current membership bid; in the area of human rights (heavily tied to the conflict in south-east Turkey); Turkey's ability to fulfil the 'respect for and protection of minorities' aspect of the Copenhagen criteria; and freedom of expression. In assessing Turkey's record in these pivotal areas, Barchard argues that:

> Western Europeans, and others, discussing human rights in Turkey need to be aware of the danger that their approach to the question is framed by prejudices of which they may personally be unconscious. European scepticism, both on Turkey's ability to abide by the laws and moral norms of Europe and on its power to reform itself, has a long pedigree and derives ultimately from the racist Turcophobic literature widespread among French and British liberals in the nineteenth century, one of whose aims was specifically to prevent the growth of friendly ties between Turkey and Europe.[1]

It is therefore worth bearing this history in mind when assessing the human rights violations which currently weigh heavily on Turkey's EU entry and which are, in fact, a relatively recent phenomenon (arising in the late 1970s), largely the product of, or certainly exacerbated by, the political violence in the south-east of the country.[2] Furthermore, it is asserted that opinion often ignores the 'parallels and similarities between Turkey's experience as a late-modernising country and the history of other Mediterranean societies …'.[3] It is worth noting that the human rights violations committed in dealing with the political violence in the south-east were, similarly, true of attempts of the British government to contain the conflict in Northern Ireland and the Russian experience in Chechnya.[4] Additionally, human rights considerations within the EU system are also a relatively recent phenomenon:

> even though the Community was originally presented as an economic entity, its wider ambitions required that a human rights discourse be deployed as a necessary ideological addition to its 'proto-constitution'.

In conjunction with other concepts, such as democracy and the rule of law, the discourse of human rights was identified as providing both the ethical direction for the Community's actions and the constraints upon its interference in the sovereignty of its Member States. The language of human rights was thus used to authenticate the Community as a site of governance.[5]

Against this backdrop, this chapter examines Turkey's compliance with the Copenhagen criteria and international human rights norms in the framework of conditionality applied by the EU to applicant states. In doing so, it assesses the extent to which the 'carrot' of EU membership has provided the catalyst for domestic legal reforms and outlines whether Turkey's accession experience in this regard has been mirrored by other applicant countries.

2   Human rights reforms and assessment of the Commission

Article 6 of the Treaty on European Union enunciates that the Union 'is founded on the principles of liberty, democracy, respect for human rights and fundamental freedoms and the rule of law'.[6] Article 7 cautions that member states that violate human rights in a 'serious and persistent' manner run the risk of forfeiting their rights under the treaty.[7] Human rights considerations are now a significant factor in any new accession to the EU and have proved to be a continuing hindrance to Turkey's membership ambitions. While this is indicative of Turkey's questionable record in terms of human rights protections, Turkey's persistence with the accession process and its implementation of substantive domestic reforms are arguably an indication that it aspires to more than simply access to a trading bloc, which the Association Agreement and Customs Union arguably already provide.

Although it has been argued that the chief factor in the reduction of human rights violations in Turkey has come about, not as a result of the EU or the accession process but due to internal demand for change in the context of receding political violence,[8] this contention is increasingly hard to sustain in light of the marked improvements in the legal protection of human rights which have coincided with Turkey's accession process.[9] Furthermore, the suggestion that Turkey's strategic importance as a NATO member and a 'buffer against political Islam' is one of the reasons why the EU has not long since closed the door of membership to Turkey for good[10] is challenged both by the rise of political Islam within Turkey itself and the concomitant continuing progression of its membership bid.

2.1   *Legislative reform*

At the Helsinki summit in December 1999, at which Turkey's candidate status was formally recognized, the European Council noted that Turkey was already in a position to open negotiations for almost all of the 35 chapters of the *acquis*. While its preparedness in areas such as economic and fiscal performance was relatively advanced, it took a further six years for human rights protections to reach the standard required for accession negotiations to begin.[11]

Although the reform process in Turkey has been under way since 1995, the implementation of legislative reforms began in earnest under the Ecevit coalition (2002–3) and accelerated after the election of the Adalet ve Kalkinma Partisi (Justice and Development Party, or AKP) in December 2002.[12] The leader of the AKP and current Prime Minister, Recep Tayyip Erdoğan, has professed his commitment to reform by calling for 'the acceptance of human rights as the common value of continents, civilizations, values, politics, strategies, East and West'[13] and has argued that countries that fail to embrace 'the universality of human rights, democracy, and the rule of law will be driven into lonliness [*sic*]'.[14] The legislative amendments have largely been facilitated by the implementation of the 'harmonization packages', which address those issues highlighted in the European Commission reports and aim to bring Turkey's laws into line with those of EU member states. The extent of the reform is evidenced by the fact that between 2001 and 2004 alone, there were two major constitutional reforms and eight legislative packages adopted, as well as an extensive revision of the penal code.[15]

There have been many significant developments relating to improved protections for civil and political rights since the reform process commenced in Turkey. The European Commission had in all of its progress reports expressed concern at the restrictions placed on freedom of expression,[16] which were substantially lifted by the repeal of Article 8 of the Anti-Terror Law and by the promulgation of the Press Law in June 2004.[17] Article 3 of the Press Law attests to the freedom of the press, which includes 'the right to acquire and disseminate information, and to criticise, interpret and create works'. In a progressive measure, Article 12 of the Law stipulates that the owner or editor of a periodical 'cannot be forced to either disclose their news sources or to legally testify on this issue'.

Reforms have also addressed cultural rights and in particular those of minorities, although this remains an area of particular contention. The adoption of the Sixth Harmonization Package in June 2003 relaxed restrictions on broadcasting in the Kurdish language by amending Article 4 of the Act on the Establishment and Broadcasts of Radio and Television Stations, sanctioning the broadcasting (on both private and public radio and television stations), in languages and dialects used by Turkish citizens traditionally in their daily lives. Additionally, in the area of education, the Regulation on Teaching Different Languages[18] regulates the teaching of different languages and dialects that Turkish citizens use traditionally in their daily lives, essentially allowing for the use of minority languages. Greater protection for rights relating to associations and freedom of assembly guarantees have also been facilitated by the implementation of the Seventh Harmonization Package.

The new Associations Law[19] stipulates that legal persons are entitled to establish associations without the need to obtain prior permission (Article 3) whereas the provision in Article 312 of the old penal code restricting those convicted of criminal offences from establishing associations has been abolished (Article 4). With regard to peaceful assembly, Article 3 of the Law on Demonstrations and Public Meetings now stipulates that citizens have the right to hold peaceful meetings and marches without prior permission.[20] Under Article 17 of the Law, demonstrations can only be banned where there is a 'clear and imminent threat of a criminal offence being committed'.

In 2001 the Council of the European Union indicated that Turkey must '[s]trengthen legal provisions and undertake all necessary measures to reinforce the fight against torture practices, and ensure compliance with the European Convention for the Prevention of Torture'[21] as a priority in its accession partnership, a sentiment echoed in the Commission's progress reports. Since this pronouncement, a number of reforms have been implemented and a purported 'zero tolerance' policy on torture adopted. According to the provisions of Supplementary Article 7 to the Code of Criminal Procedure, set out in the Seventh Harmonization Package, the investigation and prosecution of cases of alleged torture are to be treated as urgent and hearings of these cases may not be adjourned for more than 30 days, unless there are exceptional circumstances. In addition to this safeguard, Articles 94–96 of the revised penal code provide heavier penalties than previously for those found guilty of inflicting torture.[22]

Improvements in the reduction of instances of torture come largely as a result of the implementation of new procedural safeguards for detainees. In January 2003 a series of reforms were enacted, strengthening the right of access to a lawyer in cases under the jurisdiction of the state security courts.[23] In April of that year, a Human Rights Violations Investigation and Assessment Centre was established within the Gendarmerie Command and the sixth reform package repealed provisions preventing lawyers from being present during statement taking when they are defending those being tried under the competence of state security courts.[24] Changes in the rules of procedure with regard to state security courts have also been enacted to eliminate incommunicado detention.[25]

2.2 *Reports of the European Commission*

To date there has been a total of 12 formal reports on Turkey's progress towards accession to the EU. The reports are generally lengthy documents which consider all aspects of Turkey's membership bid and analyse, in particular, Turkey's compliance with the Copenhagen criteria. The analysis constitutes the basis upon which accession progress is gauged and, as such, the procedure constitutes a fundamental part of the accession process.

At the Cardiff European Council in June 1998, the European Commission confirmed that it would submit, at the end of 1998, a report on each candidate country's progress towards accession.[26] In the case of Turkey, the report was based on the decision of the 1997 Luxembourg Council which had envisaged preparing Turkey for accession by 'bringing it closer to the European Union in every field'[27] and on Article 28 of the Association Agreement which states:

> [w]hen operation of the Convention shall have permitted prospects for the full acceptance by Turkey of the commitments arising from the Treaty establishing the Community, the Contracting Parties shall examine the possibility of Turkey's accession to the Community.[28]

In the compilation of the Commission reports, the Commission considers contributions from the Turkish authorities, the evaluations of international organizations, in particular the Council of Europe, and reports from non-governmental organizations (NGOs), the European Parliament and member states.[29] In terms of the Commission's assessment of Turkey's progress in implementing political reform, the analysis 'consists of a systematic examination of the organization and functioning of the public authorities and of the systems for protecting fundamental rights'; the intention of the Commission is to present an evaluation of the effective functioning of democracy and the rule of law.[30]

The reports of the European Commission between 1998, when it published the first report on Turkey, and 2005, when the European Council decided to open formally accession negotiations, offer an insight into the effectiveness of the reform process in Turkey. The early reports' pronouncements on the state of human rights and the protection of minorities in Turkey reveal the extent to which reform was necessary. The 1998 report, for example acknowledged '[p]ersistent cases of torture, disappearances and extra-judicial executions' as well as problems with freedom of expression, association and assembly and widespread domestic violence.[31] With regard to economic, social and cultural rights, the Commission pointed to problems relating to the formation of trade unions, freedom of religion and restrictions on the use of minority languages.[32] The years 1998–2002 saw a gradual improvement in the human rights situation as evidenced by the Commission. In 1999 the Commission confirmed 'certain positive steps' since its report of the previous year but highlighted the continuing problems in relation to torture and extra-judicial killings; freedom of expression; freedom of association and assembly; women's rights; and noted no development on economic, social and cultural rights.[33] The report of 2000 recorded 'limited progress' in the area of civil and political rights and a positive development regarding economic, social and cultural rights.[34] The Commission continued to voice concerns on the case of women's rights and the protection of minorities not recognized by the Treaty of Lausanne.[35] The 2001 report highlighted a number of constitutional, legislative and administrative changes and noted that there had been a major reform of the prison system and that efforts to bring pre-trial detention provisions and other procedures such as automatic judicial review and medical examinations into line with European Convention standards were under way.[36]

Whereas the first three regular reports of the Commission could identify little in the way of progress in the protection of human rights in Turkey, the 2001 report was considerably more positive, largely as a result of the first major constitutional reform since 1982. In October 2001, 34 amendments were made to the 1982 Constitution 'introducing new provisions on issues such as freedom of thought and expression, the prevention of torture, the strengthening of civilian authority, freedom of association, and gender equality'.[37] The Commission described the constitutional amendments as 'a significant step towards strengthening guarantees in the field of human rights and fundamental freedoms and limiting capital punishment' but concern remained as to the continuing allegations of torture and ill-treatment; freedom of expression; freedom of association and assembly and violence against women.[38]

In 2002 the Commission reported progress in the area of ratification of international human rights conventions; the abolition of capital punishment in peacetime; improvements with regard to the length of pre-trial detention and further reform of the prison system.[39] Through the implementation of the reform packages, a relaxation of the law concerning broadcasts was also noted, although problems with regard to the interpretation of the law concerning freedom of expression were highlighted,[40] as well as concerns regarding freedom of association and freedom of religion among non-Muslim religious communities.[41] The 2003 report evidenced the fact that some of the concerns highlighted in 2002 had been addressed in the intervening period. The Commission pointed to Turkey's 'great determination in accelerating the pace of reforms' and noted that the powers of the National Security Council had been amended; positive changes made to the state security courts; the ratification of the ICCPR and the International Covenant on Economic Social and Cultural Rights (ICESCR); and the campaign to eradicate torture and ill-treatment had been strengthened.[42] The adoption of the reform packages had also led to the easing of restrictions on the exercise of freedom of expression and the completion of the lifting of the state of emergency in the south-east. In contrast, they maintained that problems still remained in areas such as freedom of association and functioning of the judiciary.[43] The Commission praised the 'impressive legislative efforts which constitute significant progress towards achieving compliance with the Copenhagen political criteria and urged Turkey to address the outstanding issues highlighted in the report'.[44]

Some seven years after its first progress report on Turkey, the Commission eventually recommended, in its report of October 2004, that it had sufficiently fulfilled the Copenhagen criteria, facilitating the European Council's decision in December of that year to invite Turkey to commence negotiations.[45] A number of factors influenced the Commission's decision that Turkey had satisfied the political criteria. These included efforts to achieve a comprehensive settlement to the Cyprus problem and the development of positive relations with Greece as well as Turkey's accession to most of the international and European human rights conventions and increased efforts to implement the decisions of the ECtHR.[46] The Commission also referred to Turkey's efforts to eradicate torture and progress in aligning the overall framework for the exercise of fundamental freedoms with European standards.[47] Furthermore, there was significant progress in strengthening the freedom of the press, freedom of expression and association and progress in the implementation of reforms concerning cultural rights.[48]

One year after the decision to open accession negotiations with Turkey, the Commission observed that although Turkey continued to fulfil the Copenhagen political criteria sufficiently, the pace of change slowed in 2005 and implementation of the reforms remained 'uneven'.[49] The Commission noted that further efforts were required in the areas of freedom of expression, women's rights, religious freedoms, trade union rights, cultural rights and the elimination of torture and ill-treatment. In 2006, the Commission's progress report was more critical than the preceding two years, due largely to concerns over freedom of expression. Concerns regarding freedom of expression were also evident in the reports of 2007 and 2008, which noted that 'the prosecution and conviction for the expression of non-violent opinions under certain provisions of the Turkish Criminal Code are a cause of serious concern. The number of persons prosecuted almost doubled in 2006 compared with in 2005, and there was a further increase in the number of prosecutions in 2007.'[50] The most recent report, in 2009 noted that while there had been an improvement in the protection of freedom of expression since the amendment to Article 301 of the Penal Code: 'the Turkish legal framework still fails to provide sufficient guarantees for exercising freedom of expression and, as a result, is often interpreted in a restrictive way by public prosecutors and judges'.[51] It would appear therefore, that improvements have been made on issues such as torture, freedom of association and gender equality, the main problematic issue currently is that of freedom of expression, which is essentially one of the few remaining areas of law where Turkey has yet to implement effective legislation guaranteeing its protection. Nonetheless, it is also apparent that in the post-11 September 2001 legal landscape, freedom of expression guarantees have been greatly compromised, even in those countries where the right would have traditionally rested at the apex of civil liberties protected by the state.[52] It is therefore evident that these are concerns which affect not just acceding states but are also relevant to some current member states.

3 Freedom of expression: still the issue?

Although the progress reports of the European Commission detail improvements in most areas of domestic human rights protections and reforms in Turkey, continued prosecutions for the expression of non-violent opinions protected by freedom of expression guarantees outlined in Article 10 of the ECHR and Article 19 of the CCPR, by which Turkey is bound, remain a cause for concern among EU onlookers. The sentiment, evident in recent Commission reports on progress towards accession, that freedom of expression is now the principal remaining human rights concern has also been echoed by the European

Parliament's Foreign Affairs Committee. In a 2007 resolution on Turkey's progress towards accession, the Committee welcomed positive initiatives such as the EU–Turkey Civil Society Dialogue and the establishment of financial support to encourage the economic development of the Turkish-Cypriot community, yet in relation to freedom of expression noted that it:

> Deplores the fact that a number of people are still being prosecuted under Article 301 of the Penal Code; strongly condemns the recent conviction of Saris Seropyan and Arat Dink under this article; urges the government and the newly elected parliament to make sure that all provisions of the Penal Code allowing for arbitrary restrictions on the expression of non-violent opinions are removed and that freedom of expression and freedom of the press are guaranteed; regards this as a top priority for the new government … [53]

The 2007 Report of the European Union on human rights also alluded to continuing problems in relation to the protection of freedom of expression by noting in relation to the reform process in Turkey that: '[f]urther efforts are needed, particularly in areas such as freedom of expression, where a significant number of cases are still brought against individuals for non-violent expression of opinion'.[54]

3.1 Freedom of expression and the law

The concerns outlined above are not new; there has, since the beginning of the accession process, been a certain amount of disquiet within the European Commission with regard to the adequacy of freedom of expression guarantees in Turkey. In its first report on Turkey's progress towards accession to the EU, the Commission noted that:

> freedom of expression is not fully assured in Turkey. An excessively narrow interpretation of the Constitution and other legal provisions (Articles 7 and 8 of the Anti-Terror Law, Articles 158, 159, 311 and 312 of the Criminal Code) concerning the unity of the state, territorial integrity, secularism and respect for formal institutions of the state is regularly used to charge and sentence elected politicians, journalists, writers, trade unionists or NGO workers for statements, public speeches, published articles or books that would be acceptable in EU Member States.[55]

That freedom of expression was not secured in Turkey has also been evidenced by the large number of adverse decisions received from the ECtHR, in which the Court found that Turkey had violated Article 10 of the ECHR.

Since the 1990s a substantial number of cases concerning Turkey's compliance with Article 10 of the ECHR have come before the Court. This is primarily due to the legislation enacted in response to the Kurdish conflict in the south-east, prohibiting speech deemed to constitute 'separatist propaganda', with which the majority of the cases concerning the Article are concerned.[56] Article 10 of the ECHR provides for the right to freedom of expression and outlines the permissible restrictions to the right. It states:

1. Everyone has the right to freedom of expression. This right shall include freedom to hold opinions and to receive and impart information and ideas without interference by public authority and regardless of frontiers. This Article shall not prevent States from requiring the licensing of broadcasting, television or cinema enterprises.
2. The exercise of these freedoms, since it carries with it duties and responsibilities, may be subject to such formalities, conditions, restrictions or penalties as are prescribed by law and are necessary in a democratic society, in the interests of national security, territorial integrity or public safety, for the prevention of disorder or crime, for the protection of health or morals, for the protection of the reputation or rights of others, for preventing the disclosure of information received in confidence, or for maintaining the authority and impartiality of the judiciary.

The relevant domestic legislation with which the ECtHR was concerned in the cases concerning Turkey's application of Article 10 was initially paragraphs 3 and 6 of former Article 142 of the Penal Code, which provided that:

3. A person who, prompted by racial considerations, by any means whatsoever spreads propaganda aimed at abolishing in whole or in part public-law rights guaranteed by the Constitution or undermining or destroying patriotic sentiment shall, on conviction, be liable to a term of imprisonment of from five to ten years.

[...]

6. Where the offences contemplated in the above paras are committed through publication, the penalty to be imposed shall be increased by half.

This Article was repealed by the Anti-Terror Law (Law no. 3713 of 12 April 1991), as amended by Law no. 4126 of 27 October 1995, which came into force on 30 October 1995. Subsequent cases principally concerned convictions under s. 8 of this law which stated:

1. Written and spoken propaganda, meetings, assemblies and demonstrations aimed at undermining the territorial integrity of the Republic of Turkey or the indivisible unity of the nation are prohibited. Any person who engages in such an activity shall be sentenced to not less than one and not more than three years' imprisonment and a fine of from one hundred million to three hundred million Turkish liras. The penalty imposed on a reoffender may not be commuted to a fine.

[...]

3. Where the crime of propaganda contemplated in the first paragraph is committed through the medium of printed matter or by means of mass communication other than periodicals within the meaning of the second paragraph, those responsible and the owners of the means of mass communication shall be sentenced to not less than six months' and not more than two years' imprisonment and a fine of from one hundred million to three hundred million Turkish liras ...

More recently the case law has continued to relate, directly or indirectly to the conflict, although the volume of cases has decreased significantly. As Turkey continues to reform its legislation in the area as a result of European Union prompting, it can reasonably be suggested that complaints concerning Article 10 will continue to decrease.

3.2 Recent developments

In its report of 2005 the Commission contended that:

> With regard to freedom of expression, the situation of people sentenced for the expression of non-violent opinion continues to be addressed. The Turkish authorities have reported that a significant number of persons serving prison sentences under articles of the old Penal Code have been set free. Both the authorities and a number of NGOs report that there has been a continued reduction in the number of prosecutions and particularly convictions in cases related to freedom of expression.[57]

Given that the cases referenced in the previous section all deal with the law prior to 2005, it is worth exploring how the amendments to the legislation have impacted. The repeal of Article 8 of the Anti-Terror Law and the promulgation of a new Press Law, combined with the relaxing of restrictions on the use of minority languages contributed to an overall improvement in freedom of expression. Accordingly, the progress report of the European Commission in 2004 noted that there had been 'a reduction in the number of prosecutions and convictions in cases related to freedom of expression'.[58] However, the effect of the legislative changes appears to have been greatly hindered by the entry into force on 1 June 2005 of a new Turkish Penal Code. Article 301 of the Code provides that:

> (1) A person who explicitly denigrates Turkishness, the Republic or the Turkish Grand National Assembly, shall be imposed a penalty of imprisonment for a term of six months to three years.

(2) A person who explicitly insults the Government of the Republic of Turkey, the judicial bodies of the State, the military or security organisation shall be imposed a penalty of imprisonment for a term of six months to two years.

(3) Where insulting being a Turk is committed by a Turkish citizen in a foreign country, the penalty to be imposed shall be increased by one third.

(4) Expression of opinions with the purpose of criticism does not require penalties.

Article 301 has received international attention due to the high profile nature of some of the prosecutions taken since its adoption.[59] Nobel prize-winning author Orhan Pamuk was charged (and subsequently acquitted) with insulting Turkishness under the Article for remarks made during an interview in February 2005 in which he referred to the 1915 massacres of Armenians and the killing of Kurds in south-east Turkey.[60] Another well publicized case was that taken against Hrant Dink, editor of the bilingual Armenian Turkish newspaper, *Agos*, who was convicted of insulting Turkey's national identity and given a six-month suspended sentence for publishing a series of articles in which he called on diaspora Armenians to stop focusing on the Turks and focus instead on the welfare of Armenia.[61] Dink was subsequently murdered on 19 January 2007. The European Commission in its 2006 progress report noted that:

> the prosecutions and convictions for the expression of non-violent opinion under certain provisions of the new Penal Code are a cause for serious concern and may contribute to create a climate of self-censorship in the country. This is particularly the case for Article 301 which penalises insulting Turkishness, the Republic as well as the organs and institutions of the state. Although this article includes a provision that expression of thought intended to criticise should not constitute a crime, it has repeatedly been used to prosecute non violent opinions expressed by journalists, writers, publishers, academics and human rights activists.[62]

Nonetheless, whereas Article 301 has attracted international criticism and prompted calls for its abolition from the European Parliament,[63] other lesser known Articles of the new Penal Code also represent a retroactive step in terms of freedom of expression protections and are applied particularly in the south-east of the country. Under Article 217, for example, a person who commits the crime of 'inciting people to disobey laws' can be imprisoned for nine months to three years 'but if such an offence is committed through media and press, the penalty to be imposed shall be increased by half'. Under Article 220, a person who 'makes propaganda – through the medium of press and media – about the goals of an organization which has been established in order to commit crimes' can be imprisoned for three to nine years. In addition to these and other Articles of the Penal Code, freedom of expression has also come under further threat since the adoption of amendments to the Anti-Terror Law in June 2006 which established aggravated penalties for 'propaganda' and 'praise' of terrorism.[64] The European Commission noted in its 2006 progress report that the definition of these crimes is not in line with the Council of Europe Convention for the Prevention of Terrorism and that '[f]reedom of the press and media could be undermined by provisions allowing the suspension of periodicals and introducing the liability of chief editors and of press and media owners for publishing terrorist propaganda or praise in press or media organs.'[65]

The 'routine repression of non-violent expression in Turkey' is, Yildiz asserts, '... fundamentally linked to both her strict adherence to the notion of the homogenous and secular Turkish identity, and her elevation of the idea of the state'.[66] This sentiment is also reflected in the idea that certain issues remain 'taboo' subjects within Turkey, such as the criticism of the military and discussion of the Kurdish conflict. However, the slowdown in the reform process and the regression in the area of freedom of expression may also be linked by some to the ending of the PKK ceasefire in 2004 and an escalation in tension with regard to the conflict in the south-east of the country. Nonetheless, in 2008 the Turkish Parliament voted to amend Article 301; under the amendment, the reference to 'Turkishness' in Article 301(1) was replaced with 'Turkish nation' and the prison term envisaged for violation of the Article was reduced from three to two years, thus allowing for the sentence to be suspended or converted to a fine. In an effort to make prosecution based on the Article more difficult, the provision now requires the justice minister's approval before prosecutors can launch cases and the provision in Article 301(3) that called for increased penalties in situations where the crime was committed abroad was deleted.[67] The amendment was promptly welcomed by the EU, who described its passing as 'a constructive step forward in ensuring freedom of expression' and 'an indication of Turkey's continuing commitment to the reform process',[68] although critics have argued that it does not go far enough.[69] The Progress Report of 2009 pointed to the fact that Article 301 is: 'no longer used systematically to restrict freedom of expression' and that amendments to the provision led to a 'significant decline in prosecutions compared with previous years'.[70] However, in highlighting the as yet insufficient guarantees in Turkish law to protect freedom of expression, the report pointed to the fact that other provisions of the Penal Code are routinely used to restrict freedom of expression.[71] Offences against dignity, state security, the constitutional order and public order continue to be frequently invoked as reasons for imposing restrictions and can result in 'self-censorship'.[72]

4 Minorities and Turkey

In addition to concerns over freedom of expression, the issue of minority rights protection in Turkey features as a recurring problem in the annual progress reports of the European Commission. The question of minority rights in Turkey has, in fact, always been a somewhat fraught issue:

> In Turkey, almost nothing in the lexicon of international politics provokes a more prickly reaction than the simple word 'minority'. The idea of ethnic and religious community divisions conjures up two threatening images for the majority of Turks: one of Christian powers plotting to divide, rule, and carve up the country, as happened after the fall of the Ottoman Empire, the other of non-Muslim fifth columnists conspiring to stab the Turkish majority in the back.[73]

Nevertheless, the treaty upon which the foundations of modern Turkey rests – the Treaty of Lausanne[74] – provides for minority rights protection, albeit to a limited, degree.[75]

4.1 Minority rights under the Treaty of Lausanne

Despite Turkey's commitments and obligations under the international human rights regime, its historical position that national minorities are those recognized by international treaties, remains.[76] In effect this means that the principal system of protection for minorities in Turkey is that afforded by the Treaty of Lausanne, which defines minorities exclusively on the basis of religion. Article 38 of the treaty stipulates:

> The Turkish Government undertakes to assure full and complete protection of life and liberty to all inhabitants of Turkey without distinction of birth, nationality, language, race or religion.
>
> All inhabitants of Turkey shall be entitled to free exercise, whether in public or private, of any creed, religion or belief, the observance of which shall not be incompatible with public order and good morals.
>
> Non-Moslem minorities will enjoy full freedom of movement and of emigration, subject to the measures applied, on the whole or on part of the territory, to all Turkish nationals, and which may be taken by the Turkish Government for national defence, or for the maintenance of public order.[77]

The specific reference in Article 38 to 'non-Moslem' minorities has meant the exclusion of ethnic, linguistic and Muslim minorities from governmental protection and official minority rights discourse within Turkey. The treaty does, however, grant substantial rights (negative and positive) to those protected therein 'conveying affirmative obligations on the Turkish government to undertake measures for the enjoyment of those rights'.[78] This is confirmed in Article 39 of the treaty which states that 'Turkish nationals belonging to non-Moslem minorities will enjoy the same civil and political rights as Moslems' and in Article 40 which provides for the equal rights of Turkish nationals belonging to non-Muslim minorities to 'enjoy the same treatment and security in law and in fact as other Turkish nationals' as well as the equal right 'to establish, manage and control at their own expense, any charitable, religious and social institutions, any schools and other establishments for instruction and education, with the right to use their own language and to exercise their own religion freely therein'.[79] Despite the further bolstering of these guarantees in Articles 41–43[80] and the recognition in Article 44 of the treaty that these provisions 'constitute obligations of international concern', it has been argued that non-Muslim minorities in Turkey experience continuing discrimination.[81] This, coupled with the situation that the treaty only formally acknowledges Greeks, Armenian Christians and Jews as minorities,[82] has prompted a leading study on the issue of minority rights in Turkey to conclude that '[t]he Turkish application regarding who is and who is not a minority is in breach of international standards'.[83]

In terms of ethnic and linguistic minorities, the Kurdish community is the largest ethnic minority with an estimated population of between 10 and 15 million.[84] Others include the Roma population, estimated at over 500,000; the Bosnian population at approximately 1 million; Arabs, some of whom define themselves by religion (as Alevis); Circassians, who number over 3 million; Laz, between 500,000 and 1 million; and ethnic Bulgarians, who mostly live in Thrace.[85] With regard to religious minorities, as noted above only 'non-Moslem' minorities are protected by the Lausanne Treaty, which includes an estimated 60,000 Armenian Orthodox Christians; 20,000 Jews; 2,000–3,000 Greek Orthodox Christians;[86] 15,000–20,000 Syrian Orthodox Christians; 5,000–7,000 Yezidis; and a small number of Nestorians.[87] While the great majority of Turkey's Muslims are of the Sunnī branch of Islam, there are also numerous Muslim religious minorities. These include the communities of Shīas in Eastern Turkey near the Iranian border and in Istanbul, estimated at 300,000 and the large group of Alevis consisting of 12–15 million Turks.[88]

The Constitution of 1982 seemingly copper-fastened the minority regime established under the Treaty of Lausanne and the definition of minorities therein by endorsing the treaty under Article 90(5) which gives effect to international treaties within the national legal order.[89] This was also confirmed in the constitutional amendment of 22 May 2004 which provides that:

> [i]nternational agreements duly put into effect bear the force of law ... In case of contradiction between international agreements regarding basic rights and freedoms approved through proper procedure and domestic laws, due to different provisions on the same issue, the provisions of international agreements shall be considered.[90]

The ardent nationalism that appears to permeate the Constitution[91] also suggests that minority groupings proclaiming their differences may not be altogether encouraged. This is further reflected in Article 66 which proclaims that '[e]veryone bound to the Turkish state through the bond of citizenship is a Turk', whereas the term 'minority' receives no mention in the Constitution.

4.2 The minority question in Europe

Although the idea of securing the protection of minorities has, for some time, gained a firm foothold within the framework of international law,[92] it is an issue with which the EU has only recently concerned itself. Williams even suggests that the aspect of the Copenhagen criteria requiring that applicant states guarantee 'respect for and protection of minorities' 'appears wholly arbitrary in the Community context', contending that '[t]here has been little evidence of the Community focusing previously on this particular aspect of rights'.[93] Given that 'the Community's approach to human rights has always focused on their individual application', a more consistent approach to the question, it is argued, would have been to make the elimination of all forms of discrimination a prerequisite for membership as this 'would have possessed significantly more force and identifiable content than the reference to minorities'.[94] Nonetheless, prompted undoubtedly by the events of the early nineties in the former Yugoslavia, the fulfilment of the protection of minority rights became a fundamental part of the political aspect of the Copenhagen criteria when formulated in 1993.

Following periods of relative standstill and slow progress in the area of minority protection in Europe, Türk suggests that since 1990 there has been a period of 'intensive search' consisting of work by the Council of Europe, the Organization for Security and Cooperation in Europe (OSCE) and the EU.[95] There have, therefore, been numerous attempts to codify minority rights protection within the European context, the most important of which are set forth in the following sections.

4.2.1 The European Convention on Human Rights

Following the example set by the drafters of the Universal Declaration on Human Rights (UDHR), the European Convention on Human Rights and Fundamental Freedoms (ECHR) does not contain a specific provision dealing with the rights of minorities. Protocol No. 12 to the convention, which Turkey has signed but has yet to ratify, attempted to remedy this by providing that no one shall be discriminated against on any ground by any public authority.[96] The Protocol could potentially provide protection to those minorities in Turkey not officially recognized as such under the Treaty of Lausanne or the Constitution since it is not aimed specifically at minorities.

The convention does contain a general prohibition of discrimination clause (Article 14) which prohibits discrimination on the basis of a number of criteria, including 'association with a national minority'.[97] One of the principal limitations of Article 14 is that it is limited to the prohibition of discrimination in the enjoyment of one of the other rights guaranteed by the convention. Of course, if national minorities are not recognized within member states, then Article 14 arguably does not protect against discrimination on this ground. Although the ECtHR has frequently found that Turkey violated Article 14 in conjunction with other provisions of the convention, the limitations of the convention in terms of minority protection have been noted. Baka, for example, asserts that: 'the Convention in its present form does not, and cannot – for it was not devised for this purpose – meet the present-day requirements of modern international minority protection'.[98]

4.2.2 The European Framework Convention for the Protection of Minorities

In 1998, two significant treaties for minority rights' protection came into force in Europe. The European Charter for Regional or Minority Languages was formulated in 1992 in recognition that the: 'protection and promotion of regional or minority languages in the different countries and regions of Europe represent an important contribution to the building of a Europe based on the principles of democracy and cultural diversity within the framework of national sovereignty and territorial integrity'.[99] A regional or minority language was defined in Article 1 of the charter as one which is traditionally used within a territory of the state by nationals of the state forming a numerically smaller group than the remainder of the population and different from the official language(s) of the state. The charter has now been ratified by 22 states, although Turkey has not ratified it to date.

More noteworthy for the general protection of minorities was the coming into force in 1998 of the European Framework Convention for the Protection of National Minorities. The convention was drafted in the early 1990s and derived its impetus, Steketee suggests, from a number of events; notably the collapse of the Soviet Union and the fall of the Berlin wall, the Commission on Security and Cooperation in Europe Copenhagen Declaration of 1990 and the adoption of the 1992 UN Declaration on the Rights of Persons Belonging to National or Ethnic, Linguistic and Religious Minorities.[100] While the convention has been the subject of a great deal of criticism, not least because it is a 'framework' rather than a 'normal' convention,[101] it marks a significant contribution to the existing minority rights protections.

To date, 39 member states of the Council of Europe have ratified the Framework Convention and a further four countries have signed, but not yet ratified, the treaty. Turkey is one of only four countries not to have taken any action as regards the convention and its failure to sign the convention was noted in a recent European Parliament resolution on Turkey's progress towards EU accession in which the Parliament outlined that it:

> Expects that, in order to enable the ninth package of legislative reforms to give a truly new impetus to the reform process, the Turkish Parliament

will amend and subsequently adopt this package, bearing in mind in particular the following:

[...]

international agreements such as the Council of Europe Framework Convention for the Protection of National Minorities, the European Charter for Regional or Minority Languages, the Rome Statute of the International Criminal Court (ICC) and the United Nations Convention on the Law of the Sea will be signed and ratified ...[102]

4.2.3 The Copenhagen criteria

While the mechanisms discussed above are instructive in terms of determining the prevailing legal protection of minority rights, the Copenhagen criteria are the principal standards by which EU candidate states are assessed. The political criterion requires EU applicant states to provide for stability of institutions guaranteeing democracy, the rule of law, human rights and respect for and protection of minorities. Formulated at a meeting of the European Council on 21–22 June 1993, the criteria provide:

> Membership requires that the candidate country has achieved stability of institutions guaranteeing democracy, the rule of law, human rights and respect for and protection of minorities, the existence of a functioning market economy as well as the capacity to cope with competitive pressure and market forces within the Union. Membership presupposes the candidate's ability to take on the obligations of membership including adherence to the aims of political, economic and monetary union.[103]

Given that the criteria were drafted while conflict in the Balkans continued, it is likely that the provision requiring respect for, and protection of minorities was included as an effort to avoid such conflicts in the future.[104] While undoubtedly laudable, it has been suggested that the EU demands standards of potential members that it does not stipulate for its current member states:

> While the requirement of respect for and protection of minorities is prominent in the EU accession conditionality, the fact that the Union is not well-equipped to monitor it internally leads to a paradoxical situation. The pressure to respect and protect minority rights will be less tangible for the new Member States than it was when they were candidates.[105]

The standards for minority protection in Europe have been set by the UDHR, the CCPR, the CSCE Copenhagen Document of 1990 and the Framework Convention on the Protection of National Minorities, which 'have set the guidelines for how States should provide an adequate legal framework and practical mechanisms for protecting minorities ... [and] are also the basis for interpreting the EU's accession criteria as regards minority protection'.[106] It may, therefore, appear paradoxical that Turkey should be deemed to be in compliance with the minority protection aspect of the criteria despite its failure to sign any of the major agreements on the issue. Yet Turkey's position with regard to minorities is very much akin to that of France[107] – one of the founding members of the Union – and it is not, therefore, anomalistic. There is undoubtedly merit in Ekeus's contention that:

> the standards on which the Copenhagen criteria are based are universal, in which case they should be equally – and consistently – applied to all member States ... there needs to be a more precise and consistent elaboration of minority-related standards which apply to *all* member States in order to avoid misunderstanding and arbitrariness in EU human rights policy.[108]

Ekeus's point undoubtedly highlights the double standards inherent in the human rights policies of the EU. Nonetheless, a recent study on the issue of minority rights in Turkey noted:

> Arguably, the most significant achievement of the EU process has been the way in which it has created space for various minority groups to demand recognition of their distinct identities, the reformulation of the exclusive Turkish citizenship and the removal of barriers to the free exercise of their religious, political and cultural rights ... It cannot be denied that groundbreaking reforms have been undertaken in recent years, granting limited yet significant rights to individuals belonging to minorities.[109]

Parallels also exist between Turkey's compliance with the minority rights aspect of the Copenhagen criteria and those previously encountered by the EU's newest members, Bulgaria and Romania, who joined the Union in January 2007. Bulgaria and Romania have traditionally adopted a similar position on minorities to that taken by Turkey, with both the ethnic Hungarian minorities in Romania and ethnic Turk minorities in Bulgaria 'having suffered a slow process of cultural assimilation' under communist rule:[110]

> In Romania, Ceausescu emphasized the glory of the homeland and launched a statewide campaign to celebrate Romanian history and culture to create a homogenous nation. Minority education was a principal target in this campaign. Hungarian-language schools from pre-school to university were operating during the early communist period and had their own administrators. Over time, however, teachers were replaced by individuals deemed politically trustworthy and schools were merged so that ethnic Romanians comprised a majority of the student body ... Meanwhile, in Bulgaria ethnic Turks faced what was arguably an even more stringent assimilation campaign and restrictions on education, language, and religious

rights during the communist period ... Prompted in part by Turkish resistance to the collectivization of agricultural land, the communist-led government in Bulgaria began in 1950 an expulsion of more than 250,000 ethnic Turks and a campaign to assimilate ethnic minorities into Bulgarians.[111]

It is against this historical backdrop that the European Commission declared in its report of 1998, that the protection of minorities remained a problem in Bulgaria. The Commission noted that the ethnic Turkish minority were integrated and represented in political life but that the Roma community were 'discriminated against in all spheres of social life' and that the 'economic difficulties of the country continue to affect particularly the Roma community'.[112] The report also pointed to other problems such as the situation in prisons; the number of people being held in pre-trial detention; allegations of ill-treatment against law enforcement officers; and concerns about political control of the electronic media.[113] Nonetheless, although stipulating that '[f]urther efforts [were] required to prevent the social exclusion of the Roma and to reform the judiciary' the Commission concluded that Bulgaria had fulfilled the Copenhagen political criteria.[114]

With regard to Romania's accession to the EU, similar problems relating to the protection of minorities and problems with the implementation of civil and political rights were noted in the first report of the Commission in 1998. The report highlighted, in particular, the limitations on freedom of expression, excessive use of custody and pre-trial detention and allegations of inhuman and degrading treatment.[115] In relation to the issue of minority rights, Romania's protection of minorities was found to be satisfactory 'with the major exception of the Roma'.[116] The Commission considered that discrimination and prejudice against the Roma minority was 'widespread' and noted that the protection of minority rights and the social and economic integration of the Roma required substantial additional requirements'.[117] Perhaps surprisingly then, the Commission concluded that Romania fulfilled the political criterion of the Copenhagen criteria, although it was reiterated that much remained to be done in eliminating corruption, improving the working of the courts and protecting individual liberties and the rights of the Roma.[118]

It is significant that the European Union admitted both Romania and Bulgaria in spite of the very real problems highlighted by the Commission in terms of minority rights. This suggests that the decision to do so could possibly have been motivated by one of two main factors: either human rights protections including 'respect for and protection of minorities' is not as important a criterion for accession as the fulfilment of the economic requirements, or the EU was of the opinion that having fulfilled the minimum requirements, more pressure could be brought to bear on Bulgaria and Romania in terms of improving their human rights protections when they were full members of the Union. If we are to take the various pronouncements of the

EU with regard to the importance in which it views the protection of human rights at face value, then only the latter of these two factors is a possibility and it begs the question why this approach was adopted for Bulgaria and Romania but not for Turkey.

It is evident that the problems of human rights protections in Romania and Bulgaria as assessed by the European Commission in the first progress reports of 1998, were considerably less serious than those highlighted in relation to Turkey. With regard to Turkey, the Commission had recounted regular occurrences of torture, disappearances and extra-judicial executions as well as widespread restrictions on freedom of expression, in particular of the press; freedom of association; freedom of assembly and noted that there were 'major shortcomings in the treatment of minorities'.[119] However, NGOs considering the human rights situation in Bulgaria and Romania at that time noted similar problems to those in Turkey (albeit on a slightly lesser scale). In a 1999 report, Human Rights Watch noted:

> The human rights situation in Bulgaria remained static during 1998 ... State authorities routinely infringed on freedoms of expression and religion; often state institutions and the press appeared to collaborate to increase hysteria and prejudice against minorities. Ethnic minorities continued to suffer disproportionately from widespread police brutality ... On at least four occasions in 1998, police conducted large scale raids of Roma neighborhoods; the police claimed they were searching for stolen goods, but local human rights groups and witnesses suspected the raids were intended to intimidate Roma and collectively to punish the Roma community for its perceived criminality ... Local authorities and media continued to harass the members of non-Orthodox religions ... The death penalty remained legal under Bulgarian law.[120]

In relation to Romania, the report also highlighted a number of concerns:

> Despite the government's promises and pressure from NGOs and the international community, Vasile's shaky coalition government – composed of numerous political parties with conflicting agendas – made no noticeable progress in resolving long-entrenched human rights problems such as discrimination and other ill-treatment directed at ethnic and sexual minorities. In addition, the government prosecuted critical journalists under its libel statutes, and there continued to be nearly complete impunity for police brutality, especially when the victims were unpopular minorities ... The Chamber of Deputies also failed to amend the criminal code provision prohibiting 'defamation of the nation and/or state authorities.' During 1998, these provisions were used to punish journalists who exposed corruption among public officials ... Women also faced police harassment and discrimination in Romania.[121]

With regard to Turkey, however, in deciding in 2004 that it had sufficiently satisfied the criteria in order to open accession negotiations, the European Commission was undoubtedly influenced by the volume and extent of the reform packages already instituted, some of which deal explicitly with the issue of minority rights. The revision of the Constitution in 2004, for example, details a new Article 10 which provides for a general prohibition of discrimination clause, stating:

> All individuals are equal without any discrimination before the law, irrespective of language, race, colour, gender, political opinion, philosophical belief, religion and sect, or any such considerations. Men and women have equal rights. The State shall have the obligation to ensure that this equality exists in practice. No privilege shall be granted to any individual, family, group or class. State organs and administrative authorities shall act in compliance with the principle of equality before the law in all their proceedings.

A new institutional framework, the Minority Issues Assessment Board, composed of the representatives of the Ministries of Foreign Affairs, Interior and National Education and other related institutions was also established in 2004 in order to address the problems of non-Muslim minorities.[122] It would appear, therefore, that the minority issue is one which is beginning to be addressed in Turkey. Developments such as those just mentioned therefore suggest yet another success of EU conditionality inherent in the accession process.

5 Summary

It is perhaps overly cynical to suggest that Turkey's record in providing fundamental human rights guarantees did not concern the EU when it came to establishing trade agreements through the signing of the Association Agreement in 1963 and the Customs Union in 1995. Less cynical is the proposition that the EU has employed the carrot-and-stick method to assuring the provision of human rights guarantees in a prospective member state as applied through the process of threat of exclusion and promise of acceptance, and which has been very successful in Turkey's case. Although concerns over Turkey's record in terms of fundamental human rights protections are real, it is not unique in this regard and both countries which most recently acceded to the Union, Romania and Bulgaria, shared similar problems, particularly in relation to the protection of minorities.

While support for EU membership within Turkey remains high, it has dropped somewhat[123] and as the Eurobarometer report suggests, there exists a feeling of disbelief that Turkey will ever be 'allowed' to join the Union despite its best efforts at harmonization and reform of its laws. Moreover, 'religious, cultural and historical' reasons are cited by Turkish MPs as the greatest barrier to achieving full membership of the Union.[124] Notwithstanding this perception, the current administration reaffirmed its commitment to Turkey achieving full membership and suggested a willingness to review the offending provisions of the Penal Code in an effort to secure compliance with European norms.[125]

Nonetheless, it is arguable that the extent of the reforms already achieved is such that without further incentive from the EU in terms of progression of the membership bid, reform fatigue may well set in. This sentiment was recently reflected in the statement of Turkey's Foreign Minister, Ali Babacan, suggesting that without a clear target date for membership, there is no impetus to push through further reforms.[126] In reality, it has even been suggested that not only is there a slowdown in the reform process but an actual regression in terms of human rights protections in Turkey. This is particularly so in the south-east of the country where the escalation in the conflict led to the imposition of 'military zone' status in three provinces in the south-east – Şırnak, Siirt and Hakkari – in June 2007.[127] The only information with regard to events in these provinces is therefore solely available from the military, as journalists are prohibited from reporting from 'military zones'. As early as 2006, Human Rights Watch documented a 'retrograde trend' in terms of the human rights situation in Turkey.[128] The regression has been linked to the stalling of the EU accession process, resulting in the paradoxical situation whereby a process supposedly designed to promote the protection of human rights in Turkey is possibly having the opposite result.[129]

The radical reform process implemented in response to pressures from the EU has ensured a greater deal of protection for Turkey's minorities but the Kurdish question to date remains unsolved, although the current administration showed positive signs of engagement by at least admitting to the fact of a Kurdish 'problem' in Turkey. The protracted conflict in the south-east proved a catalyst for human rights abuses for many years, perpetrated by all parties to it. The response of the Turkish government to the conflict has often been severe and has warranted criticism from both the EU and the ECtHR. The severity of the response of the Turkish authorities stems, as Evin notes:

> from a deeply felt and widely shared animosity in Turkey toward separatism. Modern Turkey had been established on the territory reclaimed and defended after the collapse of the Ottoman Empire. A deep apprehension of dismemberment had weighed heavily on the Turkish soul ever since the rapid disintegration of the Ottoman Empire at the end of the nineteenth century, followed by the partitioning and occupation of its territories after the First World War.[130]

The success of the EU reform process in Turkey has accelerated because of a period of stability in government since the parliamentary elections of 2002 and the election of the pro-EU Justice and Development Party. Apprehension surrounding the current prime minister's conservatism due to his religious fervour is not reflective of his attitude towards the EU as he has proved the most 'progressive' leader in this regard and has hastened the reform process while in office.[131] Nonetheless, concerns regarding fundamental human rights guarantees (and freedom of expression in particular) and the unresolved issues relating to the protection of minority rights in Turkey constitute but two of the questions inextricably linked to Turkey's pursuit of EU membership. A third question, which has to date eluded diplomatic resolve, is the Turkish occupation of Northern Cyprus and it is to this issue that this study now turns.

Notes

1 D. Barchard, 'The Rule of Law', in Lake, *EU and Turkey*, 89.
2 *Ibid.*, 90.
3 *Ibid.*
4 See, for example, D. Lohman, 'The International Community Fails to Monitor Chechnya Abuses', *Helsinki Monitor*, 11 (2000), 73–82, 73, noting that Europe had 'done little to stop' and did 'not even speak of an international obligation to bring an end to the very serious and systematic abuses being committed in Chechnya'. See also S. Kinzer *Crescent and Star: Turkey Between Two Worlds* (New York: Farrar, Strauss and Giroux, 2001), 113, noting that 'the eagerness with which some foreign governments have condemned Turkey, justified as condemnation may be, is more than a little disingenuous. Turkey was facing a threat to its very existence as a unified state, and it responded the way other countries in the post-war world have responded when peoples under their sovereignty rose in rebellion. The Turkish campaign against the PKK was comparable in various ways to those waged by the Dutch in Indonesia, the British in Malaya, the French in Algeria, the Americans in Vietnam, the Serbs in Bosnia and the Russians in Chechnya. Turks understandably react unpleasantly when those former imperial powers condemn them for using tactics they themselves perfected not so long ago'.
5 A. Williams, *EU Human Rights Policies: A Study in Irony* (Oxford: Oxford University Press, 2005), 129.
6 Treaty on European Union, 7 Feb. 1992, OJ C 224/1 (1992).
7 *Ibid.*
8 J. Sugden, 'Leverage in Theory and Practice: Human Rights and Turkey's EU Candidacy', in M. Uğur and N. Canefe (eds), *Turkey and European Integration: Accession Prospects and Issues* (New York: Routledge, 2004), 241–65, 242, 246. Sugden notes that '[f]rom 1995 onwards, the rate of human rights violations began to slow down. But this was a consequence of the decline in political violence rather than a product of EU influence. The PKK, presumably exhausted after years of intense fighting, made less frequent strikes against gendarmerie posts and village guards. Fewer fatal attacks on security forces meant fewer punitive security force raids involving torture and extra-judicial killing, and fewer reprisal raids on the civilian population.'
9 See N. Tocci, 'Europeanization in Turkey: Trigger or Anchor for Reform?', *South European Society and Politics*, 10(1) (2005), 73–83, 74, noting that 'the reform process coincided with the initiation of Turkey's EU accession course. Steps towards democratic change were made before the December 1999 Helsinki European Council, which accorded Turkey EU candidacy. However, until then, reforms had been largely superficial and ad hoc. They did not represent a fully-fledged and committed programme of democratic transformation.'

10 Sugden, 'Leverage in Theory', 242.
11 Barchard, 'Rule of Law', 88.
12 *Ibid.*, 89.
13 Recep Tayyip Erdoğan, address at the New Tactics in Human Rights Symposium, Ankara, Turkey, 29 September–4 October 2004 (available at: www.newtactics. org/sites/newtactics.org/files/resources/erdogan.doc) (last accessed, 20 January 2010).
14 Recep Tayyip Erdoğan, address at the Symposium on Conservative Democracy, Istanbul, 10 January 2004, available (in Turkish, at: www.akparti.org.tr/), cited in T. W. Smith, 'Civic Nationalism and Ethnocultural Justice in Turkey', Hum. Rts. Q., 27 (2005), 436–70, 437.
15 See K. Hughes, 'The Political Dynamics of Turkish Accession to the EU: A European Success Story or the EU's Most Contested Enlargement?' (Swedish Institute for European Policy Studies Stockholm 2005), 29.
16 See Section 2.
17 Law No. 5178, Published in the Official Gazette on 26 June 2004.
18 Published in the Official Gazette on 5 December 2003.
19 Law No. 5253, Published in the Official Gazette on 4 December 2004.
20 Law No. 2911.
21 European Council Decision of 8 March 2001 on the principles, priorities, intermediate objectives and conditions contained in the Accession Partnership with the Republic of Turkey (2001/235/EC), para. 4.1.
22 See 'Eradicating Torture in Turkey's Police Stations: Analysis and Recommendations', Human Rights Watch Briefing Paper 2004, 2, noting that Turkey's formal protections against torture are now among the strongest in Europe.
23 Law No. 4778.
24 See Country report on Turkey in Amnesty International Report 2005, AI Index: POL 10/001/2005, 25 May 2005.
25 State Security Courts have been abolished and replaced with 'Special Felony' Courts. See *Ibid.*
26 European Commission Regular Report on Turkey's Progress Towards EU Accession 1998.
27 Conclusions of the Presidency, Luxembourg European Council December 1997, EU Bulletin no. 12.97, para. 31.
28 Convention Establishing an Association Between the European Economic Community and Turkey, signed at Ankara, Turkey 12 September 1963.
29 European Commission Regular Report on Turkey's Progress Towards EU Accession 1998, B 1.
30 *Ibid.*
31 European Commission Regular Report on Turkey's Progress Towards EU Accession 1998, 15–17.
32 *Ibid.*, 18–19.
33 European Commission Regular Report on Turkey's Progress Towards EU Accession 1999, 11–14.
34 This concerned a ruling of the Supreme Court of Appeals, which paved the way for changes in the legislation regarding permissible names for children. See European Commission Regular Report on Turkey's Progress Towards EU Accession 2000, 15, 18.
35 *Ibid.*, 18–19.

36 European Commission Regular Report on Turkey's Progress Towards EU Accession 2001, 22.

37 *Ibid.*, 14.

38 *Ibid.*, 22–8.

39 European Commission Regular Report on Turkey's Progress Towards EU Accession 2002, 25–33.

40 The Commission stated that '[t]he interpretation of legislation is crucial to ensuring actual freedom of expression. There are as yet no signs that the interpretation of the law by judges consistently takes into account the rights of the defendant under the ECHR' (*ibid.*, 33).

41 European Commission Regular Report on Turkey's Progress Towards EU Accession 2002, 36–8.

42 European Commission Regular Report on Turkey's Progress Towards EU Accession 2003, B 1.6 (unpaginated document).

43 *Ibid.*

44 *Ibid.*

45 See Chapter 1, Section 2.

46 European Commission Regular Report on Turkey's Progress Towards EU Accession 2004, 174.

47 *Ibid.*

48 *Ibid.*, 175.

49 European Commission Regular Report on Turkey's Progress Towards EU Accession 2005, 41.

50 Turkey 2007 Progress Report, EN(COM(2007) 663), Brussels, 6 November 2007, 14. The 2008 report confirmed that provisions restricting freedom of expression remained a 'cause for concern'. See European Commission Turkey 2008 Progress Report, SEC(2008) 2699 final, Brussels, 5 November 2008.

51 Turkey 2009 Progress Report SEC(2009)1334, Brussels 14 October 2009, 18.

52 On this point see generally, C. C. Logan, 'Liberty or Safety: Implications of the USA PATRIOT Act and the UK's Anti-Terror Laws on Freedom of Expression and Free Exercise of Religion', Seton Hall L. Rev., 37 (2006–7), 863–92.

53 European Parliament Resolution of 24 October 2007 on EC–Turkey Relations, P6_TA-PROV(2007)0472, para. 13. This opinion was also reflected by the European Commission in the 2007 and 2008 progress reports on Turkey. See above n. 49 and accompanying text.

54 Council of the European Union 'EU Annual Report on Human Rights 2007', Brussels, 18 October 2007, 13288/1/07REV 1, 148.

55 European Commission Regular Report on Turkey's Progress Towards EU Accession 1998, 15.

56 See, for example, *Zana v Turkey*, application no. 69/1996/688/880, judgment of 25 November 1997; *Incal v Turkey*, application no. 41/1997/825/1031, judgment of 9 June 1998; *Arslan v Turkey*, application no. 23462/94, judgment of 8 July 1999; *Baikaya and another v Turkey*, application no. 23536/94, judgment of 8 July 1999; *Erdogdu and another v Turkey*, application no. 25067/94, judgment of 8 July 1999; *Karata v Turkey*, application no. 23168/94, judgment of 8 July 1999; *Gerger v Turkey*, application no. 24919/94, judgment of 8 July 1999; *Öztürk v Turkey*, application no. 22479/93, judgment of 28 September 1999; *Sürek v Turkey* (No. 1), application no. 26682/95, judgment of 8 July 1999. For discussion of these cases, see M. G. Kearney *The Prohibition of Propaganda*

for War in International Law (Oxford: Oxford University Press, 2007), ch. 4 B (ii).

57 European Commission Regular Report on Turkey's Progress Towards EU Accession 2005, 25.

58 European Commission Regular Report on Turkey's Progress Towards EU Accession, Brussels, 6 October 2004 COM(2004) 656 final, 37.

59 See for example Amnesty International 'Article 301 is a threat to freedom of expression and must be repealed now!' AI Index: EUR 44/035/2005 1 December 2005; 'Suppressing Academic Debate: The Turkish Penal Code' (London: KHRP, 2006) and 'Turkey on Trial: The Prosecutions of Orhan Pamuk and Others' (London: KHRP, 2006).

60 See 'Leader, In Praise Of ... Orhan Pamuk', *Guardian*, 16 December 2005.

61 See 'Dink Convicted of Insulting Turkish Identity', *Turkish Daily News*, 8 October 2005.

62 European Commission Regular Report on Turkey's Progress Towards EU Accession 2006, 14. The Commission repeated this sentiment in its 2007 report, in which it noted that '[t]he restrictive jurisprudence established in 2006 by the Court of Cassation on article 301 remains in force. Against this background, article 301 needs to be brought in line with the relevant EU standards. The same applies to other legal provisions which have been used to prosecute the non-violent expression of opinions and may limit freedom of expression' (Turkey 2007 Progress Report, EN(COM(2007) 663), Brussels, 6 November 2007, 14–15).

63 See 'European Parliament Critical of Slowdown in Turkey's Reform Process' European Parliament Press Service, 27 September 2006.

64 Again, this is perhaps reflective of the type of expression now commonly prohibited in the post-2001 legal landscape. In the UK, for example, the Terrorism Act 2006, s. 1, makes it an offence to publish a statement that is likely to be understood 'by some or all of the members of the public to whom it is published as a direct or indirect encouragement or other inducement to them to the commission, preparation or instigation of acts of terrorism'. Section 1(3) encompasses the concept of 'glorification', which includes statements which '(a) glorifies the commission or preparation (whether in the past, in the future or generally) of such acts or offences; and (b) is a statement from which those members of the public could reasonably be expected to infer that what is being glorified is being glorified as conduct that should be emulated by them in existing circumstances'.

65 Turkey 2006 Progress Report EN(COM (2006) 649 final), 6.

66 K. Yildiz, *The Kurds in Turkey: EU Accession and Human Rights* (London: Pluto Press, 2005) 50.

67 See 'Parliament Approves 301 Amendment, Eyes on Implementation', *Turkish Daily News*, 1 May 2008.

68 'EU Presidency Statement on the Changes in Article 301 of the Turkish Penal Code' (available at: www.eu2008.si/en/News_and_Documents/Press_Releases/April/0430MZZ-izjava-Turcija.html) (last accessed 20 January 2010).

69 See 'Parliament Approves 301 Amendment, Eyes on Implementation', *Turkish Daily News*, 1 May 2008.

70 Turkey 2009 Progress Report SEC(2009)1334, Brussels 14 October 2009, 18.

71 *Ibid.*

72 *Ibid.*

73 H. Pope, 'Turkey's Minority Report', Geo. J. Int'l Aff., 6 (2005), 95, 95.

74 Treaty of Lausanne.
75 Turkey is also a signatory to the majority of international human rights instruments, as well as the 1950 European Convention on Human Rights and Fundamental Freedoms. Of the main international human rights agreements, Turkey signed the Convention on the Rights of Persons with Disabilities on 30 March 2007; the International Covenant on Economic Social and Cultural Rights (CESCR) on 23 December 2003; the International Covenant on Civil and Political Rights (CCPR) on 23 December 2003; the International Convention on the Elimination of All Forms of Racial Discrimination (CERD) on 16 October 2002; the International Convention on the Elimination of All Forms of Discrimination Against Women (CEDAW) on 19 January 1988; and the Convention Against Torture (CAT) on 1 September 1988. See the website of the Office of the High Commission for Human Rights (at: http://treaties.un.org/Pages/Treaties.aspx?id=4&subid=A&lang=en) (last accessed, 13 January 2010).
76 N. Karimova and E. Deverell 'Minorities in Turkey', Occasional Papers No. 19 (2001), Swedish Institute of International Affairs, 7.
77 Treaty of Lausanne.
78 See D. Kurban, 'Confronting Equality: The Need for Constitutional Protection of Turkey's Minorities on Turkey's Path to the European Union', Colum. Hum. Rts. L. Rev., 35 (2003), 151–223, 169.
79 Treaty of Lausanne.
80 Article 41 provides:

As regards public instruction, the Turkish Government will grant in those towns and districts, where a considerable proportion of non-Moslem nationals are resident, adequate facilities for ensuring that in the primary schools the instruction shall be given to the children of such Turkish nationals through the medium of their own language. This provision will not prevent the Turkish Government from making the teaching of the Turkish language obligatory in the said schools.

In towns and districts where there is a considerable proportion of Turkish nationals belonging to non-Moslem minorities, these minorities shall be assured an equitable share in the enjoyment and application of the sums which may be provided out of public funds under the State, municipal or other budgets for educational, religious, or charitable purposes [...].

Article 42 states: 'The Turkish Government undertakes to take, as regards non-Moslem minorities, in so far as concerns their family law or personal status, measures permitting the settlement of these questions in accordance with the customs of those minorities ... The Turkish Government undertakes to grant full protection to the churches, synagogues, cemeteries, and other religious establishments of the above-mentioned minorities. All facilities and authorisation will be granted to the pious foundations, and to the religious and charitable institutions of the said minorities at present existing in Turkey, and the Turkish Government will not refuse, for the formation of new religious and charitable institutions, any of the necessary facilities which are guaranteed to other private institutions of that nature.'

Article 43 provides that:

Turkish nationals belonging to non-Moslem minorities shall not be compelled to perform any act which constitutes a violation of their faith or religious observances, and shall not be placed under any disability by reason of their refusal to attend Courts of Law or to perform any legal business on their weekly day of rest.

This provision, however, shall not exempt such Turkish nationals from such obligations as shall be imposed upon all other Turkish nationals for the preservation of public order.

81 See, for example, Kurban, 'Confronting Equality', 170, noting that: '[t]he Turkish Government's record in fulfilling its Lausanne duties towards non-Muslims has been cursory, reluctant, inconsistent, and disingenuous'. See also Karimova and Deverell, 'Minorities', 8, stating that despite Turkey's commitments under the Treaty of Lausanne: '[i]n terms of interpretation and protection of minority rights there are a plethora of problems that should be solved.

82 *Ibid.*, 7.

83 N. Kaya and C. Baldwin, 'Minorities in Turkey: Submission to the European Union and the Government of Turkey', Minority Rights Group International (July 2004), 6.

84 See O. Q. Goldman, 'The Need for an Independent International Mechanism to Protect Group Rights: A Case Study of the Kurds', Tulsa J. Comp. & Int'l L., 2 (1994), 45, 66 estimating the number of Kurds in Turkey at 10–11 million; Karimova and Deverell, 'Minorities', 13, estimating the number at about 13 million; and Kaya and Baldwin, 'Minorities', 7, estimating the number at 15 million.

85 Kaya and Baldwin, 'Minorities', 7.

86 *Ibid.*

87 N. Öktem, 'Religion in Turkey', BYU L. Rev. (2002) 371, 375.

88 *Ibid.*, 373–5.

89 'Confronting Equality', 175–6.

90 Constitution of the Republic of Turkey, Article 90.

91 See Chapter 1, section 2.3.4.

92 The modern phase in the protection of minority rights can perhaps be identified as beginning at the end of the First World War with the adoption of the League of Nations treaty system. Although the Covenant of the League of Nations did not contain specific provisions relating to the protection of minorities, its system incorporated treaties that protected designated minorities. See T. W. Simon, 'Minorities in International Law', Can J. L. & Jurisprudence, 10 (1997), 507, 508, noting that the treaties included the 1919 Treaty of Versailles with Poland; the 1919 Treaties of Saint-Germain-en-Laye with Czechoslovakia, and the Kingdom of the Serbs, Croats and Slovenes; the 1919 Treaty of Neuilly-sur-Seine with Bulgaria; the 1919 Treaty of Paris with Bulgaria; the 1919 Treaty of Paris with Romania; the 1920 Treaty of Trainon with Hungary; the 1920 Treaty of Sèvres with Greece; and the 1923 Treaty of Lausanne with Turkey. However, it wasn't until the framing of Article 27 of the ICCPR in 1966 that minorities received specific protection under the rubric of international human rights law. Article 27 states: 'In those States in which ethnic, religious or linguistic minorities exist, persons belonging to such minorities shall not be denied the right, in community with the other members of their group, to enjoy their own culture, to profess and practise their own religion, or to use their own language'. ICCPR, adopted and opened for signature, ratification and accession by General Assembly (GA) res. 2200A (XXI) of 16 December 1966. The effect of Article 27 is negated in Turkey due to its entering of a reservation to the Article on signature, stating that it

reserved the right 'to interpret and apply the provisions of Article 27 [of ICCPR] in accordance with the related provisions and rules of the Constitution of the Republic of Turkey and the Treaty of Lausanne of 24 July 1923 and its Appendixes'. See the website of the Office of the High Commission on Human Rights(at:http://treaties.un.org/Pages/ViewDetails.aspx?src=TREATY&mtdsg_ no=IV-4&ch.=4&lang=en) (last accessed 13 December 2009). It should nonetheless be noted that France also entered a reservation to Article 27 of the ICCPR on signature, stating '[i]n the light of article 2 of the Constitution of the French Republic, the French Government declares that article 27 is not applicable so far as the Republic is concerned' (Article 2 of the Constitution guarantees the equality of all citizens before the law, without distinction as to origin, race, or religion). France's position has been criticized by both the Human Rights Committee (HRC) and academic commentators. See concluding observations of the HRC: France. 04/08/97CCPR/C/79/Add. 80, para. 24, noting that the HRC was 'unable to agree that France is a country in which there are no ethnic, religious or linguistic minorities'. See generally E. M. Edelstein, 'The Loi Toubon: *Liberté, Égalité, Fraternité*, but only on France's Terms', Emory Int'l L. Rev., 17 (2003), 1127–1202.

93 Williams, *EU*, 66.
94 *Ibid.*, 67.
95 D. Türk, 'Protection of minorities in Europe', *Collected Courses of the Academy of European Law*, III–2 (1992), 143–206, quoted in G. Pentassuglia *Minorities in International Law: An Introductory Study* (Strasbourg: Council of Europe Publishing, 2002), 119.
96 Article 1 of Protocol 12 states: '1 The enjoyment of any right set forth by law shall be secured without discrimination on any ground such as sex, race, colour, language, religion, political or other opinion, national or social origin, association with a national minority, property, birth or other status. 2 No one shall be discriminated against by any public authority on any ground such as those mentioned in paragraph 1.'
97 Article 14 of the ECHR states: 'The enjoyment of the rights and freedoms set forth in this Convention shall be secured without discrimination on any ground such as sex, race, colour, language, religion, political or other opinion, national or social origin, association with a national minority, property, birth or other status.'
98 A. B. Baka, 'The European Convention on Human Rights and the Protection of Minorities Under International Law', Conn. J. Int'l L., 8 (1992–3), 227–42, 236.
99 Preamble to the European Charter for Regional or Minority Languages, European Treaty Series, No. 148.
100 F. Steketee, 'The Framework Convention: A Piece of Art or a Tool for Action?', Int'l J. on Minority and Group Rts., 8 (2001), 1–15, 2.
101 On this point, see S. Troebst 'From Paper to Practice: The Council of Europe's Framework Convention for the Protection of National Minorities', *Helsinki Monitor*, 10 (1999), 19–27, 20, noting that '[w]hilst a framework convention is a convention in the sense that it is a legally binding instrument under international law, the addition of the word "framework" indicates that the principles contained in the instrument are not directly applicable in the domestic legal orders of the member States but will have to be implemented through national legislation and appropriate government policies'. For a critical appraisal of the convention, see generally G. Alfredsson, 'A Frame with an

Incomplete Painting: Comparison of the Framework Convention for the Protection of National Minorities with International Standards and Monitoring Procedures', Int'l J. on Minority and Group Rts., 7(4) (2000), 291–304.

102 'European Parliament resolution on Turkey's progress towards accession' (2006/2118(INI)), 27 September 2006, para. 5. The other three countries not to have signed the Framework Convention are Andorra, France and Monaco.

103 European Council in Copenhagen, 21–22 June 1993, Conclusions of the Presidency, SN180/1/93 Rev. 1, 13.

104 See Williams, *EU*, 68.

105 C. Hillion, 'On Enlargement of the European Union: The Discrepancy Between Membership Obligations and Accession Conditions as Regards the Protection of Minorities', Fordham Int'l L.J., 27 (2004), 715–40, 740.

106 R. Ekeus, 'From the Copenhagen Criteria to the Copenhagen Summit: Minority Issues in an Enlarging Europe', *Helsinki Monitor*, 14 (2003), 38–41, 39.

107 See above, n. 92.

108 Ekeus, 'From the Copenhagen Criteria', 39 (emphasis in original). This view is also echoed by the EU Accession Monitoring Programme of the Open Society Institute, which has noted that 'further headway has been limited by the dearth of clear standards elaborating the political obligations embodied in the Copenhagen criteria, especially as concerns minority protection; the inconsistency of EU member States' own legislation and practice; the difficulty candidate governments have had in marshalling political will on behalf of sometimes unpopular reforms; and the failure of official bodies generally to harness the human and technical resources available in civil society organisations' (*Monitoring the EU Accession Process: Minority Protection* (Hungary: Central European University Press, 2001).

109 'A Quest for Equality: Minorities in Turkey' (London: Minority Rights Group International, September 2007), 32.

110 M. E. McIntosh, M. Abele Mac Iver, D. G. Abele and D. B. Nolle, 'Minority Rights and Majority Rule: Ethnic Tolerance in Romania and Bulgaria', *Social Forces*, 73 (1994–1995), 939–67, 942.

111 *Ibid.*, 942–3 (references omitted).

112 Regular Report from the Commission on Bulgaria's Progress Towards Accession, 1998, 11.

113 *Ibid.*, 10.

114 *Ibid.*, 11.

115 Regular Report from the Commission on Romania's Progress Towards Accession, 1998, 11.

116 *Ibid.*

117 *Ibid.*, 12.

118 *Ibid.*

119 Regular Report from the Commission on Turkey's Progress Towards Accession, 1998, 14–21.

120 Human Rights Watch World Report 1999, 'Bulgaria: Human Rights Developments' (available at: www.unhcr.org/refworld/publisher,HRW,,BGR,3ae 6a8b14,0.html) (last accessed 15 January 2010).

121 Human Rights Watch World Report 1999, 'Romania: Human Rights Developments' (available at: www.unhcr.org/refworld/publisher,HRW,,ROM,3ae 6a8b620,0.html) (last accessed 15 January 2010).

122 See K. Tsitselikis, 'How Far Have EU Policies Affected Minority Issues in Greece and Turkey?', Euroborder Conference Paper, University of Birmingham, 13 November 2004, 4.

123 The results of the sixth Eurobarometer National Report for Turkey in spring 2007 found that support for EU membership was stable at over 50 per cent; 52 per cent of respondents were of the opinion that EU membership would be a 'good thing', a drop of 2 per cent from the results recorded in autumn 2006. See European Commission 'Eurobarometer 67: Public Opinion in the European Union', June 2007 (available at: www.avrupa.info.tr/Files/eb_67_first_en.pdf) (last accessed 2 February 2010).

124 See K. Bulbul, 'Turkey and the EU: A Survey on Turkish MPs' EU Vision', *Turkish Journal of International Relations*, 5(3) (2006), 32–61, 49.

125 See '2008 to be "EU Year" in Turkey, says Foreign Minister', 6 February 2008, citing the Turkish Foreign Minister Ali Babacan reaffirming Turkey's commitment to the 'EU project', which encompasses 'all political reforms', and noting that the government could not be selective over the political criteria required to reach EU standards, whether that concerned the headscarf or Article 301 (available at: www.euractiv.com/en/enlargement/2008–eu-year-turkey-foreign-minister/article-170121) (last accessed 7 February 2010).

126 Babacan was quoted as stating that: '[s]ince a date has not been set for Turkey's membership to the EU, it is Turkey's own initiative when and how to make reforms. Whenever our membership date-timetable becomes clear, we can then display a different stance' ('Turkey Presses the EU to set a Target Date for Full Membership', *Hürriyet*, 9 May 2008. Available at www.hurriyet.com.tr/english/turkey/8896006.asp?gid=231&sz=19498 (last accessed, 9 February 2010). See also M. J. Patton, 'AKP Reform Fatigue in Turkey: What Happened to the EU Process?', *Mediterranean Politics*, 12(3) (2007), 339–58, asserting that 'reform fatigue' is already evident in Turkey.

127 See 'Reform and Regression: Freedom of the Media in Turkey' (Report) Kurdish Human Rights Project, London, October 2007, 42.

128 'Turkey: Anti-Terror Law Used Against Peaceful Activists', *Human Rights Watch*, 6 June 2006 (available at: www.hrw.org/en/news/2006/06/06/turkey-anti-terror-law-used-against-peaceful-activists) (last accessed, 07 February 2010).

129 See L. Hardy, 'Turkey and the EU: Slowly but Surely', *Common Ground News Service*, 21 October 2008 (available at: www.commongroundnews.org/article.php?id=24210&lan=en&sid=1&sp=0) (last accessed 7 February 2010).

130 A. O. Evin, 'From Özal to the Present Day', in Lake, *EU and Turkey*.

131 See Hughes, 'Political Dynamics', 29.

3   Cyprus v. Turkey

1 Introduction

The European Commission's recommendation to suspend eight of the 35 chapters in negotiations for membership in November 2006 was the result of Turkey's failure to extend aspects of the Customs Union Agreement to the Republic of Cyprus. This was not, as an initial reading might suggest, a result of a trade dispute but rather is a direct result of the protracted conflict on the island of Cyprus. A historical review of the accession process suggests that the EU has shifted the burden of conflict resolution in Cyprus to Turkey. What is surprising is the little engagement, academic or otherwise, which examines the efficacy (and integrity) of such a policy, let alone the narrative which accompanies it. Nonetheless, Turk asserts that: 'the dynamics of the Cyprus conflict need to be changed if there is to be hope of success concerning any future UN-brokered solution that might be proposed.'[1] In order to achieve this, he suggests that it requires the involvement of not just Turkey and the Turkish and Greek Cypriots but also the European Union, Greece, the United States and the United Nations. In particular, Turk contends that there is a significant onus on Greek Cypriots:

> in order to rise above the 'uncompromising position taken by the present government,' opposition forces, moderates from all political elements, and *leaders of civil society* must generate debate of the critical 'core issues'. They must understand that regional stability will result from the two-state model and accept that the 1963 actions of the Greek Cypriots against Turkish Cypriots are as responsible for the conflict as the 1974 actions of Turkey against the Greek Cypriots. They must also acknowledge that upheaval from their homes and mourning their missing apply equally to Turkish Cypriots as well as Greek Cypriots, and reconsider the advantages of implementing the bizonal and bicommunal principles to which Greek Cypriots agreed more than thirty years ago.[2]

In terms of the obligations on the other actors whom Turk contends could bring about a peaceful settlement to the conflict, the EU, he suggests, should promote the economic development and European integration of Northern Cyprus;[3] Greece should 'actively affirm to the international community its support of the Annan plan to restart negotiations and seek a solution satisfactory to both sides'; and Turkish Cypriots should ensure their laws and practice are in accordance with the EU *acquis* and should ensure that the Customs Union is extended to the north, as well as seeking an agreement from Turkey that it will reduce its numbers of military forces on the island and its population of mainland settlers.[4] Given that the Cyprus issue has featured so prominently in Turkey's EU membership aspirations, the following sections provide a brief overview of the contested history of the island of Cyprus and outlines the attempts at an internationally-brokered resolution to the conflict.

2 The Cyprus question and Turkey

The position adopted by the EU with regard to the situation in Cyprus has been unambiguous in its alignment to that of the United Nations and, as Joseph notes, the EU: 'has taken a clear and firm position on the question ... and has always considered unacceptable the status quo created by the Turkish invasion of 1974 and the continued occupation of 37 per cent of the island's territory.'[5] At its meeting in Madrid in December 1995, the European Council reiterated 'the importance which it attaches to making substantial efforts to achieve a just and viable solution to the question of Cyprus in line with the United Nations Security Council resolutions, on the basis of a bi-zonal and bi-community federation.'[6]

Although Turkey has argued that its bid for EU membership should not be linked to a resolution of the Cyprus problem, the EU has taken a different view.[7] As noted at the outset of this chapter, the European Commission's recommendation to suspend eight of the 35 chapters in negotiations for membership in November 2006 was, according to the Commission, a direct result of Turkey's failure to normalize trade relations with the Republic of Cyprus. This suggests that alongside questions relating to Turkey's human rights record (and particularly, freedom of expression), a resolution to the Cyprus conflict represents one of the principal stated barriers to Turkey's achievement of full EU membership. As Suvarierol has outlined:

> Turkish–Greek relations and the Cyprus problem following the Turkish intervention of 1974 have occupied an important place throughout the evolution of the relations between Turkey and the European Union (EU). These two issues, often linked, figured among the most difficult to handle.[8]

2.1 *Background to the Cyprus question*

The protracted conflict in Cyprus can arguably be termed a 'metaconflict'; it is not only a conflict but a conflict about the nature of the conflict.[9] As Hanf has noted: '[t]he real load of conflict, already burdened by the huge disparities in power and prosperity, is enormously increased by the fundamental ideological cleavage[s]'.[10] The Cypriot 'question' leaves little agreement as to the principal causes of the conflict, on whom the burden of resolution of the conflict rests, or even the year in which the current conflict can be said to have begun. Recognizing the minefield that is the history to the conflict, a brief engagement with the genesis and dynamics of the Cyprus–Turkey dispute is necessary.

2.1.1   The situation prior to 1974

Throughout its history, Cyprus has been occupied by various foreign powers; as noted by Ehrlich, it was 'conquered by Egypt, colonized by Greece, and annexed by Rome before the first century A.D., and for the next two thousand years a succession of absentee landlords ruled its shores'.[11] Under the terms of the 1878 Convention of Defensive Alliance between Britain and Turkey, Britain took over the administration of Cyprus from Turkey, although Turkey retained formal titular sovereignty.[12] In 1914, when Turkey entered the First World War allied with Germany, Britain renounced the Convention of 1878 and annexed Cyprus.[13] British sovereignty was recognized by Turkey under the terms of the 1923 Treaty of Lausanne and Cyprus was declared a Crown Colony in March 1925.[14] Shortly after, the first claims for union with Greece, or *enosis*, as the concept was known, were made by Greek Cypriots and in 1931 Greek Cypriots burned the British Governor's house in mass demonstrations in favour of the union.[15] Riots of this type became commonplace, particularly after the end of the Second World War and in 1949 a plebiscite among Greek Cypriots revealed that 96 per cent of eligible voters favoured union with Greece.[16]

Whereas Britain viewed retention of the island of Cyprus as an essential weapon in its military arsenal – it had been of great importance during the Second World War as an airbase and refuelling centre – the Greek-Cypriot *enosists* garnered substantial support from Greece. In 1954, the Greek Prime Minister wrote a letter to the Secretary-General of the United Nations, in which he asserted that 'Greece alone has been the lasting element, the unalterable factor, the only permanent reality in the island of Cyprus. It would not be enough to repeat that Cyprus belongs to the Greek world; Cyprus is Greece itself'.[17] The Prime Minister also urged that 'the principle of equal rights and self-determination of peoples', as outlined in Article 1(2) of the UN Charter, be applied to Cyprus; meaning, as Ehrlich suggests, that the Cypriot people should be allowed to vote, under the auspices of the UN, to decide their future.[18] Despite protests from Britain, the question of Cyprus was included on the agenda for discussion at the ninth session of the GA in 1954, it concluded that 'for the time being, it does not appear appropriate to adopt a resolution on the question of Cyprus'.[19] Over the course of the following four years, Greece was unsuccessful in its attempts to have the GA adopt a resolution in support of its position on Cyprus.

Between 1957 and 1959 new settlement proposals were made by Britain, Greece and Turkey in the midst of sporadic outbreaks of violence by the

Ethniki Organosis Kyprion Agoniston (EOKA, 'National Organization of Cyprus Fighters'), protesting British rule and Volkan ('Volcano'), a Turkish underground organization, who conducted a campaign of violence against Greek Cypriots. In February 1959, the foreign ministers of Greece and Turkey met in Zurich and outlined draft components of a final settlement, which included a 'Basic Structure of the Republic of Cyprus', a 'Treaty of Guarantee Between the Republic of Cyprus and Greece, the United Kingdom and Turkey' and a 'Treaty of Alliance Between the Republic of Cyprus, Greece and Turkey'. The 'Basic Structure' set out a series of checks and balances designed to protect the Turkish minority and rested on the premise that both sides would exercise restraint, while the 'Treaty of Guarantee' called for cooperative measures to protect the island, including a permanent tripartite military headquarters. Under the 'Treaty of Guarantee', the Republic of Cyprus, Greece, Turkey and the UK would undertake to prohibit all activity that promoted partition of the island and the three Guarantor Powers would also undertake to guarantee the independence, territorial integrity and security of the Republic of Cyprus. Immediately after the Zurich conference, representatives of Greece, Turkey, Great Britain and the Greek and Turkish communities of Cyprus met in London, where Great Britain agreed to the terms outlined in Zurich on condition that Britain would retain sovereignty over two military base areas on the island of Cyprus and that Greece, Turkey and Cyprus would respect the integrity of these areas. While these conditions were agreed to, discussion of the necessary arrangements to be put in place continued until Cyprus was formally declared independent with the signing of the Accords in Nicosia on 16 August 1960.

For the two and a half year period following the signing of the Accords, the settlement was deemed to have worked reasonably well; 'the constitutional machinery for keeping the peace between Greek and Turkish Cypriots did just that'.[20] However, this was to change in December 1963, when the President of Cyprus, Archbishop Makarios, announced to the Guarantor Powers that he proposed 13 major revisions of the Constitution. Some of these changes would in fact have instituted greater protections for Turkish Cypriots but six of the revisions, which had proved vital for Turkish accession to the agreement at Zurich and included the power of veto of the vice-president (who was required to be a Turkish Cypriot); the requirement of separate majorities in order to pass important legislation; separate municipalities for Turkish Cypriots; separate judicial systems; a limited Turkish-Cypriot security force; and the requirement that 30 per cent of the public service be Turkish Cypriot, were to the obvious detriment of the minority Turkish-Cypriot community. Unsurprisingly, the Turkish government rejected the proposals, a rejection which was refused by the President, Archbishop Makarios, and '[w]ithin days, the fighting began'.[21]

Following the outbreak of violence, the Cypriot government accepted the offer of the Guarantor Powers to establish a joint peacemaking force under British command. A conference of the Guarantor Powers and representatives of both Cypriot communities, which attempted to resolve the problems of Cyprus, quickly followed but it became apparent that there would be no easy solution. Initial British and US plans to deploy an enlarged peacekeeping force drawn from nations of the North Atlantic Treaty Organization (NATO) were discounted by Archbishop Makarios, who insisted on a UN force, which would contain neither Greek nor Turkish troops and whose mandate would be to protect the territorial integrity of Cyprus and assist it in returning to normal conditions. The United Nations Force in Cyprus (UNFICYP) became operational on 27 March 1964.

In the 10-year period that followed, the UN troops stationed themselves in buffer zones between the Greek- and Turkish-Cypriot combatants; the Turkish Cypriots withdrew from the government and the physical separation of the two communities was effected.[22] By mid-1965, the Greek Cypriots had enacted legislation giving them complete control of the government, from which the Turkish Cypriots had withdrawn, and 'temporarily' incorporated most of Makarios's 13 proposed constitutional amendments.[23] A 1964 decision taken by Greece and Cyprus to strengthen Cyprus's defences meant that by 1967, an estimated 10,000 Greek troops were stationed on the island. This, Evriviades notes, was a material breach of the Treaty of Alliance but was justified on the basis that Greece had an obligation to defend Cyprus for as long as Turkey continued to claim a right of military intervention.[24] Military intervention by Turkey was only narrowly averted in November of 1967 when the Cypriot National Guard attacked two villages, one of which was totally comprised of Turkish Cypriots. Turkey responded with military overflights of Cyprus and presented the Greek military government with a series of demands, including the withdrawal of all Greek national troops in excess of those permitted under the Treaty of Alliance; the removal of the Supreme Commander of the National Guard, General Grivas, who had commanded the attack on the villages; the eventual dismantling of the National Guard; and the reorganization of internal security within Cyprus by expanding UNFICYP's mandate.[25] Intensive negotiations at the UN, in Ankara and in Athens followed, and Greece recalled General Grivas and withdrew the Greek troops; Cyprus, however, refused to dismantle the National Guard and the issue of expanding the UNFICYP mandate was not raised at the Security Council.[26]

In 1968 the Greek- and Turkish-Cypriot communities agreed to enter negotiations in an effort to ease inter-communal tensions and while the talks 'could not bring about the reintegration of the communities, it seemed to prevent any further inter-communal violence. There was little talk of *enosis* or partition after the negotiations.'[27] A period of relative peace ensued thereafter until General Grivas, who had been recalled to Greece following the violence of 1967, secretly re-entered Cyprus and formed the EOKA-B, an extreme right-wing pro *enosis* movement.[28] The group set about enacting a campaign of violence, aimed at forcing the Makarios government to adopt a policy of *enosis*.[29]

2.1.2 *Post-1974 events*

Joseph identifies three phases in what he terms the 'Cyprus problem' and it is his 'third phase' with which the remainder of this chapter is essentially concerned. He suggests that:

> Until 1960, it was a colonial issue which was settled with the granting of independence and the establishment of the Republic of Cyprus. From 1960 to 1974, the problem was basically an internal dispute between the Greek Cypriots and the Turkish Cypriots in which external powers were involved. These powers were primarily Greece, Turkey and Britain – the guarantor powers of the independence of Cyprus under the 1960 settlement. The United States and the Soviet Union also became involved, at the political level, during the second phase by virtue of their superpower status. The third phase covers the period 1974 to the present. Following the Turkish invasion of Cyprus in 1974, the dominant element of the problem has been the *de facto* division of the island and the continuing military occupation of its northern part by Turkey.[30]

The events of 1974 are considered a defining feature of the modern Cyprus 'problem' as we now know it. Unsurprisingly, there are competing narratives as to the catalyst of the Cyprus conflict. Greek Cypriots claim that the current strife was caused by the deployment of Turkish troops in 1974 and would essentially be solved upon their withdrawal. Stephen argues persuasively, however, that this contention is a 'serious misconception, for the modern question began in 1960 and the landing of Turkish troops was the consequence, not the cause, of the problem'.[31] Tocci notes that the majority of Greek Cypriots seek the reunification of the island and the prevention of secession of northern Cyprus or its annexation to Turkey, whereas the majority of Turkish Cypriots seek political equality with and the prevention of domination by the Greek Cypriots and advocate self-rule and physical separation from the Greek Cypriots.[32] Furthermore, the majority of Greek Cypriots accept that Turkish Cypriots would be granted 'more than minority rights' but insist on the liberalization of freedom of movement, settlement and property and also call for the recognition of the right of return of displaced persons.[33] This lends weight to Stephen's argument that 1974 was the culmination rather than the catalyst for the current impasse.

The events leading to the Turkish intervention of 1974 suggests that the impetus for the invasion must be read in a broader context of the political landscape of the region at the time. In 1967 a Greek nationalist right-wing military junta came to power, a 'domestically unpopular and internationally isolated dictatorial regime', which 'abandoned the policy of independence for Cyprus and sought *enosis*'.[34] This was exacerbated by extremists in the EOKA-B movement created by General Grivas in Cyprus, who considered any political ideal short of *enosis* for Cyprus as anathema and, as Blay suggests, it was only a matter of time before a power struggle broke out among the Greek Cypriots, which culminated in the 'Greek-inspired and directed' military coup against the Makarios government in 1974.[35] President Makarios was replaced by Nicos Sampson, a member of the Cypriot Parliament, and a known advocate of *enosis*, but the new regime, calling the coup an internal matter for Cyprus, pledged to maintain Cyprus's independence and continue with the inter-communal negotiations.[36] Greece denied any involvement of its officers in the coup at a meeting of the Security Council but this assertion was rebutted by Makarios, who was still recognized as the legal head of state. Makarios denounced the coup as a flagrant violation of Cypriot independence and sovereignty, and called on the Security Council to request Greece to withdraw its troops and end its invasion of Cyprus.[37] Turkey also accused Greece of an intervention in Cyprus in violation of its treaty obligations and began consultations with Britain in accordance with the Treaty of Guarantee.[38] On failing to convince Britain that the situation necessitated joint military action, Turkish troops began landing in Cyprus on 20 July 1974, and fighting immediately broke out.[39] Blay summarizes the ensuing events as follows:

> Turkey adopted the policy that the only way to ensure Turkish Cypriot security was to re-locate them all in a clearly defined territorial base under the protection of the Turkish army. In two assaults on Cyprus, Turkey invaded and secured about 32% (i.e. virtually the entire Northern section) of the island for Turkish Cypriots. By early 1975, a reported figure of 183,000 Greek Cypriots had fled their homes in the Turkish-held north. Over 40,000 Turkish Cypriots also returned from the Greek-held Cyprus to the North.[40]

The Turkish Cypriots immediately declared the northern part of the island the 'Turkish Federated State of Cyprus', while the international community called for an end to foreign military intervention in Cyprus.[41] However, as Wippman notes: '[i]international condemnation of the Turkish invasion had little effect' and the territorial demarcation line, which since 1983 denotes the 'Turkish Republic of Northern Cyprus', recognized only by Turkey, still remains.[42] Turkish Cypriots established their own administration over the northern part of the island and continue to exercise control there, while the dividing lines between the two communities are patrolled by UN peacekeepers.

3 International attempts at a resolution to the Cyprus problem

The government of the Republic of Cyprus is recognized by the international community as the legitimate representative of the island, whereas, as noted above, the 'Turkish Republic of Northern Cyprus' is recognized only by Turkey.[43] Since the deployment of Turkish troops in 1974, the international community, through the auspices of the UN, has repeatedly called for 'an immediate end to foreign military intervention in the Republic of Cyprus' and the withdrawal of 'foreign military personnel present otherwise than under the authority of international agreements'.[44] Since this initial response of the UN to the Turkish invasion of 1974, the Security Council has issued more than 90 resolutions on the Cyprus issue, while the GA has issued seven resolutions on the matter, in which it has continually reiterated its 'full support for the sovereignty, independence, territorial integrity, unity and non-alignment of the Republic of Cyprus' and called for 'the withdrawal of all occupation forces from the Republic of Cyprus as an essential basis for a speedy and mutually acceptable solution of the Cyprus problem'.[45]

3.1 The Kofi Annan plan

As early as 1964, the Security Council had already recommended the creation of a UN Peacekeeping Force in Cyprus.[46] Subsequently, in the aftermath of the Turkish invasion of 1974 and ensuing occupation of the northern part of Cyprus, the UN Secretary-General was mandated by the Security Council to use the secretariat's 'good offices' machinery to find a resolution to the conflict and to reunify Cyprus, in accordance with the UN Charter and specific resolutions as well as the principles of international law.[47] While successive efforts at promoting a resolution to the conflict have failed, the most recent, and arguably the most concerted attempt at a resolution resulted from the good offices mission of former UN Secretary-General, Kofi Annan, which was launched at the end of 1999.[48]

The new mission of good offices was established in the context of the four guidelines set out in Security Council Resolution 1250, which 'provided a clear and realistic framework for negotiation'; the 'evolving Greek–Turkish rapprochement'; the Helsinki decision of 1999 which had recognized Turkey's candidacy for entry to the EU; and the prospect of the enlargement of the EU by ten new members, including Cyprus, on 1 May 2004.[49] The then Secretary-General was of the opinion that '[t]he European Union factor in particular offered a framework of incentives to reach a settlement as well as deadlines within which to reach it', in the hope that Cyprus would accede to the EU as a reunited island.[50] The scale and complexity of the process is apparent from the report presented to the Security Council by the Secretary-General, which outlines that in the course of the negotiations, the Secretary-General met both leaders on eleven occasions, whereas his Special Adviser hosted 54 separate meetings during the proximity phase, 72 meetings in direct format, and called on each leader on more than 100 occasions during the period.[51] Also evident in the report is the sheer difficulty of the task that the Secretary-General had undertaken:

> During the three-year period from November 1999 to November 2002, the two leaders were not able to bridge their differences on any major issue, let alone on the package of issues. This was not, in my view, because

solutions were not achievable. Rather, it was because negotiation, in the sense of give and take, almost never occurred. Instead, the process was one of procedural wrangling, verbal gymnastics, shadow boxing, and mini-crises, with only occasional promising glimmers on the substance which did not last. I and my Special Adviser sought to find ways to assist the parties to move beyond that level of dialogue and into an actual negotiation, but met with little success.[52]

Despite the reluctance of the Greek- and Turkish-Cypriot leaders, Glafcos Clerides and Rauf Denktash respectively, to engage in meaningful negotiation, there were a number of meetings between the two during this period. On 11 November 2002, Kofi Annan presented to both parties and the guarantors a 'Basis for Agreement on a Comprehensive Settlement of the Cyprus Problem'.[53] The proposal was constructed so that both leaders could sign a two-page 'Comprehensive Settlement of the Cyprus Problem', in which they would commit themselves to finalizing negotiations, with the assistance of the UN, on the basis of the substantive parts of the plan by 28 February 2003 and submit the plan to separate simultaneous referenda on both parts of the island for approval on 30 March 2003, which would have allowed a reunited Cyprus to sign the Treaty of Accession to the EU on 16 April 2004.[54] Both leaders agreed to negotiate on the proposal but Clerides sought a number of 'clarifications' and Denktash noted that there were 'serious elements of concern' on his side.[55] On 10 December 2002, Annan put forward a second version of his plan 'to bridge remaining gaps between the parties' and both the EU and the Security Council called on the parties to try to reach agreement by 28 February 2003, the date envisaged in Annan's plan for the finalization of all aspects of the plan.[56]

A three-track negotiation process was anticipated, in which the Greek- and Turkish-Cypriot leaders would focus on achieving agreement on the substantive issues: Greece and Turkey would focus on reaching agreement and finalizing the security aspects of the plan and a series of 'technical committees' would be appointed to finalize laws and the list of treaties on the basis of Annan's plan of 10 December 2002.[57] According to the report of the Secretary-General, little 'substantive progress' was made in track one as Denktash sought changes to the plan, some of which 'radically altered key concepts' of the revised plan.[58] Clerides too sought changes but they were 'by and large within the parameters of the plan' and, in any case, Clerides indicated that should they not be able to agree on changes by the end of February, he was still prepared to sign the plan as it stood.[59] Track two of the negotiations was of no greater success; the Greek government approached its Turkish counterpart twice to begin talks on security without success and when representatives did eventually meet, the discussions did not lead to any agreement or progress.[60] Reasonable progress was reported in relation to track three, with the technical committees 'particularly on the Greek Cypriot side' producing a huge number of draft laws for consideration.[61]

The negotiations outlined in the Secretary-General's report were briefly interrupted by the presidential elections in the Republic of Cyprus, in which Tassos Papadoupoulos succeeded Clerides.[62] Papadoupoulos, defying his 'rejectionist' label,[63] gave assurances of the continuity of his policy with that of Clerides and indicated that he would not reopen key concepts in the plan or matters already agreed. Annan presented the third version of his plan to the newly elected Papadoupoulos and Denktash, which contained: 'further refinements, particularly addressing the basic requirements of the Turkish side at the same time as meeting a number of Greek- Cypriot concerns in order to maintain the overall balance'.[64] At a meeting in The Hague on 10 March 2003, at which Kofi Anann met with the Greek- and Turkish- Cypriot leaders, Papadoupoulos informed the Secretary-General that he was prepared to commit himself, conditionally, to putting the plan to referendum. Denktash, however, stated that he had fundamental objections to the plan on basic points and could not, therefore, agree to put it to referendum. He also raised a further complication, indicating that Turkey was not in a position to sign the statement requested of the guarantors in the plan due to 'previously unmentioned constitutional reasons'.[65]

As Hannay has suggested, the report of the Secretary-General to the Security Council reveals that he clearly believed that the 'primary responsibility for the lengthy delays, amounting effectively to a filibuster, was Denktash's'.[66] Indeed, the frustration of the Secretary-General with the position of the Turkish-Cypriot leader is evident in his report:

> In spite of this, I tried to salvage the process – an effort in which I involved the guarantors – by proposing an extension of the deadline for finalizing negotiations until 28 March, and taking a decision at that time on the holding of separate simultaneous referenda on 6 April. To be at all realistic, such a scenario would have required a stringent work programme, including an immediate restarting of the work of the technical committees, and contingent preparations for referenda. Mr. Denktash refused all of these requirements. This meant that it would clearly not be possible to achieve a comprehensive settlement before the signature of the accession treaty to the European Union by Cyprus on 16 April 2003.
>
> Accordingly, I drew the only possible conclusion and announced that the process had reached the end of the road. I made clear, however, that my plan remained on the table, ready for the Greek Cypriots and the Turkish Cypriots to pick it up and carry it forward if they could summon the will to do so.[67]

3.2 *Revival of the negotiations*

With the failure of the meeting at The Hague, the Secretary-General informed the Security Council that he did not propose to take a new initiative on the

Cyprus question unless he believed that the political will existed for a successful outcome. This, the Secretary-General noted, should consist of 'an unequivocally stated preparedness on the part of the leaders of both sides, fully and determinedly backed at the highest political level in both motherlands', to commit themselves to finalizing the plan without reopening its basic principles by a specific date and to put the plan to separate simultaneous referenda as provided for in the plan on a date soon thereafter.[68] A number of factors contributed to a renewed interest in the plan but undoubtedly, the two most important were a change in the Turkish-Cypriot leadership in December 2003, in which the pro-unification Republican Turkish party (RTP) emerged as the largest single party,[69] and a change in policy on Cyprus on the part of the Turkish government.[70] Turkey's change in policy with regard to Cyprus was relayed to the Secretary-General in January 2004, when Prime Minister Erdoğan gave assurances that Turkey supported a resumption of negotiations.[71] The Greek-Cypriot leader had also called for the resumption of substantive negotiations on the basis of the plan and stated categorically that he sought a solution before 1 May 2004, the EU accession date.[72] With the stated willingness to renegotiate from both Cypriot leaders and support from the guarantor powers, Annan prepared the ground for the '13 February Agreement', which committed the parties to a three-phase process leading to a referendum on a finalized plan before 1 May 2004.[73]

The negotiations reconvened formally on 19 February 2004 with a briefing from the EU Commissioner for Enlargement, Günter Verheugen. He outlined the EU position concerning the accommodation of a settlement and stressed the EU's 'strong desire' for a positive outcome.[74] The report presented by the Secretary-General to the Security Council in May 2004 describes in detail the intricacies of the subsequent negotiations but it is sufficient to note here that a series of delays on both sides in outlining their proposed changes and a failure to compromise on the content of these demands coupled with public disclosure of the contents of the negotiations 'usually with a negative spin', inhibited 'frank discussions' in phase one of the process.[75] Phase two commenced on 24 March in Bürgenstock, Switzerland and was attended by the leader of the Greek Cypriots, Papadoupoulos; Talat (RTP leader) and Serdar Denktash (Democratic Party leader), negotiating on behalf of the Turkish Cypriots; and representatives of the Greek and Turkish governments. The Secretary-General's report indicates that phase two of the process was also characterized by a lack of compromise in relation to the demands of both sides and public expressions of dissatisfaction, particularly from the Greek-Cypriot side, in relation to a UN framework for signing an agreement, should one emerge.[76] After the exhaustion of opportunities for dialogue, the Secretary-General made a series of 'bridging proposals, presented in the form of a revised text', which were accepted by both the Turkish Cypriots and Turkey, who proposed some amendments but each indicated that it would be prepared to sign the plan to authenticate it as the text to be submitted to referendum.[77] However, the Greek-Cypriot side was not satisfied with the proposals, which they made clear publicly.[78]

Agreement was at this point 'clearly not achievable' and so the process moved to the third phase, as envisaged in the agreement of 13 February, which involved the finalization of the text of the plan at the discretion of the Secretary-General without the need for signature by either party.[79] Following the meeting at Bürgenstock, the Secretary-General received confirmation from the governments of Turkey, Greece and the UK that they agreed to the submission of the plan to referendum.[80] In preparation for the referenda of 24 April, Talat and Serdar Denktash, who had attended Bürgenstock on behalf of the Turkish Cypriots, advocated strongly for a 'yes' vote and remained neutral respectively, while Rauf Denktash, who had been responsible for the Turkish-Cypriot negotiations prior to December 2003, called for a 'no' vote. Prime Minister Erdoğan and Foreign Minister Gül of Turkey also 'spoke out strongly' in favour of a 'yes' vote,[81] a factor which no doubt contributed to the overwhelming 64.9 per cent to 35.1 per cent vote by Turkish Cypriots in favour of the plan. In his report to the Security Council, the Secretary-General expressed surprise at the position adopted by the Greek Cypriots, whose leader, Papadopoulos, called upon the people to reject the plan with a 'resounding No'.[82] The plan did receive support from the Greek government and Papadopoulos's two immediate predecessors as Greek-Cypriot leader, as well as from the leader of the second largest political party, DISY, but nonetheless was rejected comprehensively by Greek Cypriots at 75.8 per cent against and just 24.2 per cent voting in favour of the plan.[83]

As a result of the failure to agree on a negotiated settlement, on 1 May 2004, the Republic of Cyprus acceded to the EU, along with nine other states, but without the Turkish northern part of the island. As a consequence, as one commentator suggests, the EU inherited 'a divided island riddled with conflict and home to a Turkish Cypriot population left in limbo'.[84]

3.3 The EU position

3.3.1 EU policy on Turkey–Cyprus relations

EU policy on the Cyprus issue has undoubtedly been influenced and shaped by the UN's policies; in the 2004 report to the Security Council on his mission of good offices to Cyprus, then Secretary-General Kofi Annan praised the EU for being 'ready to throw [its] support behind the Cypriots' in working to achieve a settlement.[85] Also of relevance are the decisions of the ECtHR, particularly that in *Loizidou v Turkey*,[86] which found Turkey to be an occupying power in Northern Cyprus and, accordingly, responsible for compensating Greek Cypriots for loss of rights, particularly those relating to property. The European Commission in its first progress report on Turkey's accession to the EU adjudged the facts concerning Turkey–Cyprus relations since 1974 as follows:

> Turkey has occupied northern Cyprus since 1974, maintaining an army nearly 35,000 strong there. In 1983 this part of the island proclaimed

itself an independent republic that is not recognised by the international community, apart from Turkey. A number of UN resolutions have condemned the occupation of northern Cyprus by Turkey and the unilateral declaration of an 'independent republic' in the occupied portion in violation of the treaties which set up the Republic of Cyprus, and have judged the status quo to be unacceptable.[87]

The Cyprus question is clearly one that has concerned the EU for some time and, it would also appear, now impacts upon relations between the Union and Turkey, with the burden of resolution placed squarely and exclusively on Turkey. In 1990 the European Council, meeting in Dublin, issued a declaration in which it stated that the Council ... deeply concerned at the situation, fully reaffirms its previous declarations and its support for the unity, independence, sovereignty and territorial integrity of Cyprus in accordance with the relevant UN resolutions.[88]

The European Council also explicitly linked the Cyprus problem to its relations with Turkey, thereby implying that a resolution to the issue may be necessary in order to further advance Turkey's relations with the EU.

Reiterating that the Cyprus problem affects EC–Turkey relations and bearing in mind the importance of these relations, it stresses the need for the prompt elimination of the obstacles that are preventing the pursuit of effective intercommunal talks aimed at finding a just and viable solution to the question of Cyprus on the basis of the mission of good offices of the Secretary-General, as it was recently reaffirmed by Resolution 649/90 of the Security Council.[89]

More recently the Cyprus issue has been monitored by the European Commission, which has continued to devote a section of its progress reports on Turkey to the problem, since its first report in 1998. The Commission has in its reports consistently advocated for 'a just and fair settlement of the Cyprus issue in accordance with the relevant UN resolutions' and has called on Turkey, as the Turkish-Cypriot community's guarantor, to 'exploit its special relationship' to assist bringing about a resolution.[90] The Commission's report of 2003, in what was perhaps a reflection of Turkey's evolving policy on Cyprus, noted that the Turkish government had 'confirmed its support for efforts to find a comprehensive settlement of the Cyprus problem'.[91] The report of the Commission in 2006 was, however, highly critical of Turkey's relationship with Cyprus and its findings subsequently contributed to the decision of the Commission to recommend that eight of the 35 negotiating chapters be suspended. The report outlined that:

Turkey has not fully implemented the Additional Protocol extending the EC–Turkey Association Agreement to the ten Member States that acceded on 1 May 2004, which it had signed in July 2005 and which enabled the accession negotiations to start. Turkey has continued to deny access to its ports to vessels flying the Republic of Cyprus flag or where the last port of call is in Cyprus. Such restrictions on shipping often preclude the most

economical way of transport and therefore result in a barrier to free movement of goods and to trade. They infringe the Customs Union agreement.
Similar restrictions continued to apply in the field of air transport.

[…]

No progress has been made on any aspects of normalising bilateral relations with the Republic of Cyprus. Turkey has continued to impose a veto
on Cyprus' membership of certain international organizations such as the
OECD as well as its participation in the Wassenaar Agreement on the
Code of Conduct on Arms Exports and on Dual Use Goods.[92]

The 2006 report was also unambiguous regarding the EU's expectations of
Turkey, noting that: '[u]nder the negotiating framework and the Accession
Partnership, Turkey is expected to ensure continued support for efforts to find
a comprehensive settlement of the Cyprus problem'.[93] In 2007, the report of
the Commission continued its criticism of Turkey in relation to Cyprus and
concluded that Turkey continued to fail to implement the Additional Protocol
to the Association Agreement fully and had made no progress in normalizing
bilateral trade relations with the Republic of Cyprus, but noted that the
Turkish government continued to express its commitment to finding a comprehensive solution to the Cyprus problem.[94] However, as Brewin has noted:

What is missing from the Commission Opinions on Cyprus and Turkey
is any strong sense that it is in Europe's interest to create peace in the
Eastern Mediterranean … The island of Cyprus would be more prosper-
ous, and an example of peace instead of conflict, if the two communities
could be united in observing European Union directives on the basis that
they are united by geography. Greece and Turkey could be equals in the
European Union, united by geography despite their cultural and policy
differences.[95]

3.3.2 Recent developments

Kofi Annan concluded his final report to the Security Council on his mission
of good offices in Cyprus with an expression of hope that Cypriots would
continue to work 'with courage and determination to achieve a settlement',[96]
thus signalling the end of an opportunity for a UN-brokered agreement and
placing responsibility for a resolution squarely in the hands of the Cypriot
leaders. The possibility of such a resolution was bolstered in February 2008
with the election of the leader of the communist Akel party, Demetris
Christofias, as President of the Republic of Cyprus. Prior to the election,
Christofias advocated a departure from the policies of President Papadoupoulos,
who successfully called for a 'no' vote to the Annan plan among Greek
Cypriots.[97] Exploratory talks began between the Greek- and Turkish-Cypriot
leaders on 21 March 2008, at which both leaders agreed to work together

'in goodwill' to find a comprehensive solution which would lead to the reunification of the island.[98]

The latest phase of negotiations is based, not on the most recent version of the Annan plan, which was rejected by the Greek-Cypriot population, but on an agreement concluded by both Cypriot leaders in July 2008 in the presence of UN Undersecretary General for political affairs, Ibrahim Gambari. A joint communiqué issued after the meeting confirmed the commitment of both communities to reunification based on a bizonal, bicommunal federation and an equality policy, as laid down in the relevant UN Security Council resolutions; recognized the negative consequences of a stalemate for both communities and outlined a commitment to reach a comprehensive settlement.[99] In July 2008, the leaders of the Greek- and Turkish-Cypriot communities, Demetris Christofias and Mehmet Ali Talat, agreed to hold face-to-face peace talks to 'reunite the western world's last divided country'.[100] These negotiations continue with little sign of any significant advancement, although United Nations Secretary-General, Ban Ki-moon, in a visit to the island in February 2010 noted that the two leaders assured him of their 'shared commitment for a comprehensive solution as early as possible'.[101] The European Commission, in its most recent progress report recognized Turkey's support for the negotiations but stated that it had made 'no progress on normalising bilateral relations with the Republic of Cyprus', further underlining the role that this issue continues to play in Turkey–EU relations.[102]

4 Summary

Throughout the modern history of the Cyprus conflict, the international community has been unequivocal in its condemnation of the stance adopted by the Turkish Cypriots (and Turkey) in the northern part of the island and broadly supportive of the Republic of Cyprus. Successive attempts at determining a lasting agreement between both sides on the divided island have resulted in failure and hopes that the impending accession of the Republic of Cyprus to the EU in 2004 would spark a solution were resolutely dashed with the rejection of the Annan Plan by Greek Cypriots by a margin of three to one.

The international community has long rejected the idea that there is a shared burden between Turkey and the Republic of Cyprus (and arguably Greece and the UK) to resolve the Cyprus conflict. In addition to the employment of a framework of conditionality to promote human rights reforms, it would now appear that the progression of Turkey on the path to accession is also irretrievably connected to finding a lasting settlement to the Cyprus issue. This suggestion, regardless of any allusions to the contrary, is borne out by Prime Minister Erdoğan's enthusiasm for the ultimately doomed Annan Plan and public statements suggesting disapproval of Turkey's Cyprus policy in the last 30–40 years.[103] The benefit of this strategy adopted by the EU, or indeed its fairness, as no such condition attached to Greece joining the EU in 1981, is questionable.

Nonetheless, it has engendered a change in Turkey's policy on Cyprus, changes which have often anticipated or reflected achievements in the accession process.[104] Should a successful outcome to the present talks be forthcoming, it may yet be seen as another triumph of the carrot-and-stick policy employed by the EU on Turkey's membership bid.

The question of Cyprus and the human rights concerns addressed in the preceding chapter constitute two of the stated obstacles to membership. This study now turns to consider whether 'unstated' impediments to membership figure in Turkey's EU bid.

Notes

1 A. M. Turk, 'Rethinking the Cyprus Problem: Are Frame-breaking Changes Still Possible through Application of Intractable Conflict Intervention Approaches to this "Hurting Stalemate"?', Loy. L.A. Int'l & Comp. L. Rev., 29 (2007), 463–502, 466.

2 *Ibid.* (references omitted, emphasis in original).

3 On this point, see D. Hannay, 'Cyprus, Turkey and the EU: Time for a Sense of Proportion and Compromise', Centre for European Reform Policy Brief, 2 (July, 2006), asserting that the failure of the EU to provide promised substantial aid to Northern Cyprus and to re-establish trade links with it had been a 'sorry tale of obfuscation and bad faith'.

4 Turk, 'Rethinking the Cyprus Problem', 467. Turk also adds that Turkey should undertake unilateral confidence-building efforts to demonstrate its support of a satisfactory settlement; the US can facilitate efforts to restart negotiations for reunification of the island within the framework of the Annan plan by upgrading its diplomatic presence in the north of the island whereas the UN must call for an end to the isolation of northern Cyprus and encourage Greek Cypriots to outline their concerns regarding the Annan plan in a manner which offers some hope for a negotiated settlement.

5 J. S. Joseph Cyprus, *Ethnic Conflict and International Politics* (New York: St. Martin's Press, 1997), 124.

6 Madrid European Council, 15–16 December 1995, Conclusions of the Presidency, S. III.

7 In March 2002, then deputy Prime Minister of Turkey, Mesut Yilmaz, who was in charge of relations with the EU, told the *Turkish Daily News* that: '[Turkish] membership of the EU cannot be linked to the settlement of the Cyprus problem, a position which has been put on record in the relevant EU documents' (cited in C. Brewin, 'Turkish and European Union Interests in a Cyprus Settlement', *Journal of Ethnopolitics and Minority Issues in Europe*, 2 (2002), 1–20, 4). Additionally, Hannay has noted that: '[i]t is reasonable to assume that the Cyprus problem will have to be resolved before Turkey joins the EU, not because that is a formal legal requirement but because Turkey could not become a member of the EU while the north of the island remains in its present limbo' ('Cyprus', 1).

8 S. Suvarierol. 'The Cyprus Obstacle on Turkey's Road to Membership in the European Union', *Turkish Studies*, 4(1) (2003), 55–78, 55.

9 See J. McGarry and B. O'Leary, 'Consociational Theory, Northern Ireland's Conflict, and Its Agreement Part I: What Consociationalists Can Learn From Northern Ireland', *Government and Opposition*, 41(1) (2006), 43–63, 44, who define a 'metaconflict' as 'the intellectual conflict about the nature of the conflict and the appropriate prescriptions to tackle it'.

10 T. Hanf, 'The Prospects of Accommodation in Communal Conflicts: A Comparative Study', in H. Giliomee and L. Schlemmer (eds), *Negotiating South Africa's Future* (London: Palgrave Macmillan, 1989), 111.

11 T. Ehrlich, 'Cyprus, the "Warlike Isle": Origins and Elements of the Current Crisis', Stan. L. Rev., 18 (1965–6), 1021–98, 1021. The historical background up to 1964 in this section is drawn from Ehrlich's comprehensive article.

12 *Ibid.*, 1024–5.

13 *Ibid.*, 1025.

14 Treaty of Lausanne. Article 20 of the Treaty stated 'Turkey hereby recognises the annexation of Cyprus proclaimed by the British Government on the 5th November, 1914.'

15 Ehrlich, 'Cyprus', 1026.

16 *Ibid.*

17 UN Doc. No. A/2703 (1954), para. 2, cited in Ehrlich, 'Cyprus', 1027.

18 *Ibid.*, para. 1.

19 UN General Assembly Official Records, 9th Session, Supp. No. 21, 5, cited in Ehrlich, 'Cyprus', 1028.

20 *Ibid.*, 1040.

21 *Ibid.*, 1044. Ehrlich notes that the relatively trivial incident which sparked the fighting involved the refusal of some Turkish Cypriots to show their identity cards to two Greek-Cypriot policemen. An argument ensued and the policemen, finding themselves surrounded, fired shots, which were then returned by the Turkish Cypriots. Two Turkish Cypriots were killed and one of the policemen seriously injured. The following day, fighting broke out all over Nicosia and this quickly spread to other parts of the island.

22 M. L. Evriviades, 'The Legal Dimension of the Cyprus Conflict', Tex. Int'l L. J., 10 (1975), 227–64, 247.

23 *Ibid.*, 248.

24 *Ibid.*, 259.

25 *Ibid.*, 260.

26 *Ibid.*

27 S. K. N. Blay, 'Self-Determination in Cyprus: The New Dimensions of an Old Conflict', Aus. YBIL, 10 (1981–3), 67–100, 77–8.

28 Evriviades, 'The Legal Dimension', 261.

29 Blay, 'Self-Determination', 78.

30 Joseph, *Ethnic Conflict*, 14.

31 M. Stephen, *The Cyprus Question* (The British–Northern Cyprus Parliamentary Group 1997), 1.

32 N. Tocci, *EU Accession Dynamics and Conflict Resolution: Catalysing Peace or Consolidating Partition in Cyprus?* (Surrey, UK: Ashgate, 2004), 23–6.

33 *Ibid.*, 23–24.

34 Joseph, *Ethnic Conflict*, 51.

35 Blay, 'Self-Determination', 78.

36 Evriviades, 'The Legal Dimension', 261.

37 *The Times*, 19 July 1974, 1, col. 3, cited in 'The Legal Dimension', 261.

38 *Ibid.*, 261–2.

39 *Ibid.*, 262.

40 Blay, 'Self-Determination', 78 (references omitted).

41 UN Doc. S/RES/353 (1974) United Nations Security Council Resolution (UNSC) 353, adopted by the Security Council at its 1,771st meeting, on 20 July 1974.

42 D. Wippman, 'International Law and Ethnic Conflict on Cyprus', Tex. Int'l L. J., 31 (1996), 141–80, 147.

43 UN Doc. S/RES/541 (1983) UNSC 541, adopted by the Security Council on 18 November 1983, declared that 'the attempt to create a "Turkish Republic of Northern Cyprus", is invalid, and will contribute to a worsening of the situation in Cyprus' and called upon 'all States not to recognise any Cypriot state other than the Republic of Cyprus' (para. 7).

44 UN Doc. S/RES/353 (1974) UNSC 353, adopted by the Security Council at its 1,771st meeting, on 20 July 1974 (paras 3–4).

45 United Nations General Assembly Resolution 37/253, adopted by the GA on 13 May 1983, para. 1, 7. A full list of the UN resolutions concerning Cyprus is available at: www.un.int/cyprus/resolut.htm (last accessed, 2 February 2010).

46 See UN Doc. S/RES/186(1964), adopted by the Security Council at its 1,102nd meeting, on 4 March 1964, recommending 'the creation, with the consent of the Government of Cyprus, of a United Nations Peace-Keeping Force in Cyprus' in order to maintain 'international peace and security, to use its best efforts to prevent a recurrence of fighting and, as necessary, to contribute to the maintenance and restoration of law and order and a return to normal conditions' (paras 4–5). See also UN Doc. S/5634 UNSC, 'Agreement on the Status of the United Nations Peace-Keeping Force in Cyprus', Int'l Legal Materials, 3 (1964), 451–68.

47 The Secretary-General was requested 'to undertake a new mission of good offices and to that end to convene the parties under new agreed procedures and place himself personally at their disposal, so that the resumption, the intensification and the progress of comprehensive negotiations, carried out in a reciprocal spirit of understanding and of moderation under his personal auspices and with his direction as appropriate, might thereby be facilitated' (UN Doc. S/RES/367 (1974), adopted by the Security Council on 12 March 1975, para. 6).

48 Security Council Resolution 1250 of 22 December 1999 requested the Secretary-General to invite the Turkish- and Greek-Cypriot leaders to negotiation and called on both leaders 'to give their full support to such a comprehensive negotiation, under the auspices of the Secretary-General', and to commit themselves to the four principles of 'no preconditions; all issues on the table; commitment in good faith to continue to negotiate until a settlement is reached; full consideration of relevant United Nations resolutions and treaties' (UN Doc. S/RES/1250 (1999) UNSC 1250, adopted by the Security Council on 22 December 1999, paras 6–7).

49 UN Doc. S/2003/398, 'Report of the Secretary-General on his mission of good offices in Cyprus', 1 April 2003, para. 6.

50 *Ibid.*, paras 6–7.

51 *Ibid.*, para. 15.

52 *Ibid.*

53 *Ibid.*, para. 43.

54 *Ibid.*, para. 43. Described as 'the most detailed and elaborate proposal by the United Nations', Annan's plan proposed the establishment of a United Cyprus

Republic, 'which would be an independent state with a federal government and two equal federated constituent states, the Greek Cypriot State and the Turkish Cypriot State'. Consisting of several thousand pages, and including a Foundation Agreement; an outline of the Constitution of Cyprus; the main constitutional and federal laws; a list of international treaties binding on the United Cyprus Republic; maps with territorial arrangements; the treatment of properties; and a calendar of implementation, the plan provided that the Turkish-Cypriot federated state would comprise 28.2 per cent of the territory and the Greek-Cypriot federated state the remaining 71.8 per cent of the new Republic. See G. Vassiliou, 'Cypriot Accession to the EU and the Solution to the Cyprus Problem', Brown J. World Aff., 10(1) (2003–4), 213–22, 215. The intricate nature of the plan is evidenced in the report of the Secretary-General, which outlined that the proposal ran to 192 core pages, plus 250 pages of finalized laws. There were also draft laws running to 6,000 pages, a list of 1,954 treaties and instruments, 1,506 flag designs and 111 suggested anthems. See UN Doc. S/2003/398, 'Report of the Secretary-General on his mission of good offices in Cyprus', 1 April 2003, para. 17.

55 UN Doc. S/2003/398, para. 44.
56 *Ibid.*, paras 46, 48.
57 *Ibid.*, para. 48.
58 *Ibid.*
59 *Ibid.*, para. 49.
60 *Ibid.*, para. 50.
61 *Ibid.*, para. 51.
62 See H. Smith, 'Threat to Cyprus Deal as Hardliner Elected', *Guardian*, 17 February 2003.
63 *Ibid.*
64 UN Doc. S/2003/398, para. 54. The Secretary-General noted that he also 'filled in all the remaining gaps in the core parts of the plan, particularly those related to security on which Greece and Turkey had not been able to agree' (*ibid.*).
65 *Ibid.*, paras 56–8.
66 D. Hannay, 'Cyprus: Not Yet a Problem Solved?', in Lake, *EU and Turkey*, 165, 167. See also H. J. Barkey, 'Cyprus: Between Ankara and a Hard Place', Brown J. World Aff. Problem, 10 (2003–4), 229–40.
67 UN Doc. S/2003/398, paras 59–60. The Secretary-General also stated: '[t]here have been a good many missed opportunities over the years in the United Nations good offices efforts on Cyprus. Both sides bear a share of the blame for those failures. In the case of the latest effort, I believe that Mr. Denktash, the Turkish Cypriot leader, bears prime responsibility' (*ibid.*, para. 130).
68 *Ibid.*, para. 148.
69 See H. Smith, 'Conciliation Hopes Fade in Tied Turkish Cypriot Elections', *Guardian*, 15 December 2003.
70 See 'AKP Denktaş'la ipleri koparıyor' ['AKP Breaking Ties with Denktaş'], *Cumhuriyet*, 2 January 2003, suggesting that Prime Minister Erdoğan disapproved of previous Turkish policy on Cyprus, cited in M. Kinacioğlu and E. Oktay, 'The Domestic Dynamics of Turkey's Cyprus Policy: Implications for Turkey's Accession to the European Union', *Turkish Studies*, 7(2) (2006), 261–73.
71 UN Doc. S/2004/437, 'Report of the Secretary-General on his mission of good offices in Cyprus', 28 May 2004, para. 7.
72 *Ibid.*, para. 8.

73 *Ibid.*, para. 14.
74 *Ibid.*, para. 16.
75 *Ibid.*, paras 19–23.
76 *Ibid.*, para. 33–37.
77 *Ibid.*, para. 39.
78 *Ibid.*, para. 40.
79 *Ibid.*, para. 41.
80 *Ibid.*, para. 63.
81 *Ibid.*, para. 64.
82 *Ibid.*, para. 65.
83 *Ibid.*, paras 68, 72.
84 S. Atasoy, 'Cyprus, Turkey and the EU: The Need for a Gradual Approach', Brown J. World Aff. Problem, 10(1) (2003–2004), 257–70, 257.
85 UN Doc. S/2004/437, Annex III: 'Statement issued by the Spokesman of the Secretary-General on the outcome of the referenda in Cyprus', 24 April 2004.
86 Application no. 15318/89, judgment of 18 December 1996.
87 European Commission Regular Report on Turkey's Progress Towards EU Accession 1998, S. 1.3, 20–21.
88 Declaration on Cyprus adopted by the European Council at its meeting in Dublin, 26 June 1990, Bulletin of the European Communities, No. 6/1990, para. I.42.
89 *Ibid.*
90 European Commission Regular Report on Turkey's Progress Towards EU Accession 1998, 21.
91 European Commission Regular Report on Turkey's Progress Towards EU Accession 2003, 41.
92 SEC(2006)1390, Turkey 2006 Progress Report, 23.
93 *Ibid.* The negotiating framework of 2005 stated that Turkey's progress towards accession would be measured by a number of factors, including 'continued support for efforts to achieve a comprehensive settlement of the Cyprus problem within the UN framework and in line with the principles on which the Union is founded, including steps to contribute to a favourable climate for a comprehensive settlement, and progress in the normalisation of bilateral relations between Turkey and all EU Member States, including the Republic of Cyprus' ('Negotiating Framework: Principles Governing the Negotiations', Luxembourg, 3 October 2005, para. 6).
94 SEC(2007) 1436, Turkey 2007 Progress Report, 24. The 2008 report further urged Turkey to 'take concrete steps to contribute to a favourable climate for a comprehensive settlement' (European Commission Turkey 2008 Progress Report, SEC(2008) 2699 final, Brussels, 5 November 2008, 28).
95 Brewin, 'Turkish', 12.
96 UN Doc. S/2004/437, para. 96.
97 See H. Smith, 'Cyprus Elects its First Communist President', *Guardian*, 25 February 2008. Christofias pledged that his priority would be 'the salvation of this island, to reunify it with Turkish Cypriots under the umbrella of a bizonal, bicommunal federation'.
98 See H. Smith, 'Cyprus Takes Steps Towards Reunification', *Guardian*, 22 March 2008. The talks were welcomed by the EU Enlargement Commissioner, Olli Rehn, who praised the agreement of the two leaders 'to take full responsibility for the future conduct of the negotiations'. See 'Commissioner Rehn welcomes

Christofias–Talat meeting in Cyprus and decision to open Ledra street crossing',
21 March 2003 (available at: http://europa.eu/rapid/pressReleasesAction.do?
reference=IP/08/510&format=HTML&aged=0&language=EN&guiLanguage=
en) (last accessed 2 February 2010).

 99 See 'Bicommunal Meetings on Cyprus Problem Continue', 9 August 2006 (available
at: http://cyprusembassy.net/home/index.php?module=article&id=3752) (last
accessed 2 February 2010).

100 H. Smith, 'Cypriot Leaders Set Date for Reunification Talks', *Guardian*, 26 July
2008.

101 See S. Tisdall, 'Cyprus Leaders Vow to Reunify Island, says UN head', *Guardian*,
1 February 2010.

102 Turkey 2009 Progress Report, SEC(2009)1334, Brussels, 14 October 2010, 32.

103 See 'AKP Denktaş'la ipleri koparıyor' ['AKP Breaking Ties with Denktaş'],
Cumhuriyet, 2 January 2003, cited in Kinacioğlu and Oktay, 'Domestic Dynamics',
264. Kinacioğlu and Oktay note that in March 2003, Erdoğan, surprisingly,
'expressed his concern regarding attempts to link the Cyprus issue to the EU
membership procedure by emphasizing that although the EU kept imposing the
solution of the Cyprus question on Turkey, it was neither an issue under Copenhagen
criteria nor a precondition for EU membership'. The authors, however, attribute
Erdoğan's apparent volte-face to his 'lack of a consolidated political position'
domestically at that time (*ibid.*, 266).

104 See T. Bahcheli, 'Turkey's Quest for EU Membership and the Cyprus Problem',
in J. S. Joseph (ed.), *Turkey and the European Union: Internal Dynamics and External
Challenges* (London: Palgrave Macmillan, 2006), 161–78, 161, noting that
'[w]hile Ankara insisted that there ought to be no linkage between its EU
membership and a political settlement on the island, Greek governments
regularly reminded Ankara that the road to Brussels passed through Cyprus'.

4 Lifting the veil

1 Introduction

While a secular policy is not unusual in the European context, especially when the strict laicism advanced in France is considered, the stringent interpretation of Turkey's particular 'brand' of secularism in a country where the population is almost entirely Muslim, is somewhat remarkable.[1] With such a rigorous secularist policy in place, it may seem surprising that the issue of religion should enter into the debate surrounding Turkish accession at all. Indeed it would appear that it has remained ancillary to the more public debates taking place on issues such as Turkey's ability to fulfil requirements related to human rights protections and its willingness to resolve the Cyprus dispute, examined earlier. Yet the path of Turkey's road to EU accession suggests that this 'secular' Muslim state raises the 'clash of civilisations' debate that integration would bring.[2] Casanova makes an interesting point in this regard on the current presence of the 'other' already in Europe:

> Publicly, of course, European liberal secular elites could not share the Pope's definition of European civilization as essentially Christian. But they also could not verbalize the unspoken 'cultural' requirements that make the integration of Turkey into Europe such a difficult issue. The specter of millions of Turkish citizens already in Europe, but not of Europe, many of them second-generation immigrants caught between an old country they have left behind and their European host societies unable or unwilling to fully assimilate them, only makes the problem more visible.[3]

The question of religion in the public sphere in Europe is a complex and contentious one. It is also contended that there exists a tension between religious (and legal) pluralism and questions of 'democracy' and identity that provide a backdrop to EU–Turkish relations. This chapter will, therefore, begin by examining some of the broader questions to arise from the public sphere debate in Europe. It will outline the cases, both domestic and those emanating from the ECtHR, which deal with the manifestation of religion in the public sphere. This case law highlights the increasing tension evident in

Europe when religion enters the realm of the public sphere, particularly where this religion is Islam, one that is often perceived as 'un-European'. These questions are vital to Turkey's accession, which, as a country of more than 70 million Muslims, may find that this impacts on their EU membership bid.

2   Religion in the public sphere: the European context

Advocates of some form of special status or privileged partnership for Turkey in its relationship with the EU cite tensions between the values and objectives of the Union and those prevalent in Turkey as a reason for not awarding Turkey full membership on the same basis as the other 27 member states.[4] Furthermore, many question whether Europe is 'ready' for a *Muslim* member and whether, in fact, Turkey really 'belongs' in the EU.[5] As noted in the introduction, there are broad questions surrounding European identity in the framework of Turkish membership. So just what are the debates that frame the question of religion in the public sphere in the European context?[6]

2.1 *Religion in Europe*

Contemporary Europe is undoubtedly a largely secular region where the notion that secularism and 'progress' are intertwined has long held sway. Religion in the public sphere is, for many Europeans, associated with emergent or conservative societies, whereas secularism is equated with modernism and seen as an indispensable component of modern governance. Unlike the United States, for example, where religious belief and public expression of religious sentiment by political leaders is arguably a prerequisite for electoral success: '[a] secular liberalism is deeply ingrained in the self-understanding of most Europeans and in the interpretations of most scholars of European politics'.[7] The potential accession of a majority Muslim country to a Christian Europe, or an historically Christian Europe at the very least, has proved controversial therefore, as it not only prompts questions about the desirability of such an accession, 'but also and more fundamentally because it brings up long dormant dilemmas internal to Europe regarding how religion and politics relate to each other'.[8] If such self-examination is deemed unnecessary or undesirable by European states, then it is little wonder that Turkey's potential accession is proving contentious. As Hurd has succinctly outlined:

> Turkey's candidacy destabilises the European secular social imaginary. It involves unfinished business in the social fabric of the core EU members, including what it means to be 'secular' (both in Europe and Turkey) and how religion, included but not limited to Islam, should relate to European public life. This cultural sticking point is what the debate over Turkish accession is really about, and it is for this reason that it is culturally – in addition to economically and politically – so contentious. This argument suggests that even if economic and political obstacles to Turkish accession

are lifted, even if Turkey is deemed to be in unambiguous conformity with the Copenhagen criteria, European opposition to Turkish membership will persist.[9]

While this argument may even in fact mask a latent fear that opening the EU to a large Muslim country may result in an incursion, or even domination, by an alien culture and religion, it is somewhat incongruous given Europe's religious past and the fact that with the accession of Eastern bloc countries to the EU, religious expression in social and political life is increasing and is likely to continue doing so regardless of Turkey acceding to the EU.[10] Despite this, many in Europe and indeed in Turkey, where secularism is guarded protectively by the military,[11] continue to espouse secularist policy in a manner which is as dogmatic as the religions they seek to confine to the private sphere.

2.1.1 Europe's Christian heritage

Although the Christian tradition can be considered a crucial element in the development and evolution of modern Europe, it should be noted that it is not asserted that it is the only element in this evolution. O'Connell outlines three pivotal features in the creation and development of the entity of Europe and what is now considered 'European', namely Judeo-Christian monotheism, Greek rationalism and Roman organization.[12] The shared religious heritage of Western Europe as a decisive factor in the development of the continent of Europe as a whole also cannot be understated:[13]

> Both in historical and geographical terms, religion – or more specifically, the Christian religion – provides an example of an agency which through the promulgation of a universal and exclusive faith sought to create a commonality of values and beliefs across Europe and elsewhere. A shared religious heritage based on Christian values, therefore, may be seen as one formative cultural influence at the heart of and giving substance to 'European' civilisation.[14]

While religion is now confined to the realm of the private sphere in the majority of European countries, this has not always been the case, nor can it be argued that this is true even today of all European countries.[15] Furthermore, even in those countries where religion has been relegated to the private sphere, churches continue to act as forceful interest groups in civil society and continue to contribute to the public debate on issues of religion, law and politics. In other words, even if in terms of practicing worshippers, churches remain unoccupied or under-occupied, they continue to exert a dominant influence in the European public space.[16] McCrea has noted in this regard that 'many such denominations, most notably the Catholic Church, continue to intervene in political matters and to influence legislation in areas such as the family, abortion and homosexual equality both at Member State and EU levels'.[17]

If, as Nexon suggests, an important marker of European identity is its history 'built on the exclusion of religious heterogeneity',[18] which accounts for an overwhelmingly homogenous Christian heritage, as well as 'an historical leavening that creates an affinity among European peoples',[19] it is also true that there are many linkages which suggest that Europe is in fact composed of a set of interlocking blocs, rather than an homogenous 'European' entity. While the reasons for excluding Turkey from the EU often include the proposition that Turkey is not a 'European' country, O'Connell includes the Turks as one of the many groups which: 'have left cultural traces and communities scattered throughout south-eastern Europe, north into Romania, Bulgaria and Moldova, and west into southern parts of the former Soviet Union'.[20]

In terms of the current composition of Europe's religions, the figures allude in no small way to the continent's Christian past. It is estimated that there are at present approximately one million Jews in Western Europe, with the largest communities in France and in Britain.[21] Islam accounts for the largest 'other-faith' population in Europe with conservative estimates of around six million, accounting for approximately three per cent of most West European populations, although the estimates are inevitably related to questions about immigration, with statistics on illegal immigration being particularly problematic.[22] Theoretically then, the remainder of Europe is Christian, aside from relatively small numbers of Sikhs and Hindus in Britain and elsewhere. A 1990 European Values Study indicated that the European average for belief in 'God' was 70 per cent, with Ireland, at 96 per cent, scoring highest among the predominantly Catholic countries of Belgium, France, Ireland, Italy, Portugal and Spain; and Iceland scoring highest, at 85 per cent, among the predominantly Lutheran countries of Denmark, Finland, Iceland, Norway and Sweden.[23] While it is likely that the figures would vary somewhat given the intervening time period since this study was carried out, it is probable that the addition of countries from Eastern Europe, would keep the average figure for belief in 'God' quite high.

2.1.2 *The secularization and desecularization of Europe*

The process of privatizing religion and confining it to the sphere of civil society can be said to have begun as early as the Protestant Reformations of the sixteenth century.[24] O'Connell outlines:

> The renaissance that owed much to the rationalist cutting edge of medieval philosophy marked the secularisation of society but brought also a new humanist spirit that moved forward in art, literature, science, and voyages of discovery. The reformation marked a split in the old religious unity as had earlier the divisions between the Greek and Roman churches; and it drew in its Lutheran form on the emerging new nationalism and in its Calvinist form on the new commercial ethos of the late medieval and renaissance middle classes. The enlightenment consolidated the secularisation

of culture and saw the growth of the spirit of invention which in the next century translated into technology and production and into the extraordinary social transformation of the industrial revolution and the urbanisation of great parts of Europe.[25]

Nonetheless, it is worth noting that when commentators speak of secular Europe, they largely refer to secular Western Europe, as Eastern Europe cannot be said to have undergone the process of secularization to the same degree as countries in the West.[26] A central tenet of the secularization thesis suggests that with the onset of modernity comes the demise of traditional forms of religion. In fact the secularization thesis developed within a European framework; as Europe's economic and political life developed, religion diminished in public significance and while religious sentiment may have continued to exist, it was increasingly confined to the private sphere.[27]

While opinions may vary as to the extent to which secularization actually resulted in the abandoning of religious beliefs, there is consistent evidence to suggest that we are now in a period of desecularization, which is affecting not only Europe but is in fact a global phenomenon. As Berger suggests, the idea that modernization necessarily leads to a decline in religion, both in society and in the minds of individuals, has turned out to be false.[28] In fact, internationally, it is the more conservative or orthodox movements which have resurged in recent years, suggesting a possible backlash against modernization and its trappings.[29] What is perhaps surprising is that it is not new religious movements which are coming to the fore in this period of desecularization, or, as Casanova terms it, deprivatization of religion,[30] but rather the traditional established religions which are being reinvigorated:

> What was new and unexpected in the 1980s was not the emergence of 'new religious movements,' 'religious experimentation' and 'new religious consciousness' – all phenomena which caught the imagination of social scientists and the public in the 1960s and 1970s – but rather the revitalization and the assumption of public roles by precisely those religious traditions which both theories of secularization and cyclical theories of religious revival had assumed were becoming ever more marginal and irrelevant in the modern world.[31]

Although the re-emergence of religion in the European public sphere may not be what most secularists had predicted, it comes at a time of increasing global desecularization, prompting renewed debate on the issue. The idea of secularism is, after all, essentially a Christian construct. As Lewis has noted, the reason Muslims developed no secularist movement of their own is historical; Islam did not experience such 'epoch-making Christian events' as the Schism of Photius, the Reformation, the Holy Office of the Inquisition and the religious wars of the sixteenth and seventeenth centuries.[32] These events 'almost compelled Christians to secularize their states and societies in order to escape from the vicious circle of persecution and conflict. Muslims encountered no such problem, and therefore required no such answer.'[33] If Europe is to embrace its largest 'other faith' religion, then it may be time to reassess the motivation behind its strict secularism.[34]

2.2 *The EU and religion*

Sociologists of religion could scarcely have predicted the extent to which an increasingly secular Europe could be newly affected and concerned with issues relating to religion.[35] The increase in religion as an area of contention in the contemporary European public order has arguably been provoked by two factors; the accession of a number of Eastern European countries, which did not undergo the same process of secularization that prevailed in Western and Central European countries during the second half of the twentieth century, and the immigration to the EU of migrants of non-Christian (and specifically, Muslim) faith. While the first factor challenges the secular ethos propagated by many European countries and indeed the EU, it remains less of a perceived 'threat' than that of the increasing presence of Muslims and a concomitant increasingly visible religiosity, which threatens to catapult a religion seen as alien to many within the EU, firmly into the public sphere.[36] With European countries that would historically have been countries of emigration now hosting significant immigrant populations, it is not altogether surprising that in dealing with immigrant religions, these countries have tried to replicate their model of state regulation and separation of church and state on their newly acquired religious minorities.[37] In this vein, McCrea has pointed to the disparity in Europe in relation to the treatment of migrants, particularly Muslim migrants, who are asked to 'give explicit assurances in relation to their acceptance of liberal values in relation to issues of gender and sexuality' while, on the other hand, the EU has been 'reluctant to interfere with the important symbolic and institutional roles held by certain culturally entrenched Christian denominations in many Member States'.[38]

Relations between the EU and religious groups were formalized through the auspices of the European Commission in 1994 when the then President of the Commission, Jacques Delors, invited Catholic, Protestant and Jewish representatives to an inter-faith meeting.[39] Mohammed Arkoun, a Muslim intellectual was also invited to attend, as was Mehmet Yildrim, Secretary-General of the Turkish–Muslim Union of Germany, though the presence of Muslim leaders was, as Massignon outlines, 'considered at the last minute only' and as neither invitee claimed to represent a 'European Islam', '[t]he first attempt to include Muslims alongside other European religious leaders was not successful'.[40] Since this first meeting, a twofold process has developed:

> Firstly, a Muslim discourse on European Islam, targeting second-generation immigrants, has brought about the creation of ad hoc European-wide Muslim collectivities, though it is difficult to assess their degree of organisation at

the European level. Secondly, a growing awareness of Muslim reality in Europe has led European officials to seek representative interlocutors. Two Muslim organisations specialising in European matters are invited to the briefing conferences organised by the Counsellor for Religious Affairs of the European Commission: the Muslim Council of Cooperation in Europe (CMCE), created in 1996 and invited since 1997, and the Forum of European Muslim Youth and Student Organisations (FEMYSO), created in 1995 and invited since 2003.[41]

The process of dialogue between the Union and religious groups reflects the desire of the European Institutions to have moderate Muslim partners[42] and is, perhaps, also reflective of an increasing awareness of the desecularization which prevails in present-day Europe. A recent study commissioned by the European Parliament's committee on Culture and Education noted, however, that the: 'question of European Islam, and that of its presence in the public space of the city, represents a question which goes far beyond relations with other religions'.[43] Nevertheless, it would appear paradoxical that on the one hand the EU machinery proffers a policy of pluralism, while on the other, member states appear to maintain an increasingly unsustainable secular status quo, even where it may interfere with fundamental aspects of freedom of religion or expression rights. Cavanaugh has noted in this regard:

> While initiatives at the EU level endeavor to move (albeit, limitedly) toward a pluralist model, national jurisdictions have responded to the challenges posed, in the wake of events in the US and Europe after September 11th, by attempting to more rigorously police the public sphere of religion and religious representations while, at the same time, establish dialogue with religious minorities within their jurisdiction. More worrying is the increased state control over religious expression, proffered as a necessity to ensure and protect state stability as an essential component of religious pluralism.[44]

The consequence of this increasing trend of state control over religious expression outlined by Cavanaugh is that EU member states appear to be moving away from the well-founded principles of tolerance and freedom of religion, towards an increasingly illiberal secularist agenda despite evidence, as noted earlier, of an actual desecularization of Europe. That schisms exist among EU member states as to the proper place religion should occupy in the EU's guiding accords was aptly demonstrated by the debates surrounding the possible inclusion of a reference to 'God' or the Christian religion in the preamble to the EU Constitution (subsequently 'Reform Treaty', or 'Treaty of Lisbon'). The debates provided an interesting insight into the views of EU member states regarding the public–private divide in matters of religious expression. The text finally agreed upon omitted any reference to Europe's specifically Christian heritage or values, and opted instead for a broadly phrased provision: '[d]rawing inspiration from the cultural, religious and humanist inheritance of Europe, from which have developed the universal values of the inviolable and inalienable rights of the human person, freedom, democracy, equality and the rule of law ...'.[45]

This resulting provision was, however, much debated. Rather than the existing reference to 'cultural, religious and humanist inheritance', some argued for a more explicit reference to the 'Judeo-Christian tradition' whereas others favoured a definition of the EU that would include a 'Christian community of values' and would potentially allow the disqualification of Turkey from membership in advance.[46] While scholars such as Weiler for example, criticized the refusal to include a reference to Christian values and consequent 'Christian deficit',[47] a study of the Netherlands Scientific Council argues persuasively that it would appear strange if a union supposedly based on universal values[48] should appeal to Christian values to deny a country membership.[49]

While initiatives such as that of the European Commission noted above may go some way towards acknowledging and highlighting the existence of a more diverse religious population in Europe, when it comes to protection of actual manifestation of religious belief (by Muslims, in particular), the signs are not encouraging. Davie has suggested that one of the most urgent public-policy challenges currently facing Europe is the 'need to create and to sustain a truly tolerant and pluralist society, both in Europe as a whole and in its constituent nations'.[50] As the following sections highlight, there is still some way to go in achieving this ideal.

2.2.1 Domestic case law within the EU

Both domestic and ECtHR case law reflects the obvious tensions that arise in the manifestation of religion in the European public sphere. Two recent cases in particular – the *Teacher Headscarf Case* of the German Constitutional Court[51] and the English House of Lords' case *R (on the application of Begum (by her litigation friend, Rahman)) v Headteacher and Governors of Denbigh High School*[52] – highlight this issue.

The first of these cases concerned Fereshta Ludin, a German national of Afghan origin who, on completion of her teacher training (*Referendariat*) applied for employment in the Civil Service.[53] The relevant school authority, the state of Baden-Württemberg's board of education (Oberschulamt Stuttgart), rejected her application on the grounds of a lack of 'personal aptitude' or 'fitness' to carry out the job, which specifically related to her refusal to remove the headscarf while teaching. The headscarf, the Oberschulamt claimed, was not only a religious symbol but also a political manifestation that was incompatible with the principle of state neutrality because of its 'signalling effect' (*Signalwirkung*) and the separation of church and state as provided for in the German Basic Law (*Grundgesetz*).[54] Young children, it was asserted, were easily influenced and could be negatively affected by the presence of a headscarf-wearing teacher. Forcing impressionable young students to confront Islam would also undermine the objective of integration, notably of Muslim girls.[55] Ms. Ludin unsuccessfully appealed the decision of the Oberschulamt at all three levels of administrative courts in Germany; the administrative court (Verwaltunggsgericht) of Stuttgart, the administrative court (Verwaltungsgerichtshof) of Baden-Württemberg and the Federal Administrative Court (Bundesverwaltungsgericht). The Federal Administrative Court not only denied Ms. Ludin's appeal in upholding the board of education's denial of employment to her but also ruled that teachers in public schools must refrain from openly displaying religious symbols in class. Public school teachers, the Court emphasized, are representatives of the state and must serve as role models for students. The Islamic headscarf was a religious symbol, not simply a cultural tradition; the conflict between the religious freedom of the teacher and the fundamental rights of students and parents could therefore only be adequately resolved by a prohibition of the headscarf.[56]

Following the exhaustion of all lines of appeal before the administrative court system, Ms. Ludin lodged a constitutional complaint to the German Constitutional Court (Bundesverfassungsgericht). Insisting that she wore the headscarf as a personal symbol rather than a political provocation, Ms. Ludin alleged violations of her rights under Articles 1(1) (human dignity), 2(1) (personal freedom), 3(1) (equality before the law) and (3) (non-discrimination), 4(1) (freedom of conscience) and (2) (right to practise religion) and 33(2) (equal citizenship) and (3) (equal access to public office) of the German Basic Law.[57] Before the Constitutional Court, the applicant claimed that her right to act in accordance with her beliefs should be protected; that the Islamic headscarf in itself should not be equated with Islamic fundamentalism; and that the alleged 'signalling effect' of the headscarf was less significant than had been stated by the board of education.[58] The Baden-Württemberg board of education asserted that regardless of Ms. Ludin's motive for wearing the headscarf, the state's principal source of concern was the symbolic meaning and 'signalling effect' of the Islamic scarf itself.[59] The principle of state neutrality as well as increased immigration in Germany obliged the state to be vigilant with respect to all religious matters, and particularly with respect to schoolchildren, who, it was claimed, learn through imitation and are at a critical stage of development when entering primary and secondary schools.[60]

On 24 September 2003, by a 3:5 margin, the Constitutional Court held that the school board's rejection of Ms. Ludin's application was a violation of the Constitution.[61] Crucially though, the court refused to state that the headscarf is not a 'danger', a refusal which Gerstenberg notes, 'has enormous legal and political consequences' and essentially makes the headscarf subject to state regulation. The majority opinion of the court rejected the decision of the school board *solely* on the ground that Baden-Württemberg had no legislation in place at the time that explicitly authorized the board to ban the headscarf because of the danger it represented.[62] It would appear, therefore, that it was the manner in which the decision was reached, rather than the decision itself which the court found unconstitutional. It has also been suggested that the minority opinion of the Court was:

> even more troubling; it said that the school board's decision was the only correct response to Ms. Ludin's claim. According to the dissent, her claim did not even present an issue of freedom of conscience, which would apply at the personal level but not in the 'inner sphere of the state' that the claimant sought to enter – a sphere where private rights are 'functionally limited'. Accordingly the school board did not overstep the bounds of its administrative discretion but, rather, used that discretion in the only way possible. The head scarf, on which Ludin 'uncompromisingly' insisted, would provoke conflict, according to the dissent, and, in particular, ran counter to the state's commitment to gender equality.[63]

While the applicant in the *Teacher Headscarf Case* was ultimately successful in her case, it is arguable that securing the right to manifest Islamic religious belief in the public sphere does not emerge victorious on a broader level. The German Constitutional Court by having regard to the 'signalling effect' of the headscarf implicitly endorses the view of the Islamic headscarf as a 'powerful external symbol' with inherent proselytizing effects that is imposed on women, as proffered by the ECtHR in *Dahlab*[64] and elsewhere. That the decision does not further the cause of the right to manifest Islamic belief was borne out by the enactment in April 2004 by the parliament of Baden-Württemberg of a law providing that teachers in public schools are prohibited from demonstrating any political, religious or ideological convictions that could challenge the principle of state neutrality or endanger school peace.[65] Interestingly, as Langenfeld and Mohsen note, the law presumes (in paragraph 38(2)) that manifestations of Christian or other traditional Western beliefs do not contravene the law, and that such manifestations fulfil the educational mandate conferred on the state by the Constitution.[66] This is a clear example of the tendency within the EU to treat 'traditional' (Christian) religion more favourably than religion of the 'other' (Islam). McCrea has noted in this regard:

> The Union's attempts to protect its liberal democratic values from religious threats coupled with its explicit reluctance to tamper with the evolving and sensitive arrangements surrounding Europe's culturally-entrenched denominations has therefore led to a situation which is directly discriminatory in that 'outsider' religions such as Islam are held to more demanding standards of secularity than 'insider' religions such as mainstream Christianity.[67]

While the enactment of legislation such as that passed in numerous German states since 2003 may be one worrying consequence of the decision in the *Teacher Headscarf Case*, another troublesome aspect of the case is that the argument of the Court that the headscarf poses a 'danger' is 'to tell Ludin (and those of us not in her position) that we cannot intelligibly communicate with her as a Muslim woman and, therefore, need not listen to her interpretation of the head scarf'.[68] In many respects, this was also the issue at the heart of the case of *R (on the application of Begum (by her litigation friend, Rahman) v Headteacher and Governors of Denbigh High School*. Here, the complainant, Shabina Begum, was a 17-year-old schoolgirl who contended that her exclusion from school for wearing a *jilbab*[69] constituted a violation of her right to manifest her religion under Article 9 of the ECHR and her right to education under Article 2 of Protocol I to the ECHR.[70] The policy of the school was that pupils could wear a headscarf if desired and a *shalwar kameeze*[71] instead of the traditional school uniform should they wish to do so.

Ms. Begum had worn the *shalwar kameeze* since commencing school in September 2000 (then aged 12) and continued to do so until September 2002, when she arrived at school dressed in a *jilbab* on the basis that it concealed, to a greater extent than the *shalwar kameeze*, the contours of the female body, and was said to be appropriate for maturing girls. At this point, Ms. Begum was informed by the assistant head teacher that she would not be allowed to attend school without the correct school uniform. On the same day, the head teacher wrote to Ms. Begum's mother and brother informing them that she was required to attend school dressed in the correct school uniform and that should she fail to attend, the matter would be referred to the Education Welfare Service. In October 2002, solicitors on behalf of Ms. Begum wrote to the school contending that she had been 'excluded/suspended' from school 'because she refused to remove her Muslim dress comprising of a headscarf and long over garment'.[72] The letter highlighted that Ms. Begum believed that there was an absolute religious obligation on her to wear that dress and she was not prepared to take it off and also alleged that the school's decision to exclude her breached her human rights under UK and European human rights law. Articles 9, 8 and 14 and Article 2 of Protocol 1 of the ECHR were set out and reasons given explaining why the school's actions had breached Ms. Begum's human rights.[73]

Ms. Begum first began judicial review proceedings against the school seeking a declaration that it had unlawfully excluded her contrary to the School Standards and Framework Act 1998, ss. 64–68 and the Education Act 2002, s. 52;[74] that it had unlawfully denied her access to suitable and appropriate education in breach of Article 2 of Protocol I to the ECHR; and that it had unlawfully denied her right to manifest her religion under Article 9(1) of the ECHR.[75] In June 2004 the High Court dismissed her claim for judicial review against the school and its governors, ruling that she had not been excluded from school and that Ms. Begum's rights under Article 9 and Article 2 of Protocol I of the ECHR had not been breached. Bennett J. found that any violation of the right to freedom of religion under Article 9(1) was justified as being 'necessary in a democratic society' for the 'protection of the rights and freedoms of others' under Article 9(2) of the Convention.[76] Reminiscent of the 'signalling effect' of the headscarf as outlined in the *Teacher Headscarf Case*, Bennett J. noted:

> Furthermore, it is clear from the evidence that there are a not insignificant number of Muslim female pupils at Denbigh High School who do not wish to wear the jilbab and either do, or will, feel pressure on them either from inside or outside the school. The present school uniform policy aims to protect their rights and freedoms.[77]

Ms. Begum appealed the decision of the High Court and in March 2005 the Court of Appeal issued its judgment in which it disagreed with the judgment of the High Court and found that Denbigh High School had 'approached the issues in this case from an entirely wrong direction and did not attribute to the claimant's beliefs the weight they deserved'.[78] The appeal was therefore allowed and Ms. Begum was granted the three declarations she had sought before the High Court. The High Court had relied on the decision of the ECtHR in *Leyla Şahin*[79] in support of its judgment; the Court of Appeal, however, distinguished the decision in *Şahin* noting that the UK 'is very different from Turkey. It is not a secular State and ... we have no written Constitution.'[80] Furthermore, noting an interesting factor to which the ECtHR did not have regard in its decision in *Şahin*, Brooke LJ cautioned that:

> there are clearly potential tensions between the rights and freedoms set out in a Convention agreed more than 50 years ago between Western European countries which on the whole adhered to Judaeo-Christian traditions, and some of the tenets of the Islamic faith that relate to the position of women in society.[81]

Following the decision of the Court of Appeal, Denbigh High School won leave to appeal to the House of Lords, where the Lords unanimously reversed the findings of the Court of Appeal and restored the judgment of the trial judge on all counts. Lord Bingham of Cornhill, providing the leading judgment in the case, ruled that Denbigh High School had not intended to exclude Ms. Begum 'in the statutory sense of the word, nor believe that it was doing so'.[82]

More importantly though, the Law Lords were unanimous in their conclusion that Ms. Begum's rights under Article 9 of the Convention had not been violated. In fact, there was not even unanimous agreement that there had been an interference with Ms. Begum's rights under Article 9.[83] Nonetheless, the court proceeded to examine the justifications for interference with the rights under Article 9(1) as provided for in Article 9(2) and noted that it had not been suggested that the rules were not made for the legitimate purpose of protecting the rights and freedoms of others. The issue was therefore whether the rules and the school's insistence on them were in all the circumstances proportionate.[84] The Lords referred to numerous decisions of the ECtHR and noted in agreement the view of the ECtHR as outlined in *Kalaç v Turkey*[85] that Article 9 'does not protect every act motivated or inspired by a religion or belief. Moreover, in exercising his freedom to manifest his religion, an individual may need to take his specific situation into account.'[86] In its consideration of the interference with Ms. Begum's rights under Article 9 the court pointed to the lengths to which the school had gone in formulating its policy on the school uniform, which included a working party to consult with Imams of the three local Mosques and different sections of the school community.[87] This, in fact, appeared to be the point on which the case turned before the House of Lords. As Idriss notes: '[b]ecause great care was taken by the school to create an inclusive uniform policy, their Lordships ruled that the school was fully justified in acting as it did'.[88] This arguably suggests that as long as the lowest common denominator of religious belief is catered for, then schools, or whatever the state institution may be, will be considered as fulfilling their duty to uphold freedom of religion. This can be contrasted with the view of Brooke LJ in the decision of the Court of Appeal who considered both 'liberal' and 'strict' interpretations of Islam to be 'sincerely held'.[89]

If any common thread can be drawn from these two illustrative cases, it is that European countries appear to be invoking illiberal policies in order to maintain the requirements of strict secularism. This is against the backdrop also of outright bans on the public manifestation of religion such as that imposed in France, which was 'intended to send a powerful message to Islamists'.[90] Nonetheless, while it is a troubling trend that sees no prospect of reversal, as the following section highlights, it is not surprising given the guidance provided by the ECtHR.

2.2.2 Freedom of religion in Europe

The European Convention on Human Rights (ECHR) affords everyone the right to freedom of thought, conscience and religion but provides that the right may be subject to certain limitations as imposed by domestic authorities.[91] In matters related to religion, however, the European Court of Human Rights (ECtHR) has adopted a deferential attitude towards domestic authorities in the determination of the parameters of this right. This is reflected in the fact that it was not until 1993, some 35 years after the Court commenced operating, that a violation of Article 9 of the ECHR was found. This, as commentators have noted, suggests that: '[t]he sensitivity of religious issues has long chilled any ardour that the ECtHR might have had to address cases involving Article 9'.[92]

In its assessment of cases involving Article 9 of the ECHR, the ECtHR considers whether limitations or restrictions on the right transgressed the state's margin of appreciation by examining whether the interference was prescribed by law; whether it pursued a legitimate aim under Article 9(2); and whether the measures taken were necessary in a democratic society. In *Kokkinakis*, the Court stressed the importance of the rights protected by Article 9:

> As enshrined in Article 9 (art. 9), freedom of thought, conscience and religion is one of the foundations of a 'democratic society' within the meaning

of the Convention. It is, in its religious dimension, one of the most vital elements that go to make up the identity of believers and their conception of life, but it is also a precious asset for atheists, agnostics, sceptics and the unconcerned. The pluralism indissociable from a democratic society, which has been dearly won over the centuries, depends on it.[93]

While a comprehensive overview of the Court's jurisprudence on freedom of religion has been provided elsewhere,[94] it is worth noting that the commentary on Article 9 jurisprudence suggests that there has been a remarkable display of reticence in upholding the commitment to religious freedom outlined in Article 9 of the Convention.[95] Against this backdrop, a number of relatively recent cases, in particular, merit discussion.

3 Religion in the public sphere

The private–public sphere debate on religion has been highlighted in a number of European states (France, the Netherlands and the UK are a few that spring to mind). It is in Turkey, however, where the state policy of secularism has been most visible at the European level (both in terms of European Court jurisprudence and the accession process). It is also where, arguably, the time of confining Islamic identity to the margins has passed:

> Islamic identity in urban Turkey has emancipated itself from a feeling of 'minority' – as reflected in the form of Islamized ghettos in segregated districts of large cities – and has achieved an empowered feeling of self-confidence, declaring itself openly on the streets of modern, upmarket districts within the city.[96]

One principal reason proffered for the transformation of this Islamic identity came about through the 'emergence of new economic demands in the metropolis'[97] but it is also true that it is a transformation with which many in Europe, as well as in Turkey, may not be entirely comfortable.

3.1 'Beyond the veil'

It is the Islamic headscarf (or *hijab*) that is now the most readily identifiable visual symbol of religion in the public sphere. The jurisprudence of the ECtHR on the issue is troublesome, in that it would now appear that the wearing of the headscarf is viewed both as being incompatible with the principle of gender equality and in direct opposition to the principle of secularism.

Prior to the decision in *Leyla Şahin v Turkey*,[98] questions relating to religion in the public sphere had been raised directly before the European Convention supervisory organs.[99] These cases explored a diverse range of issues, including the impact of a dominant religion on state practice towards minority religions;[100]

limitations on religious freedom in the name of state neutrality;[101] and the wearing of the Muslim headscarf in public spaces, where this is regulated.[102] A seminal case emanating from the Court concerns the latter category and indeed the decision in *Şahin* has prompted much debate, with one commentator even going so far as to suggest that the decision:

> evidences a general fear of Islam's potential to disrupt the democratic project of the ECHR as well as a particular fear of Turkey – a distrust in Turkey's ability to Europeanise its *laik*–Muslim state and to ensure that Islamic fundamentalism does not become part of the Turkish Republic. Part of this distrust also stems from Turkey's own inability to create a symbiotic relationship between its secular state and its historic Islamic roots. With Islam searching for a definable position in the legal and political orders of Europe while continuing to challenge the *laik* nature of the Turkish state, the European Court of Human Rights simply avoided these legal ambiguities and complexities in the *Şahin* judgment by turning the headscarf into a symbolic enemy of the Court's democratic jurisprudence.[103]

The wearing of the Islamic headscarf in the public sphere has become an area of contention both within the EU and in Turkey. In March 2004, in a move that was widely perceived as targeting headscarves in particular, a law was introduced in France that banned all conspicuous religious symbols in public schools in an effort to preserve secularity.[104] Two years later, the House of Lords in the UK delivered a unanimous decision in the *Begum* case, discussed above.[105] These developments are reflective of the approach adopted by the Strasbourg machinery, which, as the following cases highlight, continually defers to domestic states' practices, in cases concerning Article 9 of the Convention.

3.1.1 Secularism and freedom of religion in public education

Prior to the *Şahin* case, the headscarf issue came before the Strasbourg machinery in two applications, both of which were declared inadmissible. In the first case, *Karaduman v Turkey*,[106] the applicant was a university graduate who could not obtain a certificate confirming her qualifications because the rules of the university required that she submit a photograph with an uncovered head in order for the certificate to be issued. The applicant alleged a breach of Article 9 of the Convention as to appear without a headscarf would have been incompatible with her religious beliefs; and Article 14 of the Convention as the administrative authorities distinguished between Turkish female students and female students of foreign nationality who were not subject to the same restrictions impinging on their freedom of religion.[107]

In the Commission's consideration of the merits of *Karaduman*'s arguments, it first looked at whether the measure complained of constituted an interference

with the exercise of freedom of religion. In doing so, it appeared to place importance on the fact that the applicant had chosen to study at a secular university
and by doing so had submitted to those university rules which may make the
freedom of students to manifest their religion subject to certain restrictions.[108]
The Commission also considered the ruling of the Turkish Constitutional Court
that had previously held that the act of wearing a headscarf in Turkish universities may constitute a challenge to those who do not wear one.[109] The Commission
was of the view that a university degree certificate is intended to certify a
student's capacities for employment purposes, with the requirement of the
photograph being for identity purposes; 'it cannot be used by that person to
manifest his religious beliefs'.[110] It followed therefore that, having regard to the
requirements of a secular university system, the regulation of students' dress
and the refusal of administrative services where they failed to comply did not
constitute an interference with freedom of religion and conscience.[111]
Accordingly, the part of the application dealing with Article 9 of the Convention
was deemed manifestly ill-founded within the meaning of Article 27(2) (now
Article 35(3)) of the Convention.[112] The applicant's allegation of discrimination
was deemed not to have been raised before the domestic proceedings and therefore was not examined by the Commission.

The reasoning of the European Commission in *Karaduman*, albeit underdeveloped, provides the first indication of the firm public–private divide that
would emerge in the Convention machinery's assessment of cases invoking
Article 9. As Vakulenko asserts, the decision in *Karaduman*:

> reinforces the perception of headscarves as an essentially political, publicly
> orientated religious statement (the reference to 'certain religious funda-
> mentalist currents' being particularly telling), discounting any possible
> ambivalence about the meaning of headscarf wearing. Second, the
> ECmHR did not appear to believe that headscarf wearing as such fell
> within the scope of Article 9 ECHR (which was the primary legal basis
> on which the case was decided). Third, the ECmHR's language of 'choice'
> suggests a firm presumption that individuals function as rational agents
> free from structural constraints. There is no discussion of whether the
> applicant had a realistic option of obtaining the same kind of education
> at a private institution, and whether any such alternatives were of the
> same quality or prestige.[113]

In 2001, the ECtHR delivered its admissibility decision in the case of *Dahlab
v Switzerland*.[114] The applicant in this case was a teacher in a public primary
school in Switzerland who had converted from Catholicism to Islam and had
worn a headscarf while working for five years before she was requested to refrain
from doing so while carrying out her professional duties by the Directorate
General for Primary Education. The basis of the Directorate's prohibition on
the wearing of the headscarf was that such a practice contravened the Public
Education Act, s. 6 and constituted 'an obvious means of identification

imposed by a teacher on her pupils, especially in a public, secular education system'.[115] The applicant appealed the decision of the Directorate to the Geneva cantonal government, which dismissed the application on the grounds that teachers must 'endorse both the objectives of the State school system and the obligations incumbent on the education authorities, including the strict obligation of denominational neutrality'.[116] This decision of the Geneva cantonal government was upheld by the Swiss Federal Court, which found that the decision was fully in accordance with the principle of denominational neutrality in schools, 'a principle that seeks both to protect the religious beliefs of pupils and parents and to ensure religious harmony'.[117]

The applicant submitted that the measure prohibiting her from wearing a headscarf in the performance of her teaching duties infringed her freedom to manifest her religion, as guaranteed by Article 9 of the Convention. She also asserted that the Swiss courts had erred in accepting that the measure had a sufficient basis in law and in finding that there was a threat to public safety and to the protection of public order.[118] The applicant further alleged a violation of Article 14 of the Convention on the grounds that the prohibition imposed by the Swiss authorities amounted to discrimination on the ground of sex because a man belonging to the Muslim faith could teach at a state school without being subject to any form of prohibition.[119] The reasoning of the Court in *Dahlab* is considerably more detailed than that offered by the Commission in *Karaduman* and, as Vakulenko suggests, 'is generally regarded as a critical point in the development of the ECHR jurisprudence on "Islamic headscarves"'.[120] It is therefore worth examining the arguments and the Court's assessment thereof in some detail.

The Swiss government submitted that the measure prohibiting the applicant from wearing a headscarf in her capacity as a teacher at a state school did not amount to interference with her right to freedom of religion as state schools were non-denominational, as provided for in Article 27(3) of the Federal Constitution given effect by the Public Education Act, ss. 6 and 120(2) in the canton of Geneva.[121] Given that the applicant had chosen to pursue her career as a teacher in a state school, it followed that when she was appointed to a permanent position in December 1990 she was required to observe the principle of secularism in accordance with these provisions and had done so by not wearing any conspicuous religious symbols.[122] Alternatively, should the ECtHR hold that the applicant's freedoms under Article 9 had in fact been interfered with, the government submitted that the interference was justified under Article 9(2) of the Convention. In support of this contention, the government proffered that the interference had a basis in law: Article 27(3) of the Federal Constitution, which made it compulsory to observe the principle of denominational neutrality in schools; the Public Education Act, s. 6, which established the principle that the state education system had to respect the religious beliefs of pupils and parents; and the Public Education Act, s. 120(2), which provided that civil servants had to be laypersons.[123] The government contended that the aims pursued were legitimate and were among those listed in Article 9(2) of the Convention; the measures prohibiting the applicant from wearing the headscarf while working were based on the principle of denominational neutrality in schools and, more broadly, on that of religious harmony.[124] The prohibition was also necessary in a democratic society because the applicant, in her work as a civil servant, represented the state and therefore her conduct should not suggest that the state identified itself with a particular religious denomination.[125] That, the government submitted, was especially valid where allegiance to a particular religion 'was manifested by *a powerful religious symbol*, such as the wearing of an Islamic headscarf'.[126]

In the applicant's submissions, she argued that the principle of secularism in state schools meant that teaching should be independent of religious faiths but should not prevent teachers from holding beliefs or from wearing any religious symbols whatever.[127] The applicant pointed to the fact that she had worn a headscarf in class since March 1991, which had not concerned the school's head teacher, his immediate superior or the district inspector whom she had met regularly; that her teaching was secular in nature and had never given rise to any problems or complaints from pupils or their parents; and that the Geneva authorities had consequently been in full knowledge of the facts in endorsing, until June 1996, the applicant's right to wear a headscarf.[128] It was only at that point and without stating any reasons, that the authorities required her to stop wearing the headscarf.[129] Additionally, the applicant argued that, contrary to the government's submissions, she had no choice but to teach within the state school system. In practice, state schools in Geneva had a 'virtual monopoly' on infant classes and the limited private schools in Geneva, were not non-denominational and were governed by religious authorities other than those of the applicant and therefore were not accessible to her.[130] The applicant further asserted that it had never been established that her clothing had had any impact on pupils and that the mere fact of wearing a headscarf was not likely to influence the children's beliefs.[131] Regarding the submission of the government that the interference was justified under Article 9(2) of the Convention, the applicant contended that the interference violated her freedom of religion because it had no basis in law and was not justified as the Public Education Act, s. 6 referred expressly to the education system alone and not to teachers themselves, and s. 120(2) of the Act did not clarify the situation.[132]

The Court began its consideration by noting that the right protected in Article 9 of the Convention represents one of the foundations of a 'democratic society' within the meaning of the Convention but that it may be necessary to restrict the right in societies in which several religions coexist within one and the same population 'in order to reconcile the interests of the various groups and ensure that everyone's beliefs are respected'.[133] The reasoning of the Court in the instant case is worrying in a number of respects.

First, the Court appeared to disregard the applicant's argument that she had worn the headscarf in class between March 1991 and June 1996 without any adverse effects or complaints from either the pupils or her employer. The ECtHR appeared content to acquiesce in the conjecture of the Swiss Federal

Court that the fact that there had been no complaints from parents or pupils to date did not mean that none of them had been affected: '[s]ome may well have decided not to take any direct action so as not to aggravate the situation, in the hope that the education authorities will react of their own motion'.[134] Second, the applicant's argument that she was the victim of discrimination on the ground of sex in contravention of Article 14 of the Convention receives but a cursory examination from the Court. By noting that 'the measure by which the applicant was prohibited, purely in the context of her professional duties, from wearing an Islamic headscarf was not directed at her as a member of the female sex but pursued the legitimate aim of ensuring the neutrality of the state primary-education system',[135] the Court seemed entirely to ignore the particular circumstances of the case. Finally, and perhaps most tellingly, is the fact that the ECtHR accepted without reservation the government's argument that the headscarf constitutes a 'powerful external symbol' and furthermore, argued that it 'cannot be denied outright that the wearing of a headscarf might have some kind of proselytizing effect, seeing that it appears to be imposed on women by a precept which is laid down in the Koran and which, as the Federal Court noted, is hard to square with the principle of gender equality'.[136] This statement not only contradicts the definition of improper proselytism advanced by the Court in *Kokkinakis v Greece*,[137] but it also sets up the headscarf as being incompatible with the abstract ideal of gender equality and clearly 'ignores the complexity and ambivalence of the applicant's attitude towards her headscarf-wearing'.[138]

With the rulings in the admissibility decisions discussed above, the fact that the *Leyla Şahin v Turkey* case came to be heard and decided on its merits must in itself be welcomed. In this case the ECtHR appeared to broaden its consideration of the reasons for which an essentially illiberal secularist agenda may be pursued by member states. In *Karaduman* and *Dahlab* the prevailing reason for allowing the restrictions rested on both the protection of the secular state education system and the protection of children from undesirable exposure to religious sentiment in the classroom. *Şahin* sees the Court move to rather paternalistic territory in which the headscarf is proffered as a powerful symbol that women may feel obliged to wear. Although this aspect of the judgment is couched in the language of gender equality, the decision of the Court undoubtedly gives credence to the increasing tendency of states parties to ban religious symbols in the public sphere, thereby encroaching on religious freedoms.

The applicant in the *Şahin* case, a 24-year-old woman in her fifth year of studies at the Faculty of Medicine at Bursa University, enrolled at the Cerrahpaşa Faculty of Medicine at Istanbul University. During her first four years of study at the University of Bursa she wore a headscarf and continued to do so until February 1998. In February 1998, the Vice Chancellor of Istanbul University issued a circular, which provided in part:

> By virtue of the Constitution, the law and regulations, and in accordance with the case-law of the Supreme Administrative Court and the European

Commission of Human Rights and the resolutions adopted by the university administrative boards, students whose 'heads are covered' (who wear the Islamic headscarf) and students (including overseas students) with beards must not be admitted to lectures, courses or tutorials. Consequently, the name and number of any student with a beard or wearing the Islamic headscarf must not be added to the lists of registered students.[139]

In accordance with the circular, the applicant was denied access to a number of examinations and lectures on the ground that she was wearing an Islamic headscarf during the period between March and April 1998. In July 1998 the applicant lodged an application for an order setting aside the circular of 23 February 1998, submitting that the circular and its implementation had infringed her rights guaranteed by Articles 8, 9 and 14 of the Convention and Article 2 of Protocol No. 1, in that there was no statutory basis for the circular and the Vice-Chancellor's Office had no regulatory power in that sphere.[140] Delivering judgment in March 1999, the Istanbul Administrative Court dismissed the application and held that under s. 13(b) of the Higher-Education Act (Law no. 2547), a university vice chancellor, as the executive organ of the university, had power to regulate students' dress for the purposes of maintaining order; and in April 2001 the Supreme Administrative Court dismissed an appeal on points of law by the applicant.[141]

Subsequent to the incidents in which the applicant was denied access to exams and enrolment, the university brought disciplinary proceedings against her for continuing to wear the headscarf to lectures and thereby failing to comply with the rules on dress and, in May 1998, the applicant was issued with a warning. In May 1999, the applicant participated in an unauthorized assembly to protest against the rules on dress, and was suspended for a semester pursuant to Article 9(j) of the Students Disciplinary Procedure Rules.[142] In June 1999, the applicant lodged an application with the Istanbul Administrative Court for an order quashing the decision to suspend her but this application was dismissed on 30 November 1999 as, in light of the material in the case file and the settled case law on the subject, the impugned measure could not be regarded as illegal.[143] In June 2000, Law no. 4584 entered into force in Turkey, which provided for students to be given an amnesty in respect of penalties imposed for disciplinary offences and for any resulting disability to be annulled. The applicant was therefore granted an amnesty releasing her from all the penalties that had been imposed on her and the resultant disabilities. Thus, in September 2000, the Supreme Administrative Court held that the entry into force of this law made it unnecessary to examine the merits of the applicant's appeal on points of law against the judgment of 30 November 1999. In the intervening period, however, the applicant left her studies in Turkey and enrolled at Vienna University, where she pursued her university education.[144]

The applicant submitted that the ban on the wearing of the headscarf in higher education constituted an infringement of her freedom of religion under

Article 9 of the Convention, and the freedom to manifest her religion in particular. The Chamber judgment had ruled that the Istanbul University regulations restricting the right to wear the Islamic headscarf and the measures taken thereunder had interfered with the applicant's right to manifest her religion but that the interference was prescribed by law and pursued one of the legitimate aims set out in the second paragraph of Article 9 of the Convention and was justified in principle and proportionate to the aims pursued and could therefore be regarded as having been 'necessary in a democratic society'.

The case was referred to the Grand Chamber, which endorsed the findings of the Chamber that 'the regulations in issue, which placed restrictions of place and manner on the right to wear the Islamic headscarf in universities, constituted an interference with the applicant's right to manifest her religion'.[145] Examining next whether the interference had been prescribed by law, the Court noted the submission of the applicant, which asserted that there had been no 'written law' to prohibit students from wearing the Islamic headscarf at university, either when she enrolled in 1993 or in the period thereafter. The applicant contended that under the Students Disciplinary Procedure Rules, it was not a disciplinary offence merely to wear the Islamic headscarf but that the first regulation to restrict her right to wear the headscarf had been the circular issued by the University Vice Chancellor on 23 February 1998, four and a half years later. Therefore, it could not validly be argued that the legal basis for that regulation was the case law of the Turkish courts, as the courts only had jurisdiction to apply the law, not to establish new legal rules.[146] The applicant further contended that the Vice Chancellor of Istanbul University had not possessed the authority or power, either under the laws in force or the Students Disciplinary Procedure Rules, to refuse students who wore the headscarf access to university premises or examination rooms. Additionally, the legislature had at no stage sought to issue a general ban on wearing religious signs in schools and universities and there had never been support for such a ban in Parliament and the fact that the administrative authorities had not introduced any general regulations providing for the imposition of disciplinary penalties on students wearing the headscarf in institutions of higher education meant that no such ban existed. The interference with the applicant's rights was therefore not foreseeable and was not based on a 'law' within the meaning of the Convention.[147] The Court considered this argument by pointing to section 17 of Law No. 2547 read in the light of the relevant case law of the domestic courts as well as the fact that Article 13 of the Turkish Constitution prohibits university authorities from placing restrictions on fundamental rights without a basis in law.[148] Section 17 of Law No. 2547 and the domestic case law constituted law which was accessible and could be considered sufficiently precise in its terms to satisfy the requirement of foreseeability in the opinion of the Court. It would have been clear to the applicant, from the moment she entered Istanbul University, that there were restrictions on wearing the Islamic headscarf on the university premises and, from 23 February 1998 that she was liable to be refused access to lectures and examinations if she continued to do so.[149]

The Court accepted that the interference with the applicant's rights under Article 9 primarily pursued the legitimate aims of protecting the rights and freedoms of others and of protecting public order, a point which was not in issue between the parties.[150] The Court therefore proceeded to examine first whether the interference was 'necessary in a democratic society'. On this point, the applicant submitted that the structure of the judicial and university systems in Turkey had been determined by the successive *coups d'état* by the military in 1960, 1971 and 1980 and that a true democracy should be based on the principles of pluralism and broadmindedness; the contracting states to the Convention should therefore have a narrow margin of appreciation in regulating students' dress. The applicant also submitted that no European state banned the wearing of the headscarf at university and that there had been no sign of tension in institutions of higher education that would have justified such a radical measure.[151] The Court reiterated its often-repeated assertion that in democratic societies, where several religions coexist within one and the same population, it may be necessary to place restrictions on freedom to manifest one's religion or belief in order to reconcile the interests of the various groups and ensure that everyone's beliefs are respected. Accordingly, 'the choice of the extent and form such regulations should take must inevitably be left up to a point to the State concerned, as it will depend on the domestic context concerned', thereby granting contracting states a wide margin of appreciation in this area.[152] Applying the supervision of the Court to Turkey's margin of appreciation in this instance, the Court noted that it must have regard to what is at stake, 'namely the need to protect the rights and freedoms of others, to preserve public order and to secure civil peace and true religious pluralism, which is vital to the survival of a democratic society'.[153] The Court also referred to the Commission decisions in *Karaduman* and *Dahlab*, discussed above, in which the Commission found that states are entitled to restrict the wearing of the Islamic headscarf if it was incompatible with the pursued aim of protecting the rights and freedoms of others, public order and public safety.[154]

In finding that there had not been a violation of the applicant's rights under Article 9 of the Convention, the Court seemed particularly swayed by the rulings of the Supreme Administrative Court and the Turkish Constitutional Court on the issue of the headscarf and secularist policy more broadly. The Court reverted to the principle established in *Valsamis v Greece*[155] that by reason of their direct and continuous contact with the education community, the university authorities are in principle better placed than an international court to evaluate local needs and conditions or the requirements of a particular course.[156] Furthermore, the Court, having found that the regulations pursued a legitimate aim, could not apply the criterion of proportionality in a way that would make the notion of an institution's 'internal rules' devoid of purpose and accordingly the interference in issue was justified in principle and proportionate to the aim pursued.[157]

The applicant had also alleged a violation of Article 2 of Protocol No. 1 to the Convention, asserting that the decision to refuse her access to the University when wearing the Islamic headscarf, amounted to a violation of her right to education under the Article read in light of Articles 8, 9, and 10 of the Convention.[158] The Court departed from the finding of the Chamber that no separate issue arose under Article 2 of Protocol No. 1 and examined the applicant's complaint under this Convention Article separately. In doing so, it first noted that there is no doubt that the right to education as provided for in the first sentence of Article 2, Protocol No. 1 refers also to higher education.[159] The applicant argued that the ban on wearing the Islamic headscarf clearly constituted interference with her right to education as it had resulted in her being refused access to oncology examinations on 12 March 1998; prevented her from enrolling with the university's administrative department on 20 March 1998; and also resulted in her being refused access to a lecture on neurology on 16 April 1998 and a written examination on public health on 10 June 1998.[160] While the applicant accepted that the right to education, by its nature, had to be regulated by the state, she submitted that the criteria to be used in the regulations should be the same as those applicable to permitted interference under Articles 8 to 11 of the Convention and that being the case, she pointed to the lack of any provision in Turkish domestic law preventing the pursuit of higher education and said that the vice-chancellor's offices had no authority or power under the laws in force to refuse students wearing the headscarf access to university.[161] Despite wearing the headscarf, the applicant had been permitted to enrol at the university and pursue her studies there without incident for four and a half years; therefore, at the time of her enrolment at the university and while pursuing her studies, there had been no domestic source of law that would have enabled her to foresee that she would be denied access to the lecture theatres a number of years later.[162] The applicant also pointed to the lack of any disciplinary proceedings taken against her, which showed that wearing the Islamic headscarf had not in any way prejudiced public order or infringed the rights and freedoms of the other students.[163] To make the pursuit of her studies conditional on her abandoning the headscarf and refusing her access to educational institutions if she refused to comply with that condition had effectively and wrongfully violated the substance of her right to education and rendered it ineffective; the state had therefore violated her right to education, read in the light of Articles 8, 9 and 10 of the Convention.[164]

The Turkish government pointed to the fact that the prohibition on the wearing of the headscarf which was put in place by the Vice Chancellor of Istanbul University had been based on the judgments of the Constitutional Court and the Supreme Administrative Court.[165] Also, the reality was that the applicant had not encountered any difficulty in enrolling at the Cerrahpaşa Faculty of Medicine, which in fact proved that she had enjoyed equality of treatment in the right of access to educational institutions. The government therefore requested that the Grand Chamber uphold the findings of the

Chamber in ruling that the regulations in issue did not contravene the Court's case law, having regard to the margin of appreciation accorded to the Contracting States.[166]

The Court noted that Contracting States enjoy a margin of appreciation in the regulation of educational institutions under Article 2 of Protocol I and are not bound by an exhaustive list of 'legitimate aims' as is the case for Articles 8–11 of the Convention.[167] Restrictions, however, must be proportionate to the legitimate aim pursued and must not conflict with other rights enshrined in the Convention and its Protocols. The Court accepted that the regulations on the basis of which the applicant was refused access to various lectures and examinations for wearing the Islamic headscarf constituted a restriction on her right to education, notwithstanding the fact that she had had access to the University and been able to read the subject of her choice in accordance with the results she had achieved in the university entrance examination.[168] Nonetheless, in the instant case, the Court noted that the right to education could not be divorced from the conclusion reached by the Court with respect to Article 9, as criticism of the regulation concerned took the same form as the restriction complained of under Article 9, which the Court had already found to be foreseeable and pursued the legitimate aim of preserving the secular character of educational institutions.[169]

With regard to the principle of proportionality, the Court had found in its examination of Article 9 that 'a reasonable relationship of proportionality between the means used and the aim pursued', placing importance on the fact that the measures in question did not hinder the students in performing the duties imposed by the habitual forms of religious observance and that the decision-making process for applying the internal regulations satisfied, so far as was possible, the requirement to weigh up the various interests at stake.[170] Lastly, the Court was of the opinion that it would be unrealistic to imagine that the applicant was unaware of Istanbul University's internal regulations restricting the places where religious dress could be worn or had not been sufficiently informed about the reasons for their introduction. Therefore, the applicant could reasonably have foreseen that she ran the risk of being refused access to lectures and examinations if, as subsequently happened, she continued to wear the Islamic headscarf after 23 February 1998.[171] As a result, the restriction did not impair the very essence of the applicant's right to education and did not conflict with other rights enshrined in the Convention or its Protocols; there was, therefore, no violation of the first sentence of Article 2 of Protocol No. 1.[172]

Regarding the applicant's alleged violations of Articles 8 and 10 of the Convention, the Grand Chamber followed the decision of the Chamber and found that no separate issue arose under these Articles as the relevant circumstances were the same as those it had examined in relation to Article 9 and Article 2 of Protocol No. 1, in respect of which it had found no violations.[173] With respect to Article 14 of the Convention, taken individually or together with Article 9 of the Convention or the first sentence of Article 2 of Protocol

No. 1, the Court noted that the applicant did not provide detailed particulars in her pleadings before the Grand Chamber. Moreover, the regulations on the Islamic headscarf: 'were not directed against the applicant's religious affiliation, but pursued, among other things, the legitimate aim of protecting order and the rights and freedoms of others and were manifestly intended to preserve the secular nature of educational institutions'.[174] Accordingly, the reasons which led the Court to conclude that there has been no violation of Article 9 of the Convention or Article 2 of Protocol No. 1 incontestably also applied to the complaint under Article 14, taken individually or together with the aforementioned provisions and therefore there was no violation of Article 14 of the Convention.[175]

The decision of the Grand Chamber undoubtedly implies that the view of the Court is that secularist policy is compatible, if not a prerequisite for achieving the Convention's fundamental aim of promoting and protecting human rights and appears to accept without question the assertion of the Turkish Constitutional Court that 'secularism, as the guarantor of democratic values, was the meeting point of liberty and equality'.[176] The *Şahin* case again aptly illustrates what is undoubtedly an overly deferential attitude of the Court to states parties' assertions in cases concerning Article 9 of the Convention. This deference is acutely evident in particular in the cases specifically concerning the wearing of the headscarf with the paradoxical result that as Turkey attempts to bring its human rights protection into line with that of EU member states, its illiberal secularist policies appear to be implicitly encouraged by the ECtHR. In the case law concerning Turkey, the Court's uncritical analysis of assertions regarding the importance of the ban on the wearing of the headscarf to upholding secularism is especially disappointing. Bleiberg suggests that the problem lies in how the Court itself views secularism:

> the ECHR merely reiterates the Turkish Constitutional Court's holding and unquestioningly accepts it at face value. The ECHR never independently analyzed Turkey's Constitution or critically inquired into the basis of the headscarf's incompatibility with secularism – an analytical flaw particularly bothersome considering that the founding father of Turkish secularism believed the headscarf did not conflict with the principle of secularism and that Turkey did not institute a headscarf ban until the 1980s. Thus, the ECHR could have found the Turkish Constitutional Court's interpretation of secularism – one that denies a right to an individual – a violation of human rights, while simultaneously upholding the importance of secularism in Turkish democracy.[177]

In fact only one of the judges of the Court was uncomfortable with the interpretation of the restriction on the applicant's right to wear a headscarf; in her dissenting opinion, Judge Tulkens expresses dissatisfaction with the Court's reasoning in relation to the two fundamental concerns on which this case was decided, secularism and gender equality. Judge Tulkens clearly did not agree with the majority opinion that the imposition of secularism is a suitable means of regulating freedom of religion and found the manner in which the Court accepted at face value the assertions of the Turkish government that the wearing of the headscarf was incompatible with the principles of secularism to be problematic. The judge further pointed to the lack of evidence that the applicant either intended to undermine the convictions of others through wearing the headscarf or that there had been any disruption in teaching or in everyday life at the University, or any disorderly conduct, as a result of the applicant wearing the headscarf.[178] Judge Tulkens also referred to that fact that in the Court's judgment in *Gündüz v Turkey*,[179] the Court held that there had been a violation of freedom of expression in a case where a Muslim religious leader had been convicted for violently criticizing the secular regime in Turkey, calling for the introduction of the shariah and referring to children born of marriages celebrated solely before the secular authorities as 'bastards': 'Thus, manifesting one's religion by peacefully wearing a headscarf may be prohibited whereas, in the same context, remarks which could be construed as incitement to religious hatred are covered by freedom of expression.'[180]

On the question of equality, Judge Tulkens also disagreed with the Court's dubious assessment that:

> where the values of pluralism, respect for the rights of others and, in particular, equality before the law of men and women are being taught and applied in practice, it is understandable that the relevant authorities should wish to preserve the secular nature of the institution concerned and so consider it contrary to such values to allow religious attire, including, as in the present case, the Islamic headscarf, to be worn.[181]

Judge Tulkens noted that she failed to see how the principle of sexual equality could justify prohibiting a woman from following a practice which, in the absence of proof to the contrary, she must be taken to have freely adopted.[182] It is evident that Judge Tulkens did not accept the arguments proffered by the Turkish government, and accepted by the majority of the Court, regarding the principles of secularism and equality as grounds for excluding the applicant. In a particularly insightful comment, she noted:

> More fundamentally, by accepting the applicant's exclusion from the University in the name of secularism and equality, the majority have accepted her exclusion from precisely the type of liberated environment in which the true meaning of these values can take shape and develop. University affords practical access to knowledge that is free and independent of all authority. Experience of this kind is far more effective a means of raising awareness of the principles of secularism and equality than an obligation that is not assumed voluntarily, but imposed. A tolerance-based

dialogue between religions and cultures is an education in itself, so it is ironic that young women should be deprived of that education on account of the headscarf. Advocating freedom and equality for women cannot mean depriving them of the chance to decide on their future. Bans and exclusions echo that very fundamentalism these measures are intended to combat. Here, as elsewhere, the risks are familiar: radicalisation of beliefs, silent exclusion, a return to religious schools. When rejected by the law of the land, young women are forced to take refuge in their own law. As we are all aware, intolerance breeds intolerance.[183]

Judge Tulkens concluded with a general argument that: 'the message that needs to be repeated over and over again is that the best means of preventing and combating fanaticism and extremism is to uphold human rights'.[184]

The ECtHR is not alone in its interpretation of the perceived perils of religious symbols in the public sphere however, and its attitude should perhaps be unsurprising considering that some of the EU member states, such as France, expressly forbid expression of religious identity in the public sphere. Parallels, for example, are often drawn between the French and Turkish models of strict secularism, or *laïcité* in this regard. But the approach of the ECtHR can be contrasted with that taken by the United Nations Human Rights Committee (HRC) in the case of *Raihon Hudoyberganova v Uzbekistan*,[185] delivered in the same year as the ECtHR's ruling in the *Şahin* case. The facts in *Raihon Hudoyberganova* were not dissimilar to those in *Şahin*. The complainant in this case alleged violations of her rights under Articles 18 and 19 of the International Covenant on Civil and Political Rights (ICCPR), which protect the rights to freedom of religion and freedom of expression respectively.[186] She was a student at the Farsi Department at the Faculty of Languages of the Tashkent State Institute for Eastern Languages since 1995 and in 1996, joined the newly created Islamic Affairs Department of the Institute.[187] In 1997, the complainant alleged that the Institute administration began to seriously limit the right to freedom of belief of practising Muslims by closing the existing prayer room and, when the students complained to the Institute's management, the administration began to harass them and 'invited' all students wearing the *hijab* to leave the courses of the Institute and to study at the Tashkent Islamic Institute instead.[188] The complainant also claimed that she had been threatened and attempts were made to prevent her attending lectures.[189] In January 1998, Ms. Hudoyberganova was informed that new regulations of the Institute had been adopted, under which students could not wear religious dress and she was requested to conform. She did so but wrote that she disagreed with the provisions which prohibited students from covering their faces and on the next day was called by the Deputy Dean on Ideological and Educational matters who showed her the new regulations again and requested that she remove her headscarf.[190] In March 1998, the complainant was informed of an order by which the Rector had excluded her from the Institute, based on her alleged negative attitude towards the professors and on a violation of the provisions of the regulations of the Institute. She was also informed that if she changed her mind about wearing the *hijab*, the order would be annulled.[191] In May 1998, following the promulgation of a new law prohibiting Uzbek nationals from wearing religious dress in public places, the complainant was informed that all students wearing the *hijab* would be expelled.[192] On failing to have her student status restored before domestic proceedings, the complainant took her complaint to the HRC, alleging violations of her rights under articles 18 and 19 of the ICCPR, as she was excluded from University because she wore a headscarf for religious reasons and refused to remove it.

In its submissions to the HRC, Uzbekistan noted that according to paragraph 2(d) of the Internal Regulations (regulating the rights and obligations of the Institute's students), in the Institute, students were forbidden to wear clothes 'attracting undue attention', and prohibited from wearing the *hijab*. This regulation was discussed at a general meeting of all students on 15 January 1998, at which the complainant was presented with the text and she made a note that she disagreed with the requirements of paragraph 2(d). On 26 January 1998, the Dean of the Faculty of History warned her that she was in violation of the provisions of paragraph 2(d) of the Institute's regulations. The complainant refused to sign the warning and a record in this respect was made on 27 January 1998. On 10 February 1998, by order of the Dean of the Faculty of History, the complainant was reprimanded for infringement of the Internal Regulations and by order of the Rector of the Institute of 16 March 1998, Ms. Hudoyberganova was excluded from the Institute. The order was grounded on the 'rough immoral attitude toward a teacher and infringement of the internal regulations of the Institute, after numerous warnings'. According to Uzbekistan, the complainant had not entered an appeal against this decision.[193]

The HRC began its consideration by noting that it considers that 'the freedom to manifest one's religion encompasses the right to wear clothes or attire in public which is in conformity with the individual's faith or religion' and that 'to prevent a person from wearing religious clothing in public or private may constitute a violation of article 18, paragraph 2, which prohibits any coercion that would impair the individual's freedom to have or adopt a religion'.[194] It also pointed to its General Comment No. 22 on the right to freedom of thought, conscience and religion, in which it stated that policies or practices that have the same intention or effect as direct coercion, such as those restricting access to education, are inconsistent with Article 18(2) of the ICCPR.[195] Echoing the pronouncements of the ECtHR in its consideration of cases arising under Article 9 of the Convention, the HRC noted that the freedom to manifest one's religion or beliefs 'is not absolute and may be subject to limitations, which are prescribed by law and are necessary to protect public safety, order, health, or morals, or the fundamental rights and freedoms of others', as per Article 18, para. 3.[196] The decision of the HRC in the instant case appeared to hinge on the lack of a justification provided by

Uzbekistan as to why the complainant was expelled, other than for the reason of wearing a *hijab*:

> The Committee notes that the State party has not invoked any specific ground for which the restriction imposed on the author would in its view be necessary in the meaning of article 18, paragraph 3. Instead, the State party has sought to justify the expulsion of the author from University because of her refusal to comply with the ban. Neither the author nor the State party have specified what precise kind of attire the author wore and which was referred to as 'hijab' by both parties. In the particular circumstances of the present case, and without either prejudging the right of a State party to limit expressions of religion and belief in the context of article 18 of the Covenant and duly taking into account the specifics of the context, or prejudging the right of academic institutions to adopt specific regulations relating to their own functioning, the Committee is led to conclude, in the absence of any justification provided by the State party, that there has been a violation of article 18, paragraph 2.[197]

The HRC was not, therefore, asserting that academic institutions did not have the right to regulate what students might wear but rather, in this case, was unconvinced by the state party's justifications for doing so. The decision of the HRC, coming as it did in the same time period as the decision of the ECtHR in *Şahin*, raises questions as to how the HRC would have dealt with the issues raised in *Şahin* were they considered under Articles 18 and 19 of the ICCPR. Boyle has suggested that the HRC 'would be likely to take a different view (to the ECtHR in *Şahin*) if it was possible to take a complaint to it', because of its reasoning in *Hudoyberganova v Uzbekistan* and also because of the fact that the HRC maintains that it does not apply a margin of appreciation.[198]

3.1.2 *The jurisprudence of fear? Recent developments at the ECtHR*

Evidence that the ECtHR is moving closer to the attitude adopted by the HRC in *Hudoyberganova v Uzbekistan* cannot be gleaned from the 2007 decision in *Kavakçi v Turkey*.[199] Although the ECtHR did not base its decision on Article 9 of the Convention, its decision is worth examining as the argument regarding the right to wear the headscarf was at issue and a violation of the Convention was in fact found.

Merve Safa Kavakçi was elected to the Turkish National Assembly in the general election of April 1999 as a candidate of the (now defunct) Fazilet Partisi (Virtue Party). On 2 May 1999, Ms. Kavakçi entered the Assembly to take her oath wearing a headscarf and was prevented from doing so and forced to leave the parliament by a group of protesting deputies. Five days after this event, an action to dissolve the Virtue Party was brought before the Constitutional Court on the ground that it had become a 'centre of activities contrary to the principle of secularism' and also that the party was in fact a continuation of the Refah party, which had previously been banned by the Constitutional Court.[200] The Speaker of the National Assembly removed the applicant's parliamentary status in March 2001, while in its judgment of 22 June 2001 the Constitutional Court dissolved Fazilet, on the ground that the party, which had based its political programme on the question of wearing of the Islamic headscarf, had become a 'centre of activities contrary to the principle of secularism'. The court also banned Ms. Kavakçi and two of her former Fazilet colleagues, Mr. Sılay and Ms. Ilıcak, from becoming founder members, ordinary members, leaders or auditors of any other political party for a period of five years.[201] Furthermore, on 13 May 1999, the applicant's Turkish citizenship had also been revoked under Article 25(a) of Law No. 403 on Nationality, although this was ostensibly on the ground that she had obtained American citizenship prior to the election without obtaining the correct formal permission from the Turkish authorities.[202] The applicant alleged violations of Articles 6, 9 and 14 of the Convention, as well as Article 3 of Protocol No. 1.[203]

Invoking Article 9 of the Convention, the applicant maintained that she was stripped of her nationality and of her parliamentary status as a result of her manifesting her religious beliefs through wearing the headscarf. She alleged that the prohibition on the wearing of the headscarf was not based on law, as the internal dress code for parliamentarians did not preclude the wearing of the headscarf. Furthermore, the applicant maintained that the interference was not justified by Article 9(2) and that a parliamentary deputy's function could not be limited by wearing religious symbols.[204] With regard to Article 6(1) of the Convention and Article 3 of Protocol No. 1, the applicant alleged that the revocation of her parliamentary mandate and the restrictions placed on her political rights as a result of her wearing the headscarf at the National Assembly, violated these provisions of the Convention. She further alleged that the decision to withdraw her Turkish citizenship was based on improper procedures and was not taken by an absolute majority of the National Assembly, as required by Article 84 of the Turkish Constitution. Finally, the applicant asserted that the courts had not considered the fact that she had recovered her Turkish citizenship by virtue of her marriage to a Turkish citizen. On the basis of these same facts, the applicant also complained of a violation of Article 14 of the Convention.[205] The Court, however, proceeded to examine all of the applicant's objections under Article 3 of Protocol No. I to the Convention.

The government submitted that a number of domestic legislative reforms had been instituted in order to harmonize Turkish law with the Convention and the jurisprudence of the Court, particularly Article 69 of the Constitution, which had been amended and now provides that the Constitutional Court, instead of dissolving a political party, may decide to partially or totally suspend its public funding depending on the seriousness of the act.[206] In this regard, the applicant argued that if the amendment of Article 69 of the Constitution shows the goodwill of the Turkish Government, it also shows that this provision, as it was at the time, did not meet the conditions listed in paragraphs 2 of Articles 9, 10 and 11 of the Convention, and in particular it did not conform to the principle of proportionality.[207] She further pointed out that Article 25 (a) of Law No. 403, on the basis of which she lost her Turkish citizenship, leaves too much discretion to the authorities and alleged that she in fact lost her citizenship and her parliamentary mandate because of wearing the Islamic headscarf when she was due to take her parliamentary oath. Also, the applicant asserted that dual nationality is not a legal impediment to holding office.[208] The withdrawal of the applicant's Turkish citizenship and the revocation of her parliamentary mandate were therefore not proportionate to the legitimate aim pursued and the contested measures were incompatible with the very substance of the right to be elected and to exercise her mandate recognized by Article 3 of Protocol No. I.[209]

The Court began its consideration by reiterating that Article 3 of Protocol No. 1 guarantees individual rights, including the right to vote and stand as candidates in elections but that these rights are not absolute and contracting states enjoy a wide margin of appreciation in the area.[210] Nevertheless, the Court affirmed that the conditions imposed on the rights under Article 3 of Protocol No. I must not be so great as to empty the rights of their very essence or deprive them of their effectiveness and the conditions must pursue a legitimate aim and be proportionate. In particular, any conditions imposed should not obstruct the free expression of the people in the choice of the legislature and they must reflect, or not thwart, the desire to maintain the integrity and effectiveness of an electoral procedure to determine the will of the people through universal suffrage.[211] The Court emphasized the relevance of the provision by noting that it enshrines a principle characteristic of a truly democratic political system and is therefore of paramount importance in the scheme of the Convention.[212] Nonetheless, although the Court ultimately found that the applicant's rights under Article 3 of Protocol No. I had been violated, its approach to the importance of secularism in Turkey is still one of deference to the opinion of the state authorities:

> The Court notes that the temporary restrictions imposed on the applicant's political rights had been intended to preserve the secular character of the Turkish political system. Given the importance of this principle for the democratic system in Turkey, the Court considers that the contested measure pursued legitimate aims, namely the prevention of disorder and the protection of the rights and freedoms of others.[213]

In assessing the proportionality of the measures imposed, the Court pointed to the very wide scope of Article 69(6) of the Turkish Constitution as it was formulated at the time. The provision did not distinguish between various levels of involvement in the impugned activities and in fact the chairman and vice-president of Fazilet had escaped sanction altogether. The sanctions imposed on the applicant were serious and could not be regarded as being proportionate to the legitimate aims pursued; therefore they violated the applicant's rights under Article 3 of Protocol No. 1 to the Convention.[214] The Court's reluctance to engage with the applicant's arguments raised under Article 9 of the Convention is perhaps yet another example of its reticence to get involved in a broader discussion about secularism in Turkey, what secularism entails and when or if the stringent protection of the principle can lead to a violation of rights under the Convention. The Court did, after all, reiterate the importance of the principle of secularism to the democratic system in Turkey,[215] as it has done in each of the cases concerning the wearing of the headscarf, discussed above. Indeed, there was no engagement at all by the Court with the fact that the applicant was ejected from parliament and prevented from taking the oath *because* she was wearing the headscarf. While the applicant in this case had a successful outcome in that the Court did rule in her favour, proponents of the freedom to wear the Islamic headscarf as a manifestation of religious belief will take little comfort from the reasoning of the Court.

3.2 En'forcing' democracy: Refah Partisi (the Welfare Party) and others v Turkey

A period of stability in Turkish government since the election of the AKP in November 2002 was threatened in July 2008 by the case brought before the Constitutional Court which sought an order to close the ruling AK party on the grounds of 'anti-secular' activities.[216] The closure of political parties in Turkey is not without precedent; the Turkish Constitutional Court dissolved or banned 38 parties between 1923 and 1996.[217] While some of these cases have come before the Strasbourg authorities, the ruling of the ECtHR in the case of *Refah Partisi (the Welfare Party) and others v Turkey*[218] in particular, which upheld the decision of the Turkish Constitutional Court to close the Refah Partisi, reflects broader European concerns regarding a possible rise in so-called 'political Islam' in Turkey.

Refah Partisi (the Welfare Party) was founded in July 1983 by former Prime Minister of Turkey, Necmettin Erbakan.[219] In the local elections of March 1989 Refah obtained about 10 per cent of the vote and its candidates were elected mayors of a number of towns and five large cities.[220] Between 1989 and 1995 the party grew immensely in power, partly, Dokupil suggests, 'because of the Islamic resurgence in the country, partly because of divisions among the centre-right parties, and partly in response to anti-western sentiment', so that in the general elections of 1995, Refah won 24 mayoral seats and a total of 158 seats in the Assembly, making it the largest political party.[221] In June 1996 Refah formed a coalition with the Doğru Yol Partisi (True Path Party).

In May 1997 the Principal State Counsel at the Court of Cassation applied to the Constitutional Court of Turkey to have Refah dissolved on the basis that it was a 'centre of activities contrary to the principles of secularism'.[222]

In support of this assertion, it was alleged that Refah chairman and other prominent members had advocated the wearing of the Islamic headscarf in state schools and buildings, thus violating the principle of secularism; that Erbakan had encouraged Muslims to join Refah by stating that only his party could establish the supremacy of the Koran and that Erbakan had assured Islamist movements of his support.[223] It was also alleged that members of Refah had called for the secular political system to be replaced by a theocratic system and that members had expressed support for introduction of shariah law in Turkey.[224]

In its defence, Refah rejected the claim that it represented a threat to the secular nature of the Turkish Republic and alleged that extracts from Erbakan's speeches had been taken out of context and distorted.[225] It was also claimed that the statements advancing political Islam[226] made by other members of Refah had been made by members who were not authorized to represent Refah and the three MPs concerned had been expelled from the party as soon as the leadership became aware of their statements.[227] Despite the defence invoked by Refah, the Turkish Constitutional Court dissolved the party on the basis that it had become a 'centre of activities contrary to the principle of secularism', basing its decision on ss. 101(b) and 103(1) of Law No. 2820 on the Regulation of Political Parties.[228]

The applicants before the ECtHR alleged that the dissolution of Refah Partisi and the order preventing its leaders, including Necmettin Erbakan, Şevket Kazan, and Ahmet Tekdal, from holding similar office in any other political party had infringed their right to freedom of association established in Article 11 of the ECHR.[229] The Court had previously stressed the importance of the rights arising from Article 11 in another case involving Turkey, in which it stated:

> an association, including a political party, is not excluded from the protection afforded by the Convention simply because its activities are regarded by the national authorities as undermining the constitutional structures of the State and calling for the imposition of restrictions. As the Court has said in the past, while it is in principle open to the national authorities to take such action as they consider necessary to respect the rule of law or to give effect to constitutional rights, they must do so in a manner which is compatible with their obligations under the Convention and subject to review by the Convention institutions ...[230]

The Court had also stated that the restrictions on Article 11, provided for in paragraph 2 of the provision, should be strictly construed where political parties are concerned; 'only convincing and compelling reasons can justify restrictions on such parties' freedom of association'.[231] It is unsurprising therefore that in four cases concerning dissolution of political parties prior to the *Refah* case, the ECtHR found violations of Article 11.[232] In its examination of the *Refah* case the Court's approach was typical; it first assessed whether or not there was an interference with the rights of Refah Partisi under Article 11 of the Convention. It concluded that there was, in fact, an interference with the applicants' right to freedom of association.[233] The Court then looked at whether this interference could be justified by looking in turn at whether it was 'prescribed by law', whether it served a 'legitimate aim' and whether the interference was 'necessary in a democratic society'.[234] In its assessment of the first element – whether the interference was 'prescribed by law' – the Court noted that Article 69 of the Turkish Constitution gave the Constitutional Court sole discretion in the issue of dissolution of political parties and the measures imposed by the Constitutional Court were based on sections 101 and 107 of Law No. 2820 on the Regulation of Political Parties, as well as Articles 68, 69 and 84 of the Constitution of Turkey.[235] The provisions in question were accessible to the applicants and given the status of Refah as a large political party with legal advisors familiar with constitutional law and the rules applicable to political parties, the applicants were reasonably able to foresee that they ran the risk of dissolution of the party if they or the party's members engaged in anti-secular activities.[236] The interference was therefore prescribed by law.

Regarding whether the interference served a legitimate aim, the Turkish government asserted that it pursued several, namely the protection of public safety, national security, the rights and freedoms of others and the prevention of crime.[237] The applicants argued, however, that the real reason for Refah's dissolution was that its economic policy, which included reducing the national debt to zero, would threaten the interests of major businesses and the military.[238] With a 'notably brief analysis',[239] the ECtHR concluded that the applicants had not presented sufficient evidence to suggest that Refah had been dissolved for reasons other than those cited by the Constitutional Court and having taken into account 'the importance of the principle of secularism for the democratic system in Turkey' agreed with the position advanced by the government and concluded that Refah's dissolution pursued several of the legitimate aims listed in Article 11.[240]

Lastly, with regard to whether the interference was 'necessary in a democratic society', the applicants submitted a number of arguments. In the first instance, they argued that the speeches advancing political Islam had been made several years prior to the institution of dissolution proceedings and therefore Refah could not be said to constitute a threat to secularism and democracy in Turkey at the time of the proceedings.[241] In its thirteen-year existence it had taken on many responsibilities of local and central government and accordingly in coming to its decision, the Court should assess all of the factors that had led to the decision to dissolve the party and all of the party's activities since it had come into existence.[242] The applicants also pointed to the fact that during the year in which it was in power (from June 1996 to July 1997), it made no attempt to introduce legislation that would facilitate a regime based on Islamic law.[243] Furthermore, Refah had expelled the members who had made the inflammatory statements and Erbakan's comments, when read in context, contained no apologia for violence; nor did Refah's constitution or programme make any reference to either shariah or Islam.[244] To sanction the dissolution of Refah; the imposition of restrictions on the political activities of its members; and the financial losses the party would suffer as a result would, the applicants argued, constitute an interference which was disproportionate to the legitimate aims pursued.[245]

The Turkish government refuted the applicants' arguments by alleging that had Refah been the sole party in power in the government, it 'would have been quite capable of implementing its policy and thus putting an end to democracy'.[246] A number of other arguments were also advanced, including the assertion that certain aspects of the party's activities and speeches indicated that the party would in fact seek to introduce shariah if it held power; would introduce a plurality of legal systems based on religious affiliation; and would 'do away with' the principle of secularism altogether.[247] Additionally, the government alleged that some members of Refah advocated the use of violence in order to resist certain government policies or to gain power, constituting incitement to a popular uprising.[248]

The ECtHR's assessment of the arguments posited by both parties broke with past precedent for a number of reasons, including the Court's failure to use Refah's constitution to determine if there was a specific exception to Article 11(1); assessing Refah's actions while it was the controlling party in government;[249] placing too great an emphasis on the extremists within Refah; and imposing additional requirements before finding a violation of Article 11.[250] In beginning its consideration of the case, the Court repeated its ruling in *United Communist Party of Turkey v Turkey* that democracy is an important feature of the European public order.[251] In the *United Communist Party* case, the Court had made an interesting statement, indicative perhaps, of the lengths to which it would go to 'uphold democracy' in the future. The Court contended:

> Democracy is without doubt a fundamental feature of the European public order ... That is apparent, firstly, from the Preamble to the Convention, which establishes a very clear connection between the Convention and democracy by stating that the maintenance and further realisation of human rights and fundamental freedoms are best ensured on the one hand by an effective political democracy and on the other by a common understanding and observance of human rights ... The Preamble goes on to affirm that European countries have a common heritage of political tradition, ideals, freedom and the rule of law. The Court has observed that in that common heritage are to be found the underlying values of the Convention ... it has pointed out several times that the Convention was designed to maintain and promote the ideals and values of a democratic society ... In addition, Articles 8, 9, 10 and 11 of the Convention require that interference with the exercise of the rights they enshrine must be assessed by the yardstick of what is 'necessary in a democratic society'. The only type of necessity capable of justifying an

interference with any of those rights is, therefore, one which may claim to spring from 'democratic society'. Democracy thus appears to be the only political model contemplated by the Convention and, accordingly, the only one compatible with it.[252]

In *Refah*, the Court also reaffirmed that freedom of thought, conscience and religion, protected by Article 9 of the Convention is one of the foundations of a 'democratic society' within the meaning of the Convention.[253] Nonetheless, the Court noted that the principle of secularism is 'one of the fundamental principles of the state which are in harmony with the rule of law and respect for human rights and democracy'[254] and went on to justify the dissolution of Refah as being within the power of preventive intervention on the part of the state and as being consistent with a state's positive obligations under Article 1 of the Convention to secure the rights and freedoms of persons within their jurisdiction.[255] Furthermore, the dissolution of Refah was deemed to have met the 'pressing social need' of averting the danger to democracy which Refah was found to hold and accordingly the decision to dissolve the party was a proportionate response to the legitimate aim of upholding democracy and the principles of secularism.[256] In agreeing with the decision of the Turkish Constitutional Court, the ECtHR followed 'the logic of collapsing unity, democracy and progress' employed by the domestic court, which had indicated that Refah was a 'political representation of the general Islamist threat':[257]

> The root of the Islamist threat was in its being backward-looking, threatening to steer Turkey away from the road of progress. According to the Court, the major threat Refah represented was to the laicism principle of the constitution. At the hands of the Court, laicism became not merely the tenet of separation of religious and governmental spheres, or even of state control over religion, but also a crucial embodiment of the idea of progress. In turn, laicism functioned as a means of enhancing national unity.[258]

A number of concerns have been raised about the ECtHR's reasoning in the *Refah* case. Among these are the fact the Court paid no attention to the constitution of Refah Partisi, which made no reference to either shariah or Islamic law forming the basis of the Turkish system; and also the contention that even if the proposals of Refah were inconsistent with the principle of secularism set out in the Turkish Constitution, the ECtHR should refrain from being 'the judge of secularism' and concentrate instead on ensuring the freedom to associate and publicly debate ideas, as provided for in Article 11.[259] Schilling further asserts that the Court added two additional obstacles to its consideration of Refah's arguments that were not present in previous dissolution cases, namely the likelihood that Refah would have been successful in its attempts to impose its own programme were it to achieve an overall majority as opposed to functioning within coalition government and the assumption that Refah's leaders knew the risk associated with their conduct.[260]

It follows, then, that the approach of the ECtHR in *Refah* may set the same precedent for other cases from Turkey or any other country grappling with issues relating to religion in the public sphere, particularly if the religion in question is Islam. That the Court will continue to adopt an inflexible approach to this issue was left in little doubt by its endorsement of the Chamber's opinion on shariah, which found it to be incompatible with the fundamental principles of democracy as set forth in the Convention:

> Like the Constitutional Court, the Court considers that sharia, which faithfully reflects the dogmas and divine rules laid down by religion, is stable and invariable. Principles such as pluralism in the political sphere or the constant evolution of public freedoms have no place in it. The Court notes that, when read together, the offending statements, which contain explicit references to the introduction of sharia, are difficult to reconcile with the fundamental principles of democracy, as conceived in the Convention taken as a whole. It is difficult to declare one's respect for democracy and human rights while at the same time supporting a regime based on sharia, which clearly diverges from Convention values, particularly with regard to its criminal law and criminal procedure, its rules on the legal status of women and the way it intervenes in all spheres of private and public life in accordance with religious precepts ... In the Court's view, a political party whose actions seem to be aimed at introducing sharia in a State party to the Convention can hardly be regarded as an association complying with the democratic ideal that underlies the whole of the Convention.[261]

There is much to criticize in the Court's judgment in *Refah* but this statement in particular appears entirely to go beyond the bounds of what the Court was being asked to examine in this case. Boyle has suggested that it was 'unnecessary and unhelpful' for the Court to engage with shariah at all but, since it had apparently been convinced of such a necessity:

> it might have sought expert pleadings, for example by means of an amicus curiae brief, which at the very least would have brought to the Court's attention the considerable ongoing debate within Islam on shariah and democracy and those aspects of Islamic law that are in conflict with international human rights standards. It might have understood better the difference between political Islam and the faith of the vast majority of followers of Islam.[262]

Boyle has also rightly criticized the Court's 'incidental assessment of Islam' and its 'intemperate and injudicious language' in which it: 'indulged in a wholly unnecessary and inappropriate critique of this religion, which has over 100 million followers in the European legal space of forty-five States over which the Court exercises jurisdiction'.[263] For all the importance the Court purports to attach to democracy, the decision to uphold the dissolution of an elected party in government that, it is suggested, 'did not challenge democracy as such, but rather sought to question an ideology imbued in the institutions of the State and enforced by the Turkish military'[264] undoubtedly led to one of the Court's most undemocratic results to date.

4 Summary

While the issues raised, formally, in Turkey's accession process are real and certainly merit remark, equally there are additional fundamental undeclared concerns within EU member states. These relate, as Casanova has argued, to a collective Christian (but secular) identity, which now must confront the possible accession of almost 70 million *Muslims* to the EU. It is clear that a type of cultural, or even specifically religious, requirement is another obstacle on Turkey's route to membership.

In Europe, the privatization of religion is considered a sine qua non for a modern secular democracy (signalled by an embracing of the concept of militant democracy) and events in Turkey, such as the election of the AKP, rest uneasily with some European neighbours, who have, since the Enlightenment, assumed religion's relegation to the private sphere, despite the very real evidence to the contrary in numerous EU states. While this attitude is somewhat surprising given the strictly secular nature of official government policy in Turkey since the early twentieth century, the issue is of course complicated even further when the public manifestation of religious beliefs are those of Islam as it is perceived as an essentially 'un-European' religion.[265] As Casanova rightly notes:

> when it comes to Islam, secular Europeans tend to reveal the limits and prejudices of modern secularist toleration. One is not likely to hear among liberal politicians and secular intellectuals explicitly xenophobic or anti-religious statements. The politically correct formulation tends to run along such lines as 'We welcome each and all immigrants irrespective of race or religion as long as they are willing to respect and accept our modern liberal secular European norms.'[266]

Thus, while the European Commission may criticize the inadequate protection of religious rights in Turkey,[267] it is evident from the case law of the ECtHR, that Europe's guarantee of religious freedoms is hardly the appropriate yardstick by which such protection should be measured. The paradoxes in the triangular EU–Religion–Turkey discussion are all too apparent. In 2003, for example, the European Parliament issued a resolution on Turkey's application for EU membership, which considered that 'a relaxed attitude to Islam and to religion in general will counteract the rise of antidemocratic movements such as intolerant and violent religious extremism'.[268] This is despite numerous ECtHR decisions sanctioning Turkey's stringent application of secularist policy; the EU's implicit encouragement of this policy; as well as the very obvious point that the EU's own attitude to Islam and to religion in general has been anything but 'relaxed'. It would appear that Turkey's policies with regard to religion in the public sphere are at once too secular, as demonstrated by the European Parliament resolution, yet not secular enough for those who fear that Turkey's accession may herald an unthinkable return to religion in Europe's public sphere. It is also likely that the debate provoked by Turkey's potential accession to the EU as well as the accession of the more outwardly religious countries of Eastern Europe (such as Poland) is one which is viewed as undesirable by many of Europe's secularists. As Casanova persuasively argues:

> It is this 'secular' identity shared by European elites and ordinary people alike that paradoxically turns 'religion' and the barely suppressed Christian European identity into a thorny and perplexing issue when it comes to delimiting the external geographic boundaries and to defining the internal cultural identity of a European Union in the process of being constituted.[269]

If Casanova's contention is correct, then it may prove exceptionally difficult for Turkey to overcome perceptions with regard to the limits of the EU, both geographic and conceptual.

Notes

1 As noted in Chapter 1, Turkey is one of only 11 countries with a predominantly Muslim population to prescribe secularism in its Constitution. See Chapter 1, n. 45 and accompanying text.
2 The 'clash of civilisations' debate refers to the thesis put forward by Samuel P. Huntington, which suggests that cultural and religious identities are the primary source of conflict in a post Cold War world. See 'The Clash of Civilisations?', Foreign Aff., 72(3) (1993), 22–49.
3 J. Casanova, 'Religion, European Secular Identities, and European Integration', in T. A. Byrnes and P. J. Katzenstein (eds), *Religion in an Expanding Europe* (New York: Cambridge University Press, 2006), 65–93, 74.
4 For example, French President, Nicolas Sarkozy, has frequently cited the fact that Turkey is not 'European' and is not 'in Europe' as reasons for not offering it full EU membership. See M. Almond 'A Friend in Need: Turkey Is a Strategically Crucial Country, at an Important Juncture. Can Western Countries Afford to Snub Its EU Application?', *Guardian*, 10 June 2008, noting that: 'French President Nicolas Sarkozy's insistence that a referendum should be held on Turkey's admission suggests that years of painful adjustment to EU norms will never produce the payoff of membership.'
5 See generally, W. Schäuble, 'Talking Turkey: Is Europe Ready for a Muslim Member?', Foreign Aff., 83 (2004), 134–7, 136, noting that '[t]he EU is, after all, European. Although Australia or Japan could fulfil its accession criteria, no one has proposed them as potential EU members. Similarly, countries such as Turkey and

Russia only partly share Europe's heritage and geography; in other parts, they definitely do not.' See also L. Lugo, 'Does "Muslim" Turkey Belong in "Christian" Europe?', Pew Forum on Religion and Public Life, National Press Club, Washington, 13 January 2005 (event transcript), noting: '[i]nterestingly, opposition to Turkish accession is coming from secular as well as religious quarters in Europe. Some nonreligious Europeans worry that bringing a large Muslim country into the EU could endanger the Continent's tradition of gender equality and tolerance of alternative lifestyles, for instance. For traditionalists, Turkish accession threatens the very idea of Europe as a Christian civilization.' Former President of France, Valéry Giscard d'Estaing is one such traditionalist, who, in November 2002, told French newspaper, *Le Monde*, that admitting Turkey to the EU would mean 'the end of Europe' and accused those who backed Turkey's membership as being 'adversaries of the European Union'. See 'Turkey Entry Would Destroy EU', BBC News World Edition, 8 November 2002 (available at: http://news.bbc.co.uk/2/hi/europe/2420697.stm) (last accessed, 2 February 2010). D'Estaing's reasoning is not without historical precedent however; in 1917, J. A. R. Marriott published *The Eastern Question: An Historical Study in European Diplomacy* (Oxford: Clarendon Press, 1917), in which he noted: 'The primary and most essential factor in the problem … is the presence, embedded in the living flesh of Europe, of an alien substance. That substance is the Ottoman Turk. Akin to the European family neither in creed, in race, in language, in social customs, nor in political aptitudes and traditions, the Ottomans have for more than five hundred years presented to the other European powers a problem, now tragic, now comic now bordering almost on burlesque, but always baffling and paradoxical' (cited in C. Morris, *The New Turkey: The Quiet Revolution on the Edge of Europe* (London: Granta Books, 2005), 11).

6 On the distinction between the public and private spheres in the context of religion, see Casanova, *Public Religions in the Modern World* (Chicago, IL: University of Chicago Press, 1994), ch. 2. He notes: '[o]f all dichotomous pairs of relational terms few are as ambiguous, multivocal, and open to discursive contestation as the private/ public distinction. Yet the private/public distinction is crucial to all conceptions of the modern social order and religion itself is intrinsically connected with the modern historical differentiation of private and public spheres. As inaccurate as it may be as an empirical statement, to say that "religion is a private affair" is nonetheless constitutive of Western modernity in a dual sense. First it points to the fact that religious freedom, in the sense of freedom of conscience, is chronologically "the first freedom" as well as the precondition of all modern freedoms. Insofar as freedom of conscience is intrinsically related to "the right to privacy" – to the modern institutionalization of a private sphere free from governmental intrusion as well as free from ecclesiastical control – and inasmuch as "the right to privacy" serves as the very foundation of modern liberalism and of modern individualism, then indeed the privatization of religion is essential to modernity' (*ibid.*, 40, references omitted).

7 P. J. Katzenstein, 'Multiple Modernities as Limits to Secular Europeanization', in Byrnes and Katzenstein, *Religion*, 1–34, 7. See also T. Inglis, 'Understanding Religion and Politics', in T. Inglis, Z. Mach and R. Mazanek *Religion and Politics: East–West Contrasts from Contemporary Europe* (Dublin: University College Dublin Press, 2000), 1–15, 1, noting that secularists see any relation between religion and politics in contemporary society as: 'a lingering residue of religious fundamentalism which, under the strain of Western rationality, will eventually fade and disappear'.

8 E. S. Hurd, 'Negotiating Europe: The Politics of Religion and the Prospects for Turkish Accession', *Review of International Studies*, 32 (2006), 401–18, 402 (reference omitted).

9 *Ibid.*

10 Katzenstein, 'Multiple Modernities', 2, noting; '[t]he core of secular Western Europe has preserved Christianity largely as glimmering embers that are no longer able to generate, on their own, much heat. European enlargement, however, is infusing renewed religious vitality into Europe's political and social life, thus chipping away at its exceptional secularism.'

11 For a detailed discussion of secularism in Turkey, see Chapter 1, Section 2.

12 J. O'Connell, 'The Making of Modern Europe: Strengths, Constraints and Resolutions', University of Bradford Research Report No. 26 (1991), cited in G. Davie, 'Is Europe an Exceptional Case?', *Hedgehog Review* (2006), 23–34, 24. Davie notes that these three factors 'shift and evolve over time, but their combinations can be seen in forming and reforming a way of life that we have come to recognize as European'.

13 See G. Davie, *Religion in Modern Europe: A Memory Mutates* (Oxford: Oxford University Press, 2005), 6.

14 O'Connell, 'Making of Modern Europe', cited in G. Davie, 'Is Europe an Exceptional Case?', 7.

15 Some European countries retain religious references in their Constitutions. The drafting of the *Bunreacht na hÉireann* (Constitution of Ireland) 1937, for example, was greatly influenced by Catholic teaching and in fact retained a reference to the 'special position of the Holy Catholic Apostolic and Roman Church as the guardian of the Faith professed by the great majority of the citizens', in Article 44(2) until this section was deleted from the Constitution by virtue of the Fifth Amendment of the Constitution Act, 1972. The Preamble to the Irish Constitution acknowledges 'all our obligations to our Divine Lord, Jesus Christ, Who sustained our fathers through centuries of trial'. Similarly the Constitution of Poland, adopted by the National Assembly on 2 April 1997, refers in its Preamble to a 'responsibility before God'.

16 Davie asserts that churches in Europe remain 'highly significant players at a different level of social reality. As voluntary organizations they are both influential and effective and compete successfully with comparable institutions in European society. They are, for example, considerably more successful in terms of recruitment than most political parties or industrial organizations (trade unions) and continue to hold their own ...' (*Religion*, 38).

17 R. McCrea, 'Limitations on Religion in a Liberal Democratic Polity: Christianity and Islam in the Public Order of the European Union', LSE, Society and Economy Working Papers (18/2007), 2.

18 D. Nexon, 'Religion, European Identity, and Political Contention in Historical Perspective', in Byrnes and Katzenstein, *Religion*, 256–82, 256.

19 J. O'Connell, 'The Making of Europe: The Foundations of Unity and the Elements of Belonging' (copy on file with author), 4.

20 *Ibid.*, 5. O'Connell suggests that the interlocking and overlapping blocs comprising European groups consist of groups from western Europe; central Europe; the Mediterranean world; the Nordic/Baltic countries; the Slav peoples: the British Isles; and the former Ottoman territories.

21 Davie, *Religion*, 13.

22 *Ibid.*

23 Cited in *ibid.*, 10.

24 Nexon, 'Religion', in Byrnes and Katzenstein, *Religion*, 256–82, 261. Nexon notes that the doctrines of Martin Luther involved a 'privatization of religion, and a strong separation of the profane from the sacred' (emphasis omitted).

25 O'Connell, 'Making of Europe', 3.

26 Nexon, 'Religion', in Byrnes and Katzenstein, *Religion*, 256–82, 256.

27 Davie, *Religion*, 26.

28 P. L Berger, 'The Desecularization of the World: A Global Overview', in P. L. Berger (ed.), *The Desecularization of the World: Resurgent Religion and World Politics* (Washington, DC: Ethics and Public Policy Center and Eerdmans Publishing Co., 1999) 1–19, 2.

29 Berger asserts that religious movements and institutions that have tried to conform to a perceived modernity are in decline almost everywhere. For example, in the United States, mainline Protestantism has declined while Evangelicalism has risen concomitantly, whereas the conservatism of John Paul II resulted in an increase in converts and a renewed enthusiasm among native Catholics. Equally, following the collapse of the Soviet Union, there was a revival of the Orthodox Church in Russia while the most rapidly growing Jewish groups in Israel and the Diaspora, are Orthodox. Also, '[t]here have been similarly vigorous upsurges of conservative religion in all the other major religious communities – Islam, Hinduism, Buddhism – as well as revival movements in smaller communities (such as Shinto in Japan and Sikhism in India)' (*ibid.*, 6).

30 Casanova defines 'deprivatization of religion' as meaning that 'religious traditions throughout the world are refusing to accept the marginal and privatized role which theories of modernity as well as theories of secularization had reserved for them' (*Public Religions*, 5).

31 *Ibid.*

32 B. Lewis, *What Went Wrong?: Western Impact and Middle Eastern Response* (London: Phoenix, 2002), 115.

33 *Ibid.*, 115–16.

34 Fokas asserts that Islam in Europe is in a state of flux, but so is religion in general 'and it is useful to recognise how these two dimensions affect one another: understanding, in other words, how European policies impact upon Muslim communities and individuals, but also how activities and discourse of Muslim individuals and groups influence changing conceptions and policy considerations on the place of religion in the European public sphere. Discussion of religion's proper place in the European public sphere have not found much of a formal discursive space within the EU thus far, but one may wonder how long these conversations will be delayed, given their increasing salience in so many EU member states' ('Introduction', in A. Al-Azmeh and E. Fokas (eds), *Islam in Europe: Diversity, Identity and Influence* (Cambridge: University Press Cambridge, 2007), 1–16, 3).

35 Casanova notes that the majority of sociologists of religion have abandoned the paradigm of increasing and unfettered secularization 'with the same uncritical haste with which they previously embraced it ... sociologists of religion now feel confident to predict bright futures for religion' (*Public Religions*, 11).

36 For a historical overview of the relations between Muslims and Christians in Europe, see T. Mitri, 'Christians and Muslims: Memory, Amity and Enmities', in Al-Azmeh and Fokas, *Islam*, 16–34.

37 Casanova, *Public Religions*, 75.

38 McCrea, 'Limitations', 2.

39 B. Massignon, 'Islam in the European Commission's System of Regulation of Religion', in Al-Azmeh Fokas, *Islam*, 125–48, 129. Massignon traces the 'symbolic birth' of relations between the EU and religious actors to a speech delivered by Jacques Delors to the representatives of the Evangelical Church of Germany (EKD) in 1992, in which he stated: '[i]f in the next ten years we haven't managed to give a Soul to Europe, to give it spirituality and meaning, the game will be up'. A Soul for Europe now operates on a permanent basis as a non-profit organization and is described as 'an initiative with the aim of giving a spiritual and ethical dimension to the European Union'. It is comprised of six members 'who are all communities of faith and conviction with a European structure' and include the Commission of the Bishops' Conferences of the European Community; the Church and Society Commission of the Conference of European Churches; the Orthodox Liaison Office; the Conference of European Rabbis; the European Humanist Federation; and the Muslim Council for Cooperation in Europe (see http://ec. europa.eu/dgs/policy_advisers/archives/activities/dialogue_religions_ humanisms/sfe_en.htm) (last accessed, 2 February 2010).

40 Massignon, 'Islam', in Al-Azmeh and Fokas, *Islam*, 129.

41 *Ibid.*

42 *Ibid.*, 130.

43 F. Dassetto and S. Ferrari, 'Islam in the EU: What's at Stake in the Future?', IP/B/CULT/ST/2006_061, 14 May 2007, 63.

44 K. Cavanaugh, 'Islam and the European Project', *Muslim World Journal of Human Rights*, 4(1) (2007), 1–20, 5.

45 Treaty of Lisbon amending the Treaty on European Union and the Treaty establishing the European Community, signed at Lisbon, 13 December 2007, Official Journal of the European Union, 17 December 2007, 2007/C 306/01, Article 1(1) (a).

46 Netherlands Scientific Council for Government Policy (WRR), *The European Union, Turkey and Islam* (Amsterdam: Amsterdam University Press, 2004), 27.

47 See J. Weiler, *Un'Europa Cristiana: Un Saggio Esplorativo* (Milan: BUR Saggi, 2003).

48 Article 6 of the Treaty on European Union states that the Union is: 'founded on the principles of liberty, democracy, respect for human rights and fundamental freedoms, and the rule of law, principles that are common to the Member States'.

49 Netherlands Scientific Council for Government Policy, *European Union*, 27. See also S. Cvijic and L. Zucca 'Does the European Constitution Need Christian Values?', *Oxford Journal of Legal Studies*, 24(4) (2004), 739–48, 743, suggesting that the framers of the Constitution 'did well not to concede to the inclusion of God or Christian values in the Preamble'.

50 Davie, 'Europe: The Exception that Proves the Rule?', in Berger, *Desecularization*, 65–85, 73.

51 BVerfG, 2BvR 1436/02 of 24 September 2003 (available at: www.bundesverfa ssungsgericht.de/en/decisions/re20030924_2bvr143602en.html) (last accessed, 2 February 2010).

52 [2006] UKHL 15.

53 For an overview of this case, see C. Langenfeld and S. Mohsen, 'Germany: The Teacher Head Scarf Case', Int'l Journal of Constitutional Law, 3(1) (2005), 86–94.

54 The concept of a State Church in Germany was rejected through the incorporation into the *Weimarer Reichsverfassung* (Weimar Reich Constitution) of 11 August

1919 of Article 137 (1), which states 'Es besteht keine Staatskirche' ('There is no State Church'). Article 137 is added as an appendix to the Basic Law (*Grundgesetz*). See C. R. Barker, 'Church and State Relationships in German "Public Benefit" Law', *International Journal of Not-for-Profit Law*, 3(2) (2000) (available at: www.icnl. org/KNOWLEDGE/ijnl/vol3iss2/art_1.htm) (last accessed, 2 February 2010).

55 BVerfG, 2BvR 1436/02 of 24 September 2003, para. 2. See C. Skach, 'Religious Freedom – State Neutrality – Public Order – Role of International Standards in Interpreting and Implementing Constitutionally Guaranteed Rights [decisions]', Am. J. Int'l L., 100 (2006), 186–96.

56 Decision of 4 July 2002 BverwGE 116, 359. See Langenfeld and Mohsen, 'Germany', 87.

57 The relevant Articles provide: Art. 1(1): 'Human dignity shall be inviolable. To respect and protect it shall be the duty of all state authority'; Art. 2(1): 'Every person shall have the right to free development of his personality insofar as he does not violate the rights of others or offend against the constitutional order or the moral law'; Art. 3(1): 'All persons shall be equal before the law'; Art. 3(3): 'No person shall be favoured or disfavoured because of sex, parentage, race, language, homeland and origin, faith, or religious or political opinions. No person shall be disfavoured because of disability'; Art. 4(1): 'Freedom of faith and of conscience, and freedom to profess a religious or philosophical creed, shall be inviolable'; Art. 4(2): 'The undisturbed practice of religion shall be guaranteed'; Art. 33(2): 'Every German shall be equally eligible for any public office according to his aptitude, qualifications, and professional achievements'; Art. 33(3); 'Neither the enjoyment of civil and political rights, nor eligibility for public office, nor rights acquired in the public service shall be dependent upon religious affiliation. No one may be disadvantaged by reason of adherence or non-adherence to a particular religious denomination or philosophical creed.'

58 See Skach, 'Religious Freedom', 189.

59 *Ibid.*

60 *Ibid.*

61 BVerfG, 2BvR 1436/02 of 24 September 2003.

62 O. Gerstenberg, 'Germany: Freedom of Conscience in Public Schools', Int'l Journal of Constitutional Law, 3(1) (2005), 94–106, 96.

63 *Ibid.*

64 *Dahlab v Switzerland*, application no. 42393/98, admissibility decision of 15 February 2001.

65 Amended law of 1 April 2004, GVBl. Baden-Württemberg 178 (2004). Cited in Langenfeld and Mohsen, 'Germany', 90.

66 *Ibid.* Langenfeld and Mohsen also note that other German states have followed suit and enacted similar legislation. For example, the amended school law of Niedersachsen was adopted on 29 April 2004 and contains a provision stipulating that a teacher's outward appearance should leave no doubt as to his or her fitness to convey the state's educational values. Administrative practice interprets, the authors note, the wearing of the headscarf as raising such doubts. Also, an amendment passed by the parliament of Saarland in June 2004 suggests that the lawmakers 'clearly consider the garment impermissible'. Another issue the Baden-Württemberg law raises is whether it should be left to local authorities to legislate on pertinent issues such as the manifestation of religion in the public sphere. While the ECtHR defers to domestic States' opinions on the regulation of religion,

it is questionable whether it is acceptable for contracting States to delegate to regional legislatures the power to regulate fundamental rights such as freedom of religion.

67 McCrea, 'Limitations', 2 (references omitted).

68 Gerstenberg, 'Germany', 106.

69 Described in the House of Lords' judgment as 'a long coat-like garment'. *R (on the application of Begum (by her litigation friend, Rahman)) v Headteacher and Governors of Denbigh High School* [2006] UKHL 15, para. 10.

70 Article 9 provides: '1. Everyone has the right to freedom of thought, conscience and religion; this right includes freedom to change his religion or belief, and freedom, either alone or in community with others and in public or private, to manifest his religion or belief, in worship, teaching, practice and observance. 2. Freedom to manifest one's religion or beliefs shall be subject only to such limitations as are prescribed by law and are necessary in a democratic society in the interests of public safety, for the protection of public order, health or morals, or the protection of the rights and freedoms of others.' Article 2 of Protocol No. 1 states: 'No person shall be denied the right to education. In the exercise of any functions which it assumes in relation to education and to teaching, the State shall respect the right of parents to ensure such education and teaching in conformity with their own religions and philosophical convictions.'

71 Described in the judgment as 'a combination of the kameeze, a sleeveless smock-like dress with a square neckline, revealing the wearer's collar and tie, with the shalwar, loose trousers, tapering at the ankles. A long-sleeved white shirt is worn beneath the kameeze and, save in hot weather, a uniform long-sleeved school jersey is worn on top' (*Begum*, above n. 69, para. 6).

72 *Ibid.*, para. 12.

73 *Ibid.*

74 The relevant provisions of the Schools Standards and Framework Act 1998 deal with the exclusion of pupils from school and the responsibilities of the school. Section 64 is entitled 'Power of head teacher to exclude pupils'; s. 65 'Exclusion of pupils: duty to inform parents etc.'; s. 66 'Functions of governing body in relation to excluded pupils'; s. 67 'Appeals against exclusion of pupils'; and s. 68: 'Exclusion of pupils: guidance' (Act available at: www.opsi.gov.uk/Acts/acts1998/ukpga_19980031_en_1) (last accessed, 2 February 2010). Section 52 of the Education Act 2002 also deals with 'Exclusion of pupils' (Act available at: www.opsi.gov.uk/ACTS/acts2002/ukpga_20020032_en_6#pt3–ch3–pb2–l1g52) (last accessed, 2 February 2010).

75 See M. M. Idriss '*R (Begum) v Headteacher and Governors of Denbigh High School*: A Case Note', Jud. Rev., 10 (2005), 296–302.

76 [2004] EWHC 1389 (Admin).

77 *Ibid.*, para. 90.

78 [2005] EWCA Civ 199, para. 78, per Brooke LJ.

79 Application no. 44774/98, judgment of 10 November 2005.

80 [2005] EWCA Civ 199, para. 73, per Brooke LJ.

81 *Ibid.*, para. 72.

82 *Begum*, above n. 69, para. 38. For an overview of the ruling, see M. M. Idriss, 'The Defeat of Shabina Begum in the House of Lords', *Liverpool Law Rev.*, 27 (2006), 417–36.

83 *Ibid.*, para. 25, per Lord Bingham.

84 *Ibid.*, para. 26.

85 Application no. 61/1996/680/870, judgment of 1 July 1997.

86 *Ibid.*, para. 27.

87 *Begum*, above n. 69, para. 7.

88 Idriss, '*R (Begum)*', 426. See also M. Ssenyonjo, 'The Islamic Veil and Freedom of Religion, the Rights to Education and Work: A Survey of Recent International and National Cases', Chinese J. Int'l L., 6(3) (2007), 653–710, 680, noting that: '[d]eferring to the school authorities granted to the school an almost unlimited "margin of discretion" thereby enabling the court to avoid the "difficult" jilbab question and its failure to recognize the rights of the most marginalized individuals within minority groups – in this case being the rights of a female Muslim pupil wearing a jilbab at school.'

89 See [2005] EWCA Civ 199, para. 48, per Brooke LJ, noting '[O]ne can see clearly the two main schools of thought (I exclude, for instance, those who rely on the interpretation of other ancient texts for their belief that a woman's face should also be covered). The first, which represents mainstream opinion among South Asian Muslims, from whom most of this country's Muslim population are descended, is that a garment like the shalwar kameeze (coupled with a headscarf) complies sufficiently with Islamic dress requirements, and that there is no need to go any further. The other, which is a minority view among Muslims in this country, but is nevertheless sincerely held, is that the shalwar kameeze, even when it goes down to mid-calf, is not compliant, and that a garment like the jilbab, which disguises the shape of the wearer's arms and legs, is required.'

90 J. R. Bowen, *Why the French Don't Like Headscarves: Islam, the State, and Public Space* (Princeton and Oxford: Princeton University Press, 2006), 243.

91 For the text of Article 9, see above, n. 70.

92 M. W. Janis, R. S. Kay and A. W. Bradley, *European Human Rights Law: Text and Materials* (Oxford: Oxford University Press, 3rd edn, 2008), 323. The case concerned was *Kokkinakis v Greece*, judgment of 23 May 1993, 17 EHRR 397. For a comprehensive overview of freedom of religion under the ECHR, see C. Evans, *Freedom of Religion Under the European Convention on Human Rights* (Oxford: Oxford University Press, 2001).

93 *Kokkinakis v Greece*, judgment of 23 May 1993, 17 EHRR 397, para. 31.

94 See, for example, Evans, *Freedom*; J. Martínez-Torrón, 'Limitations on Religious Freedom in the Case Law of the European Convention on Human Rights', Emory Int'l L. Rev., 19 (2005), 587–636; C. Ovey and R. C. A. White, *The European Convention on Human Rights* (Oxford: Oxford University Press, 4th edn, 2006), 300–17; Cavanaugh, 'Islam', 11–17; Janis *et al.*, *European Human Rights*, 323–73.

95 Ovey and White assert that while most commentators would agree with the Court's view that governments should work to promote pluralism and tolerance in situations of religious tension and therefore be allowed a wide margin of appreciation to place restrictions on the freedom to manifest religion of belief, 'it is the more mundane cases – the teacher who wishes to wear the Islamic headscarf to school, the children whose Jehovah's Witness parents do not wish them to attend a militaristic parade – that the Court has demonstrated a certain lack of empathy for the believer, and has appeared only to pay lip-service to the commitment to religious freedom proclaimed in such judgments as *Kokkinakis v Greece*' (*European Convention*, 316).

96 S. Genel and K. Karaosmanoğlu, 'A New Islamic Individualism in Turkey: Headscarved Women in the City', *Turkish Studies*, 7 (2006), 473–88, 473.

97 *Ibid.* For an interesting account of the changing contexts of veiling in Turkey, see A. Saktanber and G Çorbacioğlu, 'Veiling and Headscarf – Skepticism in Turkey', *Social Politics: International Studies in Gender, State and Society*, 15(4) (2008), 514–38.

98 Application no. 44774/98, judgment of 10 November 2005.

99 For an overview of these cases, see Cavanaugh, 'Islam', 11–17.

100 *Kokkinakis v Greece*, application no. 14307/88, judgment of 23 May 1993.

101 *Metropolitan Church of Bessarabia v Moldova*, application no. 45701/99, judgment of 13 December 2001; *Serif v Greece*, application no. 38178/97, judgment of 14 December 1999; *Agga v Greece*, application no. 38178/97, judgment of 14 December 1999; *Supreme Holy Council of the Muslim Community v Bulgaria*, application no. 39023/97, judgment of 16 December 2004; and *Hasan and Chaush v Bulgaria*, application no. 30985/96, judgment of 26 October 2000.

102 *Karaduman v Turkey*, application no. 16278/90, admissibility decision of 3 May 1993; *Dahlab*, above n. 64 ; and *Leyla Şahin v Turkey*, application no. 44774/98, judgment of 10 November 2005.

103 C. D. Belelieu, 'The Headscarf as a Symbolic Enemy of the European Court of Human Rights', 'Democratic Jurisprudence: Viewing Islam through a European Legal Prism in Light of the *Şahin* Judgment', Colum. J. Eur. L., 12 (2005–6), 573–623, 623. See also A. Vakulenko, 'Islamic Dress in Human Rights Jurisprudence: A Critique of Current Trends', *Human Rights Law Review*, 7(4) (2007), 717–39.

104 Loi no. 2004–228 du 15 mars 2004 encadrant, en application du principe de laïcité, le port de signes ou de tenues manifestant une appartenance religieuse dans les écoles, collèges et lycées publics (Law No. 2004–228 of 15 March 2004 concerning, as an application of the principle of the separation of church and state, the wearing of symbols or garb which show religious affiliation in public primary and secondary schools.) For an interesting account of the reasoning behind the introduction of the law and its repercussions, see Bowen, *Why the French*.

105 See *Begum*, above n. 69.

106 Application no. 16278/90, admissibility decision of 3 May 1993.

107 *Karaduman v Turkey*, application no. 16278/90, admissibility decision of 3 May 1993, 104. Article 14 states: 'The enjoyment of the rights and freedoms of set forth in this convention shall be secured without discrimination on any ground such as sex, race, colour, language, religion, political or other opinion, national or social origin, association with a national minority, property, birth or other status.'

108 *Karaduman*, above n. 107, 108.

109 *Ibid.*

110 *Ibid.*, 109.

111 *Ibid.*

112 *Ibid.*

113 A. Vakulenko, '"Islamic Headscarves" and the European Convention on Human Rights: An Intersectional Perspective', *Social and Legal Studies*, 16(2) (2007), 183–99, 187.

114 Application no. 42393/98, admissibility decision of 15 February 2001.

115 *Dahlab*, above n. 64, 2. Section 6 of the Public Education Act of 6 November 1940 stated: 'The public education system shall ensure that the political and religious beliefs of pupils and parents are respected.'
116 *Dahlab*, above n. 64.
117 *Ibid.*
118 *Ibid.*, 7.
119 *Ibid.*, 8.
120 Vakulenko, '"Islamic Headscarves"', 188.
121 *Dahlab*, above n. 64, 9.
122 *Ibid.*
123 *Ibid.*
124 *Ibid.*
125 *Ibid.*
126 *Ibid.* (emphasis added).
127 *Ibid.*, 10.
128 *Ibid.*
129 *Ibid.*
130 *Ibid.*
131 *Ibid.*
132 *Ibid.*
133 *Ibid.*, 11.
134 *Ibid.*, 4.
135 *Ibid.*, 14.
136 *Ibid.*, 13
137 Application no. 14307/88, judgment of 23 May 1993. In *Kokkinakis*, the Court defined improper proselytism as including 'the form of activities offering material or social advantages with a view to gaining new members for a Church or exerting improper pressure on people in distress or in need; it may even entail the use of violence or brainwashing; more generally, it is not compatible with respect for the freedom of thought, conscience and religion of others' (para. 48). There was certainly no allegation that *Dahlab* and ever engaged or intended to engage in such activity nor that it would be possible to do so through simply wearing a headscarf and so the comments of the Court in this regard appear wholly arbitrary.
138 Vakulenko, '"Islamic Headscarves"', 189.
139 *Leyla Şahin v Turkey*, application no. 44774/98, judgment of 10 November 2005, para. 16.
140 *Ibid.*, para. 18.
141 *Ibid.*, para. 20.
142 *Ibid.*, para. 24. The Students Disciplinary Procedure Rules, published in the Official Gazette of 13 January 1985, prescribe five forms of disciplinary penalty: a warning, a reprimand, temporary suspension of between a week and a month, temporary suspension of one or two semesters and expulsion. Paragraph 9(j) provides that students who organize or take part in unauthorized meetings on university premises are liable to one or two semesters' suspension.
143 *Leyla Şahin*, above n. 139, para. 25.
144 *Ibid.*, paras 26–28.
145 *Ibid.*, para. 78.
146 *Ibid.*, paras 79–80.

147 *Ibid.*, para. 82.

148 Article 13 of the Constitution of Turkey states: 'Fundamental rights and freedoms may be restricted only by law and on the grounds set out in special provisions of the Constitution, provided always that the essence of such rights and freedoms must remain intact. Any such restriction shall not conflict with the letter or spirit of the Constitution or the requirements of a democratic, secular social order and shall comply with the principle of proportionality.'

149 *Leyla Şahin*, above n. 139, paras 84–98.

150 *Ibid.*, para. 99.

151 *Ibid.*, para. 100.

152 *Ibid.*, paras 106, 109.

153 *Ibid.*, para. 110.

154 *Ibid.*, para. 111.

155 Application no. 74/1995/580/666, judgment of 18 December 1996.

156 *Leyla Şahin*, above n. 139, para. 121.

157 *Ibid.*, paras 121, 122.

158 Article 2 of Protocol No. 1 to the Convention provides: 'No person shall be denied the right to education. In the exercise of any functions which it assumes in relation to education and to teaching, the State shall respect the right of parents to ensure such education and teaching in conformity with their own religions and philosophical convictions.' Article 8 provides:

> 1. Everyone has the right to respect for his private and family life, his home and his correspondence. 2. There shall be no interference by a public authority with the exercise of this right except such as is in accordance with the law and is necessary in a democratic society in the interests of national security, public safety or the economic well-being of the country, for the prevention of disorder or crime, for the protection of health or morals, or for the protection of the rights and freedoms of others.

Article 10 provides:

> 1. Everyone has the right to freedom of expression. this right shall include freedom to hold opinions and to receive and impart information and ideas without interference by public authority and regardless of frontiers. This article shall not prevent States from requiring the licensing of broadcasting, television or cinema enterprises. 2. The exercise of these freedoms, since it carries with it duties and responsibilities, may be subject to such formalities, conditions, restrictions or penalties as are prescribed by law and are necessary in a democratic society, in the interests of national security, territorial integrity or public safety, for the prevention of disorder or crime, for the protection of health or morals, for the protection of the reputation or the rights of others, for preventing the disclosure of information received in confidence, or for maintaining the authority and impartiality of the judiciary.

159 *Leyla Şahin*, above n. 139, paras 134–41.

160 *Ibid.*, para. 143.

161 *Ibid.*, para. 144.

162 *Ibid.*, para. 145.

163 *Ibid.*, para. 146.

164 *Ibid.*, paras 147–8.

165 *Ibid.*, para. 150.
166 *Ibid.*, para. 151.
167 *Ibid.*, para. 154.
168 *Ibid.*, para. 157.
169 *Ibid.*, paras 157–8.
170 *Ibid.*, para. 159.
171 *Ibid.*, para. 160.
172 *Ibid.*, paras 161–2.
173 *Ibid.*, para. 163.
174 *Ibid.*, para. 165.
175 *Ibid.*, paras 165–6.
176 *Ibid.*, para. 113.
177 B. D. Bleiberg, 'Unveiling the Real Issue: Evaluating the European Court of Human Rights' Decision to Enforce the Turkish Headscarf Ban in *Leyla Şahin v Turkey*', Cornell L. Rev., 91 (2005–6), 129–70, 152 (references omitted).
178 *Leyla Şahin*, above n. 139, dissenting opinion of Judge Tulkens, para. 8.
179 Application no. 35071/97, judgment of 4 December 2003.
180 *Leyla Şahin*, above n. 139, dissenting opinion of Judge Tulkens, para. 9.
181 *Ibid.*, para. 116.
182 *Ibid.*, dissenting opinion of Judge Tulkens, para. 11.
183 *Ibid.*, para. 19.
184 *Ibid.*, para. 20.
185 Communication No. 931/2000, UN Doc. CCPR/C/82/D/931/2000 (2004).
186 ICCPR, GA res. 2200A (XXI), 21 UN GAOR Supp. (No. 16) at 52, UN Doc. A/6316 (1966), 999 UNTS 171, entered into force 23 Mar. 1976. Article 18 provides:

> 1. Everyone shall have the right to freedom of thought, conscience and religion. This right shall include freedom to have or to adopt a religion or belief of his choice, and freedom, either individually or in community with others and in public or private, to manifest his religion or belief in worship, observance, practice and teaching. 2. No one shall be subject to coercion which would impair his freedom to have or to adopt a religion or belief of his choice. 3. Freedom to manifest one's religion or beliefs may be subject only to such limitations as are prescribed by law and are necessary to protect public safety, order, health, or morals or the fundamental rights and freedoms of others. 4. The States Parties to the present Covenant undertake to have respect for the liberty of parents and, when applicable, legal guardians to ensure the religious and moral education of their children in conformity with their own convictions.

Article 19 of the Covenant states:

> 1. Everyone shall have the right to hold opinions without interference. 2. Everyone shall have the right to freedom of expression; this right shall include freedom to seek, receive and impart information and ideas of all kinds, regardless of frontiers, either orally, in writing or in print, in the form of art, or through any other media of his choice. 3. The exercise of the rights provided for in paragraph 2 of this article carries with it special duties and responsibilities. It may therefore be subject to certain restrictions, but these shall only be such as are provided by law

and are necessary: (a) For respect of the rights or reputations of others; (b) For the protection of national security or of public order (ordre public), or of public health or morals.

187 Communication No. 931/2000, above n. 185, para. 2.1.
188 *Ibid.*
189 *Ibid.*, para. 2.2.
190 *Ibid.*, para. 2.3.
191 *Ibid.*, para. 2.4.
192 *Ibid.*, para. 2.6. According to Article 14 of the legislation, entitled 'On the Liberty of Conscience and Religious Organisations', Uzbek nationals cannot wear religious dress in public places.
193 *Raihon Hudoyberganova v Uzbekistan*, Communication No. 931/2000, above n. 185, paras 4.2, 4.3.
194 *Ibid.*, para. 6.2.
195 General Comment No. 22: The right to freedom of thought, conscience and religion (Art. 18), CCPR/C/21/Rev.1/Add.4, General Comment No. 22, 30 July 1993, para. 5. The Committee also noted in this Comment that '[t]he observance and practice of religion or belief may include not only ceremonial acts but also such customs as the observance of dietary regulations, the wearing of distinctive clothing or headcoverings, participation in rituals associated with certain stages of life, and the use of a particular language customarily spoken by a group'.
196 *Raihon Hudoyberganova v Uzbekistan*, Communication No. 931/2000, above n. 185, para. 6.2.
197 *Ibid.*
198 See 'Interview with Professor Kevin Boyle', in *'Leyla Şahin v Turkey'* (at: www. zaman.com), cited in D. McGoldrick, *Human Rights and Religion: The Islamic Headscarf Debate in Europe* (Oxford: Hart Publishing, 2006), 169. But cf. McGoldrick's assertion that the non-resort to the margin of appreciation by the HRC may be 'no more than a matter of semantics' and also that notwithstanding the decision of the HRC in *Hudoyberganova*, 'it is unlikely that the HRC's interpretation of the ICCPR would give significantly different answers to the headscarf-*hijab* issue in Turkey to those the European Convention institutions have given, and in particular, to the 22 judges of the Court who found no violation'. It is currently not possible to make a complaint against Turkey to the HRC, as Turkey has not ratified the individual complaint procedure under the First Optional Protocol to the Covenant.
199 Application no. 71907/01, judgment of 5 April 2007 (judgment only available in French; translations provided in this section are that of the author and are unofficial).
200 *Kavakçi v Turkey*, application no. 71907/01, judgment of 5 April 2007, para. 11. The *Refah* case is discussed in Section 3.2 of this chapter.
201 *Ibid.*, paras 11–12.
202 *Ibid.*, paras 13–16. Article 25(a) states that the Council of Ministers may revoke the citizenship of anyone who acquires the citizenship of a foreign state intentionally without permission.
203 Article 6 states:

1. In the determination of his civil rights and obligations or of any criminal charge against him, everyone is entitled to a fair and public hearing within a

reasonable time by an independent and impartial tribunal established by law. Judgement shall be pronounced publicly by the press and public may be excluded from all or part of the trial in the interest of morals, public order or national security in a democratic society, where the interests of juveniles or the protection of the private life of the parties so require, or the extent strictly necessary in the opinion of the court in special circumstances where publicity would prejudice the interests of justice. 2. Everyone charged with a criminal offence shall be presumed innocent until proved guilty according to law. 3. Everyone charged with a criminal offence has the following minimum rights: (a) to be informed promptly, in a language which he understands and in detail, of the nature and cause of the accusation against him; (b) to have adequate time and the facilities for the preparation of his defence; (c) to defend himself in person or through legal assistance of his own choosing or, if he has not sufficient means to pay for legal assistance, to be given it free when the interests of justice so require; (d) to examine or have examined witnesses against him and to obtain the attendance and examination of witnesses on his behalf under the same conditions as witnesses against him; (e) to have the free assistance of an interpreter if he cannot understand or speak the language used in court.

Article 3 of Protocol No. 1 states: 'The High Contracting Parties undertake to hold free elections at reasonable intervals by secret ballot, under conditions which will ensure the free expression of the opinion of the people in the choice of the legislature.' For the text of Articles 9 and 14 see above nn. 70 and 98 respectively.

204 *Kavakçi*, above n. 200, para. 29.
205 *Ibid.* Article 84 of the Constitution of Turkey, entitled 'Loss of Membership' (as amended on 23 July 1995) states:

The loss of membership of a deputy who has resigned shall be decided upon by the plenary of the Turkish Grand National Assembly after the Bureau of the Turkish Grand National Assembly attests to the validity of the resignation. The loss of membership, through a final judicial sentence or deprivation of legal capacity, shall take effect after the final court decision in the matter has been communicated to the plenary of the Turkish Grand National Assembly. The loss of membership of a deputy who insists on holding a position or continues an activity incompatible with membership according to Article 82, shall be decided by a secret plenary vote, upon the submission of a report drawn up by the authorized commission setting out the factual situation. Loss of membership by a deputy who fails to attend without excuse or permission, five meetings in a period of one month shall be decided by an absolute majority of the total number of members after the Bureau of the Turkish Grand National Assembly determines the situation. The membership of a deputy whose statements and acts are cited in a final judgment by the Constitutional Court as having caused the permanent dissolution of his party shall terminate on the date when the decision in question and its justifications are published in the Official Gazette. The speaker of the Turkish Grand National Assembly shall immediately take the necessary action concerning such decision and shall inform the plenary of the Turkish Grand National Assembly accordingly.

206 *Kavakçi*, above n. 200, para. 31. Article 69 of the Constitution of Turkey, entitled 'Principles to be Observed by Political Parties' (as amended on 17 October 2001) states:

> The activities, internal regulations and operation of political parties shall be in line with democratic principles. The application of these principles is regulated by law. Political parties shall not engage in commercial activities. The income and expenditure of political parties shall be consistent with their objectives. The application of this rule is regulated by law. The auditing of the income, expenditure and acquisitions of political parties as well as the establishment of the conformity to law of their revenue and expenses, methods of auditing and sanctions to be applied in the event of unconformity shall also be regulated by law. The Constitutional Court shall be assisted in performing its task of auditing by the Court of Accounts. The judgments rendered by the Constitutional Court as a result of the auditing shall be final. The dissolution of political parties shall be decided finally by the Constitutional Court after the filing of a suit by the office of the Chief Public Prosecutor of the Republic. The permanent dissolution of a political party shall be decided when it is established that the statute and programme of the political party violate the provisions of the fourth paragraph of Article 68. A political party shall be deemed to become the centre of such actions only when such actions are carried out intensively by the members of that party or the situation is shared implicitly or explicitly by the grand congress, general chairmanship or the central decision-making or administrative organs of that party or by the group's general meeting or group executive board at the Turkish Grand National Assembly or when these activities are carried out in determination by the above-mentioned party organs directly. Instead of dissolving them permanently in accordance with the above-mentioned paragraphs, the Constitutional Court may rule the concerned party to be deprived of State aid wholly or in part with respect to intensity of the actions brought before the court. The foundation and activities of political parties, their supervision and dissolution, or their deprival of State aid wholly or in part as well as the election expenditures and procedures of the political parties and candidates, are regulated by law in accordance with the above-mentioned principles.

207 *Kavakçi*, above n. 200, para. 32.
208 *Ibid.*, paras 33, 35.
209 *Ibid.*, para. 36.
210 *Ibid.*, para. 40.
211 *Ibid.*, para. 41.
212 *Ibid.*
213 *Ibid.*, para. 43. The original French text states: 'La Cour note que les limitations temporaires apportées aux droits politiques de la requérante avait pour finalité de préserver le caractère laïc du régime politique turc. Vu l'importance de ce principe pour le régime démocratique en Turquie, elle estime que la mesure litigieuse visait les buts légitimes de défense de l'ordre et de protection des droits et libertés d'autrui.'
214 *Ibid.*, paras 45–47.
215 *Kavakçi*, above n. 200, para. 43.
216 A majority of the Constitutional Court voted in favour of closing the party but the court was one vote short of the required consensus necessary to order the closure.

Eleven judges voted by 6:5 for closure but the rules of the court stipulate that at least seven votes in favour are needed for a dissolution ruling. The court did, however, vote to strip the AKP of state funding. See R. Tait, 'Turkey's Governing Party Avoids Being Shut Down for Anti-Secularism', *Guardian*, 31 July 2008.

217 See E. Yuksel, 'Cannibal Democracies, Theocratic Secularism: The Turkish Version', Cardozo J. Int'l & Comp. L., 7 (1999), 423–67, 423. See also D. Koğacioğlu, 'Progress, Unity, and Democracy: Dissolving Political Parties in Turkey', *Law and Society Review*, 38(3) (2004), 433–62.

218 Application no. 41340/98 and 41342–4/98, judgment of 13 February 2003. The case was taken by four applicants; Refah Partisi, Necmettin Erbakan, the chairman of Refah Partisi, Şevket Kazan, a vice-chairman of Refah and Ahmet Tekdal, also a vice-chairman of Refah.

219 *Refah Partisi and Others v Turkey*, application no. 41340/98 and 41342–4/98, judgment of 13 February 2003, para. 10.

220 *Ibid.*, para. 11

221 S. Dokupil, 'The Separation of Mosque and State: Islam and Democracy in Modern Turkey', W. Va. L. Rev., 105 (2002–3), 53–129, 105.

222 *Refah Partisi*, above n. 219, para. 12.

223 *Ibid.*

224 *Ibid.*

225 *Ibid.*, paras 14, 17.

226 The Turkish government alleged that members of Refah had made speeches calling for the replacement of the secular system with a theocratic one and had stated that 'blood would flow' if any attempt was made to close the 'İmam-Hatip' theological colleges. *Refah Partisi*, above n. 219, para. 12.

227 *Ibid.*, para. 18.

228 *Ibid.*, para. 23. Section 101(b) of Law No. 2820 stated:

The Constitutional Court shall dissolve a political party... (b) where its general meeting, central office or executive committee ... takes a decision, issues a circular or makes a statement ... contrary to the provisions of Chapter 4 of this Law [This ch. (from ss. 78–97), which concerns restrictions on the activities of political parties, provides, *inter alia*, that such activities may not be conducted to the detriment of the democratic constitutional order (including the sovereignty of the people and free elections), the nature of the nation State (including national independence, national unity and the principle of equality), and the secular nature of the State (including observance of the reforms carried out by Atatürk, the prohibition on exploiting religious feelings and the prohibition on religious demonstrations organised by political parties), or where the chairman, vice-chairman or general secretary makes any written or oral statement contrary to those provisions.'] Section 103(1) of the Law stated 'Where it is found that a political party has become a centre of activities contrary to the provisions of sections 77 to 78 ... of the present Law, the party shall be dissolved by the Constitutional Court'.

229 *Refah Partisi*, above n. 219, para. 49. Article 11 of the Convention provides:

1. Everyone has the right to freedom of peaceful assembly and to freedom of association with others, including the right to form and to join trade unions for the protection of his interests. 2. No restrictions shall be placed on the exercise of

these rights other than such as are prescribed by law and are necessary in a democratic society in the interests of national security or public safety, for the prevention of disorder or crime, for the protection of health or morals or for the protection of the rights and freedoms of others. This article shall not prevent the imposition of lawful restrictions on the exercise of these rights by members of the armed forces, of the police or of the administration of the State.

230 *United Communist Party of Turkey and Others v Turkey*, application no. 133/1996/752/951, judgment of 30 January 1998, para. 27.
231 *Ibid.*, para. 46.
232 See *Yazar and Others v Turkey*, application nos. 22723/93, 22724/93 and 22725/93, judgment of 9 April 2002; *Socialist Party and Others v Turkey*, application no. 20/1997/804/1007, judgment of 25 May 1998; *Freedom and Democracy Party (Özdep) v Turkey*, application no. 133/1996/752/951, judgment of 8 December 1999; *United Communist Party of Turkey*, above n. 230.
233 *Refah Partisi*, above n. 219, para. 50.
234 *Ibid.*, para. 51.
235 *Ibid.*, para. 56, 59.
236 *Ibid.*, paras 62, 63.
237 *Ibid.*, para. 65.
238 *Ibid.*, para. 66.
239 D. Schilling, 'European Islamaphobia and Turkey – *Refah Partisi (the Welfare Party) v Turkey*', Loy. L.A. Int'l & Comp. L. Rev., 26 (2003–4), 501–15, 510.
240 *Refah Partisi*, above n. 219, para. 67. The aims included protection of national security and public safety, prevention of disorder or crime and protection of the rights and freedoms of others.
241 *Ibid.*, para. 68.
242 *Ibid.*, para. 69.
243 *Ibid.*, para. 71.
244 *Ibid.*, paras 71, 73.
245 *Ibid.*, para. 77.
246 *Ibid.*, para. 78
247 *Ibid.*, paras 81, 83.
248 *Ibid.*, para. 84.
249 On this point, see K. Boyle, 'Human Rights, Religion and Democracy: The *Refah Party* Case', *Essex Human Rights Review*, 1(1) (2004), 1–16, 2, noting the particular seriousness of sanctioning the closure of a party serving in government: 'By any standard, the dislodging of a government from office is a radical intervention in democratic political life by a national court. It took the notion of "militant democracy", the measures permissible to defend democracy from being subverted through electoral politics, to a new level' (references omitted).
250 Schilling, 'European Islamaphobia', 511.
251 *Refah Partisi*, above n. 219, para. 86.
252 *United Communist Party of Turkey and others*, above n. 230, para. 45.
253 *Refah Partisi*, above n. 219, para. 90.
254 *Ibid.*, para. 93.
255 *Ibid.*, para. 103.
256 *Ibid.*, paras 132, 135.
257 Koğacioğlu, 'Progress', 454.

258 *Ibid.*, 455.

259 Schilling, 'European Islamaphobia', 511–12.

260 *Ibid.*, 513.

261 *Refah Partisi*, above n. 219, para. 123. Boyle notes that the 'stridency of the European Court's assessment of Islamic law and shariah is regrettable. In effect the Court seems to say that shariah, *tout court*, is incompatible with universal rights, or at least European ideas of democracy and rights ... the judgment represents an unsympathetic dismissal of what is a central element of a 1400-year-old civilization, comprising today the cultures of in excess of a billion people, and the religion of at least 100 million Muslims in the Council of Europe countries. The Court makes no effort, in its thinking or language, to separate the vast majority of Muslim people and their religious practices from extremists' ('Human Rights', 12).

262 Boyle, 'Human Rights', 13.

263 *Ibid.*, 4.

264 *Ibid.*, 12.

265 Casanova, 'Religion', 78.

266 *Ibid.*

267 The 2008 report of the European Commission on Turkey's Progress Towards Accession concluded: 'A legal framework in line with the ECHR has yet to be established, so that all non-Muslim religious communities and Alevis can function without undue constraints. Turkey needs to make further efforts to create an environment conducive to full respect for freedom of religion in practice and to carry out consistent initiatives aimed at improving dialogue with the various religious communities' (Turkey 2008 Progress Report, SEC(2008) 2699 final, Brussels, 5 November 2008, 19).

268 European Parliament Resolution on Turkey's Application for Membership of the European Union (COM(2002) 700–C5–0104/2003– 2000/2014(COS), 5 June 2003, para. 10.

269 Casanova, 'Long, Difficult, and Tortuous', 245.

Conclusion

This study set out to examine the aspects of Turkey's accession to the European Union that have been cited as problematic. A key aspect of this examination was to determine, through the lens of assessing the stated obstacles to membership, whether there are unstated obstacles hampering Turkey's accession prospects that are not acknowledged in the public debates. The chapters in this study have therefore provided the backdrop to Turkish membership and assessed the stated and potentially unstated obstacles to the achievement of EU accession.

The evidence points to a lack of engagement in official discourse with what is an important obstacle in Turkey's membership bid. This obstacle takes the form of a religious requirement, which although an unspoken obligation, plays a large part in the unease surrounding Turkey's potential accession. Through critically analysing the principal stated obstacles to membership[1] – human rights concerns, the Kurdish conflict and the failure to resolve the Cyprus issue – this study suggests that Turkey's candidacy, although affected by these issues, also raises fundamental questions regarding the limits of religious and legal pluralism in Europe. In this chapter, several aspects of Turkey's accession process that has emerged from this study are highlighted. Some of the factors that have blocked Turkish membership in the EU will be briefly reviewed before situating one of the 'veiled' factors in the larger context of tensions that arise when religion endeavours to encroach into the public space in Europe.

1 Turkey's path to membership and the broader question of Islam in Europe

The historical trajectory of Turkey–EU relations suggested that achieving accession would not be an easy task. The length with which Turkey has been engaged with the EU and its previous incarnations spans some five decades and has been characterized by a reluctance on the part of some EU actors to endorse Turkey's accession aspirations in spite of the determined efforts of successive Turkish administrations to this end.

1.1 *Factors preventing membership*

While this study acknowledged from the outset that there are legitimate concerns regarding Turkey's membership of the EU, such as human rights concerns and the Cyprus stalemate (but also the position occupied by the military in public life and the economic and fiscal state of Turkey), it is contended that there is an additional factor to Turkey's membership which is inextricably linked to the question of religion and whether Turkey as an EU member would conflict with a supposed European 'identity', examined in the introduction. Baykal makes an interesting point in this regard, suggesting that we would do well, if discussions about 'identity' must continue, to distinguish between European identity and that of the EU:

> 'Europe' might be a cultural, geographical, historical, ethnic or even religious concept depending on various perceptions. Some of its values, such as democracy, rule of law and human rights are universal, whereas some, such as individualism, Enlightenment, secularism, and maybe to a certain extent, Christianity, are mainly Western. 'European Union', on the other hand, is a specific regional project, a process of coming together and sharing sovereignty by like minded states and their peoples in order to attain the common good which is depicted in the founding treaties and their amendments, including the Constitutional Treaty, in a minimalist fashion. That common good is identified and substantiated by the shared objectives and projects that are laid down in the founding legal documents of the integration process.[2]

This work addressed three of the main issues frequently cited as reasons why Turkey is not yet 'ready' for EU membership. Two of these factors, human rights concerns and the Kurdish conflict, are inextricably linked due to the fact that many of the human rights abuses complained of in Turkey emerged through the state authorities' response to the conflict. But this is hardly unusual in the broader European context where countries have dealt with conflict either internally or on its borders; human rights abuses perpetrated by the UK in its containment of the conflict in Northern Ireland as well as by Russia during the more recent conflict in Chechnya are well documented.[3] What is notable, however, is the 'element of schizophrenia that afflicts the Union between its internal and external policies'[4] which subjects Turkey, as an applicant state, to a more critical assessment of its human rights performance than states that are already members. Williams observes in this regard that:

> the notion that states may be subjected to a different regime of scrutiny and intervention on the cusp of entry to the Union from that which applies when full membership is achieved, is both dangerous and potentially divisive. At heart, the distinction suggests a 'bifurcation' of human rights which infers a sub-text of discrimination and exclusion.[5]

It is unsurprising, therefore, that public opinion in Turkey now reflects the belief that the reasons for keeping Turkey out of the Union have more to do with cultural differences than Turkey's human rights track record, resulting in a decline in support for membership.[6] The effectiveness of the carrot–stick approach adopted by the EU towards Turkish accession can now also be called into question, as it is unlikely that concessions will continue to be made domestically unless they are seen to result in tangible progress on the path to membership.[7] In fact the carrot-stick approach adopted by the EU in relation to Turkey may have counter-intuitively resulted not just in a slowdown in reform but in a rollback in the human rights improvements achieved earlier in the accession process. It is clear that the carrot–stick approach can only work if there is a genuine advancement towards membership. Without this, the policy may in fact be (unintentionally) detrimental to Turkey's human rights reforms.

The policy adopted by the EU in pursuit of a resolution to the conflict in Cyprus is yet another area of contention in Turkey's road to accession. As highlighted earlier in this study, the burden of moving the conflict towards a resolution has been placed almost exclusively on Turkey. This policy rests uneasily with many in Turkey, who feel that they have been unfairly treated over the Cyprus issue:

> The EU's treatment of Turkey during the Cyprus stalemate has hit a raw nerve. Its stipulation that Turkey must budge on Cyprus is viewed as an unfair demand for one-sided concessions. From a Turkish perspective it is unreasonable to insist that the Turks should have to bend over backwards to please the EU when the solution to any political dispute requires at minimum a two-sided effort as well as compromise on the part of all the parties. It is further argued that the Turkish government already made concessions on Cyprus, having backed the Annan Plan to reunite the divided island in the April 2004 referendum, and that it is not Turkey's fault that the Greek Cypriot community rejected the plan. EU bullying to either recognize Cyprus or forget EU membership has proven to be highly counterproductive and has countenanced a perception among Turks that the Cyprus issue is a zero-sum game with the deck unfairly stacked and in which there can be only one winner.[8]

Thus the stated obstacles to membership involve primarily human rights concerns and the impasse relating to the Cyprus conflict. Less clear, however, is whether membership also hinges on factors less to do with Turkey's performance on these issues and more related to Europe's own tensions regarding pluralism and democracy.

2.2 Pluralism and the public space

The nature of the relationship between religion and state in Turkey has always been that of a tense coexistence. Atatürk's rigidly enforced programme of strict secularization since the beginning of the twentieth century left little room for expression of religious sentiment in the public sphere. While some indications of a change in the relationship between religion and state in the mid-1980s may have been evident[9], not even the election of the Islamic AKP in two general elections has prompted a relaxation in the policies of enforced secularism, which continues to be strictly guarded by Turkey's military.[10] Similarly, Europe has been grappling with issues related to religion in the public sphere, which have been brought to the forefront by both the accession of more openly religious Eastern European countries to the EU and also the immigration to Europe of 'other faith' religions, most notably Muslims.

The presence of Islam in the public sphere in Europe is viewed equally as problematic (as it forces a re-evaluation of the question of 'public religions') and as a threat (both to secularism and the 'European' way of life). But it is also apparent, at least from a European viewpoint, that public expression of Islam is now synonymous with 'political Islam'. As Salvatore notes:

> The politicization of the Islam issue from a European viewpoint has a long history. It is more immediately related to the specific twist that the long-term European perspective on Islam, nurtured by rivalry and competition, has taken since the colonial era. Attempts to deliver a typology of 'political Islam' are thus inherently volatile, because they rest on contingent interests, viewpoints and emotions. These are in turn parasitic on the least balanced and most essentialized views of the relations between Islam and modernity within the European sociology of religion and social theory at large. The politicization of Islam not only depends on what Muslims do or do not do in their various collective action or inaction, but also, if not more so, on the simultaneous and mutual construction of the imagined realities termed 'Europe' and the 'Islamic world'... This is particularly evident in how, below the level of public discourse proper, the issue of the Islamic 'veil' ... has increasingly become an icon of the politicization of Islam in European eyes.[11]

The fear of 'political Islam' and the fact that the public expression of Islam is often viewed as a political statement as much as a demonstration of piety is perhaps part of the reason why its manifestation has been provided with minimum protection at the domestic level in Europe. This narrative has been reinforced at the European level by the ECtHR.

The approach of the ECtHR in the *Refah* case, as it relates to Islam,[12] while surprising at first reading, may in fact reflect domestic debates taking place in a number of European countries, as highlighted in the domestic jurisprudence discussed in the previous chapter. Since the attacks of 11 September 2001 in particular,[13] the (relatively) pluralist model represented by the European Union in which some attempt was made to promote inter-cultural dialogue and exchange has given way to an increasingly illiberal secularism in member states, highlighted by domestic case law concerning representations of religion in the public sphere. Two domestic cases in particular, examined in the previous chapter, are instructive in attempting to determine the nature of restrictions on the manifestation of religion in the public sphere in Europe – the *Teacher Headscarf Case* of the German Constitutional Court[14] and the English House of Lords' decision in *R (on the application of Begum (by her litigation friend, Rahman)) v Headteacher and Governors of Denbigh High School*.[15]

The decision of the ECtHR to uphold the banning of the Refah party and the debates provoked by the potential accession of Turkey, with an Islamic party in government, have prompted a re-evaluation of the limits to both religious and legal pluralism in Europe. That strict limitations on religious pluralism exist in Europe is evident from both rulings of the ECtHR and domestic courts but with regard to legal pluralism, it appears that having acquired 'a measure of normative and political legitimacy unimagined by the architects of the Europe that emerged from the ashes of world war'[16] it is now considered a phenomenon which must be prevented at any cost. The ECtHR's narrative in the *Refah* case affirms this contention by asserting that the purported plan of Refah to introduce a 'plurality of legal systems' would be incompatible with the Convention and 'would introduce into all legal relationships a distinction between individuals grounded on religion, would categorise everyone according to his religious beliefs and would allow him rights and freedoms not as an individual but according to his allegiance to a religious movement.'[17] The ECtHR was of the opinion that a plurality of legal systems would be incompatible with the Convention for two reasons:

> Firstly, it would do away with the State's role as the guarantor of individual rights and freedoms and the impartial organiser of the practice of the various beliefs and religions in a democratic society, since it would oblige individuals to obey, not rules laid down by the State in the exercise of its above-mentioned functions, but static rules of law imposed by the religion concerned. But the State has a positive obligation to ensure that everyone within its jurisdiction enjoys in full, and without being able to waive them, the rights and freedoms guaranteed by the Convention ...
>
> Secondly, such a system would undeniably infringe the principle of non-discrimination between individuals as regards their enjoyment of public freedoms, which is one of the fundamental principles of democracy. A difference in treatment between individuals in all fields of public and private law according to their religion or beliefs manifestly cannot be justified under the Convention, and more particularly Article 14 thereof, which prohibits discrimination. Such a difference in treatment cannot maintain a fair balance between, on the one hand, the claims of certain religious groups who wish to be governed by their own rules and on the other the interest of society as a whole, which must be based on peace and on tolerance between the various religions and beliefs ...[18]

While the opinion of the Court on legal pluralism seems clear from this statement, it fails to take account of the fact that within Europe, 'differential treatment up to and including forms of legal pluralism'[19] is already provided for through a variety of mechanisms in numerous countries. Several European states, for example, have entered into bilateral treaties protecting the rights of national minorities sharing an historical affiliation who live outside the state and, furthermore, the EU itself has committed to legal pluralism 'both in its respect for the sovereign authority of its members as well as for the rights of persons belonging to minorities'.[20] Nonetheless, the determining factor for the Court in *Refah* appeared to be the possibility that to allow legal pluralism in Turkey, or at least the kind envisaged by *Refah*, might result in some form of Islamic law coming into force. The Court's fears in this regard were highlighted in its subsequent discussion of shariah.[21]

2 Final remarks

The cases on religious freedom examined by the ECtHR, particularly those relating to the headscarf, highlight 'the way in which the members of the Court find it difficult to move outside the religious paradigms that are most common in Europe (that is, either broadly Christian or secular) and to deal with non-Christian religions in a manner that is respectful and culturally sensitive.'[22] Indeed, if Yavuz's contention that one of the reasons 'Islamic groups' have supported Turkey's full integration into the EU is the belief that religious freedoms in Turkey would be protected better under the EU than under the Turkish Constitution as interpreted by the Constitutional Court and the military,[23] then there is undoubtedly great concern at the rulings of the ECtHR in both the *Refah* case and the Islamic headscarf jurisprudence.

Although it is not the conclusion of this study that human rights considerations play no part in the accession process – there are undoubtedly numerous outstanding issues relating to the lack of fundamental protections in Turkey – what is suggested is that there is an element of disingenuousness on the part of the EU in its treatment of Turkey's bid.[24] This, it is proposed, manifests itself in the form of a 'religious' requirement which Turkey, by virtue of its almost exclusively *Muslim* population and in spite of its European-style secular policy, cannot fulfil regardless of the extent of human rights reforms instituted. One of the principal reasons for this, which is borne out through the domestic cases and the case law of the ECtHR discussed in the previous chapter, is an underlying apprehension that Islam is in some way incompatible with the modern liberal democratic state. This is despite the fact that Islam–state interaction is not dissimilar to other faiths which endeavour to encroach on the public sphere (notably the Christian right in the US).[25] Nonetheless, it is because of this perceived incompatibility that the conduct of numerous domestic courts in Europe and certainly the ECtHR in attempting to uphold secularism at any cost can perhaps be said to be sanctioning, even engaging in, the actions associated with militant democracies.[26] Moreover, as

Harvey notes, one of the dangers inherent in a 'militant democracy' is that a government can deny political actors their rights simply by labelling them 'anti-democratic'; the label of 'anti-democratic' can then be used as a pretext for banning those whose political activism amounts to no more than a challenge to the prevailing national ideology.[27]

Accordingly, in the *Refah*[28] case, the dislodging of a government from office, described by Boyle as taking the notion of militant democracy 'to a new level'[29] was permissible in order to uphold the 'democratic' secular nature of the Turkish State. The principle of secularism is after all, in the opinion of the Court 'one of the fundamental principles of the State which are in harmony with the rule of law and respect for human rights and democracy'.[30] However, as the Court has never made similar pronouncements in any of the Article 9 cases concerning Christianity, this suggests that the Court has placed Islam in a particularly unique position.[31] Nor had the Court allowed Turkey to be seen to act in a 'militant' manner prior to the decision in *Refah*. In *United Communist Party of Turkey v Turkey*,[32] the Court had found that banning a party which called for a debate on the Kurdish question and constitutional recognition of the Kurds, had violated Article 11 of the Convention. In *Socialist Party and Others v Turkey*,[33] Turkey was found to be in violation of the Convention for banning a party that had advocated a form of internal self-determination for the Kurdish people. Similar decisions were reached in the cases of *Freedom and Democracy Party (Özdep) v Turkey*,[34] and *Yazar and others v Turkey*.[35] The fundamental difference, it would appear, was that none of these cases expressly involved an issue concerning Islam.[36] In *Refah*, however, the threat (albeit one that had not materialized) was deemed so grave that 'preventive intervention' was required. This approach, as Macklem suggests, is problematic:

> Militant democracy – what the Court terms 'preventive intervention' – involves steps to prevent the peaceful accession to power of those with political agendas that would, if implemented, dismantle democracy itself. Until it becomes policy, however, a radical political agenda – whether advanced by an individual or a political party – represents freedom of expression and association in action. The traditional democratic approach to such an agenda is to determine its constitutionality when it begins to conflict with the rights of others. In the absence of accompanying violence or criminal activity, there is no legal conflict until the party comes to power and begins to introduce legislation or policies or otherwise engages in actions that represent the realization of such an agenda; the task of democratic institutions is to restrain the government of the day from acting in an unconstitutional manner. Militant democracy constitutes a stark departure from this traditional democratic stance.[37]

The approach of the Court is worrying, not least because of the fact that EU members states are also members of the Council of Europe and therefore under the jurisdiction of the Court but also because the Court is supposed to be the upholder of fundamental rights and freedoms and challenge states to do the same, rather than acquiesce in the flawed reasoning put forward by states who engage in actions which prima facie constitute a violation of the Convention.

Since undertaking this study, Turkey has experienced a relatively stable period of government, with the successive election of the AKP in 2002 and 2007 coinciding with progression on the path to EU membership. Despite Turkey's long and difficult path to accession, as detailed in Chapter 1, the use of the carrot–stick approach by the EU had resulted in the implementation of a series of human rights reforms. Yet with each new impasse we have concomitantly seen a rollback in human rights reforms suggesting a reform fatigue or too much 'stick' and not enough genuine incentive by the EU. As it stands, the earliest date at which Turkey can achieve full membership remains 2014, as provided by the Negotiating Framework of 2005. The stated arguments for keeping Turkey out of the EU, most notably because of its lack of human rights protections, can be countered with an assertion that it would be easier to track Turkey's human rights performance as a member state than an applicant state. In any event, with little progression on the road to membership in recent years, the impetus for proceeding with reforms may well dissipate entirely.

While centred on the specific example of Turkey's accession to the EU, this study has wider application in determining the parameters of the requirements of accession and in particular whether a form of cultural, or specifically religious, requirement now attaches to successful accessions. Moreover, Turkey's path to accession can be viewed as reflecting the tensions inherent in a European public space which is grappling with issues of secularism and religious and legal pluralism, not to mention the perceived 'clash' between Islam and democracy. Suggestions that it is, in fact, Europe, and not Turkey, which is the 'torn country,'[38] are therefore unsurprising. Perhaps the most worrying trend to emerge from this study is the fact that these tensions have also been subsumed into the reasoning of the ECtHR that has, in what could be termed its 'jurisprudence of fear', grafted the critically flawed 'clash of civilisations' thesis.[39]

Notes

1 Other obstacles, largely economic factors, are also relevant but these have been considered elsewhere and are in any case relatively clear-cut. See, for example, Z. Y. Herschlag, *The Contemporary Turkish Economy* (Routledge: London, 1988); I. Saăba, 'Central–Local Fiscal Relations in Turkey: A Technical Analysis of Fiscal Equalization', *Turkish Studies*, 2(2) (2001), 121–42; M. Eder, 'Implementing the Economic Criteria of EU Membership: How Difficult is it for Turkey?', Turkish Studies, 4(1) (2003), 219–244; A. M. Lejour, R. A. de Mooij and C. H. Capel, 'Assessing the Economic Implications of Turkish Accession to the EU', CPB Netherlands Bureau for Economic Policy Analysis, No. 56 (2004); N. B. Gültekin and K. Yilmaz, 'The Turkish Economy before the EU Accession Talks', in Lake, *The EU*, 61–79 and J. T. McCarthy, 'Turkey's Financial Sector: A Practitioner's

View of a Work in Progress', in *ibid.*, 79–87; A. Hadjit and E. Moxon-Browne, 'Foreign Direct Investment in Turkey: The Implications of EU Accession', *Turkish Studies*, 6(3) (2005), 321–40; I. Isik and D. Uysal, 'The Sources of Productivity Growth in Turkish Banks by Ownership: The Initial Responses of Public, Private, and Foreign Banks to Liberalization', *Turkish Studies*, 7(3) (2006), 365–403; M. Ugur, 'The Economic Dimension of Turkey's EU Membership: A Stock-Taking Exercise at the Start of Accession Negotiations', in J. S. Joseph (ed.), *Turkey and the European Union: Internal Dynamics and External Challenges* (New York: Palgrave Macmillan, 2006), 16–42.

2 S. Baykal, 'Unity in Diversity? The Challenge of Diversity for the European Political Identity, Legitimacy and Democratic Governance: Turkey's EU Membership as the Ultimate Test Case', Jean Monnet Working Papers Series 09/2005, 56–57.

3 See Chapter 2, n. 4 and accompanying text.

4 P. Alston and J. H. H. Weiler, 'An "Ever Closer Union" in Need of a Human Rights Policy: The European Union and Human Rights', in Alston *et al.*, 3–69, 9.

5 A. Williams, 'Enlargement of the Union and Human Rights Conditionality: A Policy of Distinction', Eur. L. Rev., 25(6) (2000), 601–17, 602.

6 The Eurobarometer report of spring 2007 noted that in Turkey trust in the EU (at 38 per cent) was lower than in Member States (57 per cent) and continued to fall. Positive evaluations of the 'image of the EU' had also fallen. See 'Eurobarometer 67: Public Opinion in the EU', spring 2007 (available at: http://ec.europa.eu/public_opinion/archives/eb/eb67/eb67_en.htm) (last accessed, 2 February 2010).

7 See M. J. Patton, 'AKP Reform Fatigue in Turkey: What Happened to the EU Process?', Mediterranean Politics, 12(3) (2007), 339–58, 355, noting that: '[r]eform fatigue has been brought on by a confluence of factors, both external and internal. The EU, once considered a catalyst of reform, now looks to be unreliable. Modalities of EU behaviour toward Turkey, mixed signals about its commitment to full Turkish membership and demands for unilateral concessions have soured Turkish public opinion.'

8 *Ibid.*, 346

9 See F. Acar, 'Islam in Turkey', in Balkir and Williams *Turkey*, 219–38, 222 noting: 'Since the mid-1980s some indications of a significant chance in the nature of the relationship between religion and state can be discerned in Turkish society. In other words, the direction of the main axis of interaction between Islamists and secular forces has begun to shift from open antagonism and confrontation to toleration. This change is primarily exemplified in the secular camps' discourse on Islamists. At present, the conventional conception of Islam and secularism as polar opposites, incompatible with one another, shows signs of giving way to the alternative conception of coexistence of the two ideologies and their supporters in the institutional framework of a pluralist democracy and/or civil society.'

10 Yavuz asserts that the Islamic presence in public spaces in Turkey is presented by the military as a threat to national security and the Kemalist way of life, which is claimed to be the only legitimate one, a phenomenon which he refers to as the 'securitization' of Islam. See H. Yavuz, *Islamic Political Identity in Turkey* (Oxford: Oxford University Press, 2003), 244–5.

11 A. Salvatore 'Authority in Question: Secularity, Republicanism, and "Communitarianism" in the Emerging Euro-Islamic Public Sphere', *Theory, Culture and Society*, 24 (2007), 135–60, 136.

12 See Chapter 4, Section 3.2.
13 On this point, see Cavanaugh, 'Islam', 2–3, noting that the 'events of September 11th woke a previously dormant political establishment to face the challenges posed by the cultural and social background of religious diversity (private domain versus public space and political community) and the obvious legal and political implications that Europe must now address'.
14 BVerfG, 2BvR 1436/02 of 24 September 2003.
15 [2006] UKHL 15. See Chapter 4, Section 2.2.1.
16 P. Macklem, 'Militant Democracy, Legal Pluralism, and the Paradox of Self-Determination', Int'l J. Con. Law, 4(3) (2006), 488–516, 490. Macklem also notes that domestic, regional and international human rights law has 'blunted' the challenge of legal pluralism. 'Rights bearers overwhelmingly are individuals, and their entitlements protect a zone of individual liberty from the exercise of public power. Although not blind to the significance of social and cultural interests, international human rights law – in particular, jurisprudence under the European Convention on Human Rights (ECHR) – emphasises the protection of individual freedoms (of expression, opinion, religion, and association) as essential to liberty and the rule of law. Diverse forms of legal pluralism, however, have become increasingly legitimate institutional possibilities in the face of real or potential religious, cultural, or national conflict' (*ibid.*, 489).
17 *Refah Partisi and others* v. *Turkey,* application no. 41340/98 and 41342–4/98, judgment of 13 February 2003, para. 119.
18 *Ibid.*
19 Macklem, 'Militant Democracy', 496.
20 *Ibid.* Macklem also contends that the 'asymmetrical devolution of power to the various autonomous regions in Spain also offers another example of legal pluralism'. The same could possibly be said of the devolved governments of Northern Ireland, Wales and Scotland within the UK.
21 See Chapter 4, Section 3.2.
22 C. Evans, 'The "Islamic Scarf" in the European Court of Human Rights', Melb. J. Int'l L., 7 (2006), 52–73, 54 (references omitted).
23 See Yavuz, *Islamic Political Identity*, 249. Yavuz contends that the other reasons full EU integration has been supported by Islamic groups in Turkey centre on 'the rise of a new bourgeoisie from Anatolia with economically liberal and socially religious values; … the European National Outlook Movement's encouragement of Turkey's integration into the EU; and the increasing influence of a new generation of Muslim politicians and intellectuals … The public realised that, to reduce the influence of the military and to establish a democratic state in Turkey, the European option had become the *only* option' (emphasis in original, references omitted).
24 An example of this is the statement in May 2007 of EU Enlargement Commissioner, Olli Rehn, in which he noted that: '[i]f a country wants to become a member of the EU, it needs to respect the principle of democratic secularism, part of our Copenhagen criteria' (O. Rehn, European Commissioner for Enlargement, 'Open Debate on Enlargement', European Parliament Foreign Affairs Committee, SPEECH/07/287, Brussels, 7 May 2007, 3). This, as McCrea contends, served to identify secularism as part of the Copenhagen criteria, 'something which had not been done in relation to the application of any other state' ('Limitations on Religion in a Liberal Democratic Polity: Christianity and Islam in the Public

Order of the European Union', London School of Economics and Political Science Law, Society and Economy Working Papers 18/2007 14).

25 Teitel cites the emergence of the Christian right as illustrative of the 'impossibility of religious commitment being distinct from public life … Primarily evangelical Protestant, its platform called for political involvement on a variety of social issues: abortion, feminism and school prayer' (R. Teitel, 'A Critique of Religion as Politics in the Public Sphere', Cornell L. Rev., 78 (1992–3), 747–821, 760–1, references omitted).

26 The phrase 'militant democracy' was coined by the German constitutional lawyer Karl Loewenstein in an essay entitled 'Militant Democracy and Fundamental Rights', American Political Science Rev., 31 (1937), 418–32. It refers to the restricting of certain rights in order to uphold these same rights for the greater good; 'a form of constitutional democracy authorized to protect civil and political freedom by preemptively restricting the exercise of such freedoms' (Macklem, 'Militant Democracy', 488). See also M. Klamt, 'Militant Democracy and the Democratic Dilemma: Different Ways of Protecting Democratic Constitutions', in F. Bruinsma and D Nelken (eds), *Explorations in Legal Cultures* (Amsterdam: Elsevier, 2007), 133–58.

27 P. Harvey, 'Militant Democracy and the European Convention on Human Rights', European L. Rev., 29(3) (2004), 407–20, 409, 414–15.

28 *Refah Partisi and Others*, above n. 17.

29 Boyle, 'Human Rights', 2.

30 *Refah Partisi and Others*, above n. 17, para. 93.

31 McCrea notes that '[d]espite the fact that many biblical passages relating to gender equality and sexuality are as patriarchal and interventionist as the sharia, the Court has never detected a threat to democracy in the official status of certain Christian denominations as state churches or in the presence in the legislatures and governments of explicitly Christian political parties in many member states' ('Limitations on Religion', 18).

At the time of writing, a case involving the mandatory display of the crucifix in public schools in Italy has been referred to the Grand Chamber of the Court. In *Lautsi v Italy*, Application number 30814/06, judgment of 3 November 2009, the Court found violations of Articles 9 and Article 2 of Protocol No. 1 to the Convention. The judgment appeared to hinge on the Court's assertion that the state has a duty to be neutral in the provision of public services, in particular education (para. 57).

32 Application no. 133/1996/752/951, judgment of 30 January 1998.

33 Application no. 20/1997/804/1007, judgment of 25 May 1998.

34 Application no. 133/1996/752/951, judgment of 8 December 1999.

35 Application nos. 22723/93, 22724/93 and 22725/93, judgment of 9 April 2002.

36 Additionally, Macklem suggests that: '[i]n none of these cases had the political party proposed or sought to implement an agenda in a way that, according to the Court, ran counter to convention values of liberty and democracy. The Court's jurisprudence implies that a state can act in a militant manner to preserve these values in the face of political agenda that seeks their destruction' ('Militant Democracy', 507).

37 *Ibid.*, 514.

38 Casanova, 'Long, Difficult, and Tortuous', 241.

39 S. P. Huntington, *The Clash of Civilisations and the Re-making of World Order* (New York: Touchstone, 1997). For a critique of Huntington's thesis, see, for example, D. J. D. Sandole, 'The "Fog of War" on Terrorism: US Policy, Deception, and the Continuing Slide into the Clash of Civilisations', ILSA J. Int'l & Comp. L., 13 (2006–7), 149–70.

Bibliography

Abela, Anthony M. 'Solidarity and Religion in the European Union: A Comparative Sociological Perspective', in Peter Xuereb (ed.) *The Value(s) of a Constitution for Europe*, (Malta European Documentation and Research Centre University of Malta 2004), 71–101.

Addis, Adeno (1992) 'Individualism, Communitarianism, and the Rights of Ethnic Minorities', *Notre Dame Law Review*, 67: 615.

Adıvar, Halide Edip (1930) *Turkey Faces West: A Turkish View of Recent Changes and Their Origins*, New Haven: Yale University Press.

Ahdar, Rex and Leigh, Ian (2005) *Religious Freedom in the Liberal State*, Oxford: Oxford University Press.

Ahmad, Feroz (1993) *The Making of Modern Turkey*, London and New York: Routledge.

Al-Azmeh, Aziz and Fokas, Effie (eds) (2007) *Islam in Europe: Diversity, Identity and Influence*, Cambridge: Cambridge University Press.

Alfredsson, Gudmundur (2000) 'A Frame with an Incomplete Painting: Comparison of the Framework Convention for the Protection of National Minorities with International Standards and Monitoring Procedures', *International Journal on Minority and Group Rights*, 7(4): 291.

Allain, Jean (2004) *International Law in the Middle East: Closer to Power than Justice*, Surrey, UK: Ashgate Publishing Limited.

Almond, Mark (2008) 'A Friend in Need: Turkey Is a Strategically Crucial Country, at an Important Juncture. Can Western Countries Afford to Snub Its EU Application?', *Guardian* 10 June.

Alston, Philip (ed.) (1999) with Bustelo, Mara and Heenan, James *The EU and Human Rights*, Oxford: Oxford University Press.

Altinay, Hakan and Nicolaïdis, Kalypso (2008) 'Why the European Union Strengthens Turkish Secularism', Open Democracy, 3 September.

Amnesty International (1995) 'Turkey: A Policy of Denial', AI Index: EUR 44/24/95.

— (1996) 'No Security without Human Rights', Amnesty International AI Index: EUR 44/084/1996.

— (1999) 'Turkey: The Duty to Supervise, Investigate and Prosecute', AI Index: EUR 44/24/99.

— (2005) 'Country report on Turkey', AI Index: POL 10/001/2005.

— (2005) 'Article 301 Is a Threat to Freedom of Expression and Must Be Repealed Now!', AI Index: EUR 44/035/2005.

— (2008) AI Report 2008, State of the World's Human Rights.

Andrews, Peter A. (ed.) (1989) *Ethnic Groups in the Republic of Turkey*, Weisbaden: Reichert.

Arat, Zehra F. Kabasakal (ed.) (2007) *Human Rights in Turkey*, Pennsylvania, PA: University of Pennsylvania Press.

Arikan, Harun (2002) 'A Lost Opportunity? A Critique of the European Union's Human Rights Policy Towards Turkey', *Mediterranean Politics*, 7(1): 19.

— (2006) *Turkey and the EU: An Awkward Candidate for EU Membership?*, 2nd edn, Surrey, UK: Ashgate.

Arvanitopoulos, Constantine (ed.) (2009) *Turkey's Accession to the European Union: An Unusual Candidacy*, New York: Springer.

Asad, Talal (1993) *Genealogies of Religion: Discipline and Reasons of Power in Christianity and Islam*, Baltimore and London: John Hopkins University Press.

Atasoy, Seymen (2003–4) 'Cyprus, Turkey and the EU: The Need for a Gradual Approach', *Brown Journal of World Affairs*, 10(1): 257.

Ayubi, Nazih (1991) *Political Islam: Religion and Politics in the Arab World*, London: Routledge.

Baka, Andras B. (1992–3) 'The European Convention on Human Rights and the Protection of Minorities Under International Law', *Connecticut Journal of International Law*, 8: 227.

Balibar, Etienne (2002) *Politics and the Other Scene*, London and New York: Verso.

Balkir, Canan and Williams, Allan M. (eds) (1993) *Turkey and Europe*, London and New York: Pinter Publishers Limited.

Banani, Dinesh D. (2003) 'Reforming History: Turkey's Legal Regime and its Potential Accession to the European Union', *Boston College International and Comparative Law Review*, 26: 113.

Bañkowski, Zenon and Christodoulidis, Emilios (1998) 'The European Union as an Essentially Contested Project', *European Law Journal*, 4(4): 341.

Barber, Tony (2009) 'Van Rompuy against Turkey Membership' *Financial Times*, 19 November.

Barker, Christine (2000) 'Church and State Relationships in German "Public Benefit" Law', *International Journal of Not-for-Profit Law*, 3(2).

Bauman, Zygmunt (2004) *Europe: An Unfinished Adventure*, London: Polity Press.

Baykal, Sanem (2006) 'Unity in Diversity? The Challenge of Diversity for the European Political Identity and Democratic Governance: Turkish Membership as the Ultimate Test Case', Lake Mary, FL: Vandeplas Publishing.

BBC World News Edition (2002) 'Turkey Entry Would Destroy EU', 8 November.

Beck, Ulrich (2003) 'Understanding the Real Europe', *Dissent*, 50(3): 32.

Beck, Ulrich and Grande, Edgar (2007) 'Cosmopolitanism: Europe's Way Out of Crisis', *European Journal of Social Theory*, 10(1): 67.

Belelieu, Christopher D. (2005–6) 'The Headscarf as a Symbolic Enemy of the European Court of Human Rights. Democratic Jurisprudence: Viewing Islam Through a European Legal Prism in Light of the *Şahin* Judgment', *Columbia Journal of European Law*, 12: 573.

Bellamy, Richard and Warleigh, Alex (eds) (2001) *Citizenship and Governance in the European Union*, London: Continuum Publishing.

Bennhold, Katrin (2006) 'Turkey Assails EU's Decision to Partially Suspend Entry Talks', *International Herald Tribune*, 12 December.

Berger, Peter L. (ed.) (1999) *The Desecularization of the World: Resurgent Religion and World Politics*, Washington, DC: Ethics and Public Policy Center and Eerdmans Publishing Co.

Berkes, Niyazi (1998) *The Development of Secularism in Turkey*, 2nd edn, New York: Routledge.

Birch, Nicholas (2005) 'Turkey Looks for Peace with Kurds', *Guardian*, 13 August.

Black, Ian (2003) 'Doubting North wins battle to leave God out of it', *Guardian* 29 May.

Blay, Sam K. N. (1981–3) 'Self-Determination in Cyprus: The New Dimensions of an Old Conflict', *Australian Yearbook of International Law*, 10: 67.

Bleiberg, Benjamin D. (2005–6) 'Unveiling the Real Issue: Evaluating the European Court of Human Rights' Decision to Enforce the Turkish Headscarf Ban in *Leyla Şahin v Turkey*', *Cornell Law Review*, 91: 129.

Bogdandy, Armin von (2000) 'The European Union as a Human Rights Organisation? Human Rights and the Core of the European Union', *Common Market Law Review*, 37: 1307.

— (2005) 'The European Constitution and European Identity: Text and Subtext of the Treaty Establishing a Constitution for Europe', *International Journal of Constitutional Law*, 3(2–3): 295.

Bowen, John R. (2006) *Why the French Don't Like Headscarves: Islam, the State, and Public Space*, Princeton and Oxford: Princeton University Press.

Boyle, Kevin (2004) 'Human Rights, Religion and Democracy: The *Refah Party* Case', *Essex Human Rights Review*, 1(1): 1.

Braude, Benjamin and Lewis, Bernard (eds) (1982) *Christians and Jews in the Ottoman Empire: The Functioning of a Plural Society*, New York: Holmes and Meier.

Bredt, Stephan (2006) 'The European Social Contract and the European Public Sphere', *European Law Journal*, 12(1): 61.

Brewin, Christopher (2002) 'Turkish and European Union Interests in a Cyprus Settlement', *Journal of Ethnopolitics and Minority Issues in Europe*, 2: 1.

Bruinessen, Martin van (1992) *Shaikh and State: The Social and Political Structures of Kurdistan*, London: Zed Books Ltd.

Bruinsma, Fred and Nelken, David (eds) (2007) *Explorations in Legal Cultures*, Amsterdam: Elsevier.

Bulbul, Kudret (2006) 'Turkey and the EU: A Survey on Turkish MPs' EU Vision', *Turkish Journal of International Relations*, 5(3): 32.

Bulloch, John and Morris, Harvey (1992) *No Friends But the Mountains: The Tragic History of the Kurds*, Oxford: Oxford University Press.

Búrca, Gráinne de (2001) 'Drafting the EU Charter on Fundamental Rights', *European Law Review*, 26(2): 126.

— (2004) 'Beyond the Charter: How Enlargement has Enlarged the Human Rights Policy of the European Union', *Fordham International Law Journal*, 27: 679.

Byrnes, Timothy A. and Katzenstein, Peter J. (eds) (2006) *Religion in an Expanding Europe*, New York: Cambridge University Press.

Calhoun, Craig (ed.) (1992) *Habermas and the Public Sphere*, Cambridge, MA: MIT Press.

Caporaso, James A. (2005–6) 'The Possibilities of a European Identity', *Brown Journal of World Affairs*, 12: 65.

Capotorti, Fancesco (1991) 'Study on the Rights of Persons Belonging to Ethnic, Religious and Linguistic Minorities', Geneva: United Nations.

Çarkoğlu, Ali and Rubin, Barry (eds) (2003) *Turkey and the European Union: Domestic Politics, Economic Integration and International Dynamics*, London: Frank Cass.

Casanova, José (1994) *Public Religions in the Modern World*, Chicago, IL: University of Chicago Press.

— (2006) 'The Long, Difficult, and Tortuous Journey of Turkey into Europe and the Dilemmas of European Civilization', *Constellations*, 13(2): 234.

Cassese, Antonio (2004) *International Law*, 2nd edn, Oxford: Oxford University Press.

Cavanaugh, Kathleen (2007) 'Islam and the European Project', *Muslim World Journal of Human Rights*, 4(1): 1.

Çelik, Ayşe and Rumelili, Bahar (2006) 'Necessary But Not Sufficient: The Role of the EU in Resolving Turkey's Kurdish Question and the Greek–Turkish Conflicts', *European Foreign Affairs Review*, 11: 203.

Chaliand, Gerard (ed.), M Pallis (tr.) (1993) *A People Without a Country: The Kurds and Kurdistan*, 2nd edn, London: Zed Books.

Chalmers, Damian (2003) 'The Reconstitution of European Public Spheres', *European Law Journal*, 9(2): 127.

Clapham, Andrew (1990) 'A Human Rights Policy for the European Community', *Yearbook of European Law*, 10: 309.

Craig, Paul and de Búrca, Gráinne (2002) *EU Law: Texts, Cases and Materials*, 3rd edn, Oxford: Oxford University Press.

Cvijic, Srdjan and Zucca, Lorenzo (2004) 'Does the European Constitution Need Christian Values?', *Oxford Journal of Legal Studies*, 24(4): 739.

Cyprus Embassy (2006) 'Bicommunal Meetings on Cyprus Problem Continue', 9 August (available at http://cyprusembassy.net/home/index.php?module=article &id=3752).

Dartan, Muzaffer and Nas, Çiğdem (eds) (2002) *The European Union Enlargement Process and Turkey*, Istanbul: Marmara University European Community Institute.

Dassetto, Felice and Ferrari, Silvio (2007) 'Islam in the EU: What's at Stake in the Future?', IP/B/CULT/ST/2006_061, 14 May.

Dauses, Manfred (1985) 'The Protection of Fundamental Rights in the Community Legal Order', *European Law Review*, 10: 398.

Davie, Grace (2005) *Religion in Modern Europe: A Memory Mutates*, Oxford: Oxford University Press.

Davison, Andrew (1998) *Secularism Revivalism in Turkey*, New Haven: Yale University Press.

Dawson, Christopher (1953) *Understanding Europe*, London and New York: Sheed and Ward.

Dehousse, Renaud (2006) 'The Unmaking of a Constitution: Lessons from the European Referenda', *Constellations*, 13(2): 151.

Delanty, Gerard (1995) *Inventing Europe: Idea, Identity, Reality*, London: Macmillan Press.

— (2005) 'The Idea of a Cosmopolitan Europe: On the Cultural Significance of Europeanization', *International Review of Sociology*, 15(3): 405.

Diez, Thomas (2002) 'Why the EU Can Nonetheless Be Good for Cyprus', *Journal of Ethnopolitics and Minority Issues in Europe*, 1: 1.

— (2007) 'Expanding Europe: The Ethics of EU–Turkey Relations', *Ethics and International Affairs*, 21(4): 415.

Doğan, Nejat (2006) 'Human Rights and Turkey's Bid for EU Membership: Will "Fundamental Rights of the Union", Bring Fundamental Changes to the Turkish Constitution and Turkish Politics?', *Turkish Studies*, 7(2): 243.

Dokupil, Susanna (2002) 'The Separation of Mosque and State: Islam and Democracy in Modern Turkey', *West Virginia Law Review*, 105: 53.

Edelstein, Elizabeth Manera (2003) 'The Loi Toubon: *Liberté, Égalité, Fraternité*, But Only on France's Terms', *Emory International Law Review*, 17: 1127.

Eder, Mine (2003) 'Implementing the Economic Criteria of EU Membership: How Difficult Is It for Turkey?', *Turkish Studies*, 4(1): 219.

Ehrlich, Thomas (1965–6) 'Cyprus, the "Warlike Isle": Origins and Elements of the Current Crisis', *Stanford Law Review*, 18: 1021.

Ekeus, Rolf (2003) 'From the Copenhagen Criteria to the Copenhagen Summit: Minority Issues in an Enlarging Europe', *Helsinki Monitor*, 14: 38.

Elsuwege, Peter van (2002) 'The Baltic States on the Road to EU Accession: Opportunities and Challenges', *European Foreign Affairs Review*, 7: 171.

Engle Merry, Sally (1988) 'Legal Pluralism', *Law and Society*, review, 22(5): 869.

Erdoğan, Birsen (2007) 'Turkey's Compliance with European Union Democratic Conditionality: Resistance or Transformation of Identity?', *Netherlands Quarterly of Human Rights*, 25(1): 21.

Erdoğan, Recep Tayyip (2004) address at the 'New Tactics in Human Rights' Symposium, Ankara, Turkey, 29 September–4 October (available at www.newtactics.org/sites/newtactics.org/files/resources/erdogan.doc).

Eriksen, Thomas Hylland (1993) *Ethnicity and Nationalism: Anthropological Perspectives*, London: Pluto Press.

Euractiv (2008) '2008 to be "EU Year" in Turkey, Says Foreign Minister', 6 February (available at www.euractiv.com/en/enlargement/2008-eu-year-turkey-foreign-minister/article-170121).

Europa (2003) 'Commissioner Rehn Welcomes Christofias–Talat Meeting in Cyprus and Decision to Open Ledra Street Crossing', 21 March (available at http://ec.europa.eu/enlargement/index_en.htm).

European Stability Initiative (2006) 'Beyond Enlargement Fatigue?: The Dutch Debate on Turkish Accession', (report), Berlin, Istanbul and Brussels, 24 April.

Evans, Caroline (2001) *Freedom of Religion Under the European Convention on Human Rights*, Oxford: Oxford University Press.

— (2006) 'The "Islamic Scarf" in the European Court of Human Rights', *Melbourne Journal of International Law*, 7: 52.

Evriviades, Marios L. (1975) 'The Legal Dimension of the Cyprus Conflict', *Texas International Law Journal*, 10: 227.

Ewald, Gregory J. (1993–4) 'The Kurds' Right to Secede Under International Law: Self-Determination Prevails Over Political Manipulation', *Denver Journal of International Law and Policy*, 22: 375.

Fossum, John Erik (2003) 'The European Union: In Search of an Identity', *European Journal of Political Theory*, 2(3): 319.

Furtado, Charles F., Jnr. (2002–3) 'Guess Who's Coming to Dinner? Protection for National Minorities in Eastern and Central Europe Under the Council of Europe', *Columbia Human Rights Law Review*, 34: 333.

Genel, Sema and Karaosmanoğlu, Kerem (2006) 'A New Islamic Individualism in Turkey: Headscarved Women in the City', *Turkish Studies*, 7: 473.

Gerhards, Jürgen (2007) *Cultural Overstretch? Differences Between Old and New Member States of the EU and Turkey*, London: Routledge.

Gerstenberg, Oliver (2005) 'Germany: Freedom of Conscience in Public Schools', *International Journal of Constitutional Law*, 3(1): 94.

Gilbert, Geoff (2002) 'The Burgeoning Minority Rights Jurisprudence of the European Court of Human Rights', *Human Rights Quarterly*, 24(3): 736.

Giliomee, Hermann and Schlemmer, Lawrence (eds) (1989) *Negotiating South Africa's Future*, London: Palgrave Macmillan.

Goldman, Olivia Q. (1994) 'The Need for an International Mechanism to Protect Group Rights: A Case Study of the Kurds', *Tulsa Journal of Comparative and International Law*, 2: 45.

Göle, Nilüfer (1997) 'Secularism and Islamism in Turkey: The Making of Elites and Counter-Elites', *Middle East Journal*, 51(1): 46.

Gönenç, Levent (2004) 'The 2001 Amendments to the 1982 Constitution on Turkey', *Ankara Law Review*, 1(1): 89.

Goody, Jack (2004) *Islam in Europe*, Cambridge: Polity Press.

Grabbe, Heather (2004) 'EU Expansion and Democracy', *Georgetown Journal of International Affairs*, 5: 73.

Griffiths, John (1986) 'What is Legal Pluralism?', *Journal of Legal Pluralism*, 24: 1.

Guardian (2005) 'Leader, In Praise of ... Orhan Pamuk', 16 December.

Guardian (2007) 'EU Calls on Turkey to Halt Strikes in Northern Iraq', 17 December.

Gülalp, Haldun (2003) 'Whatever Happened to Secularization? The Multiple Islams of Turkey', *South Atlantic Quarterly*, 102(2/3): 381.

Gunter, Michael M. (1990) *The Kurds in Turkey: A Political Dilemma*, Boulder, CO: Westview Press.

—— (1997) *The Kurds and the Future of Turkey*, New York: St. Martin's Press.

Habermas, Jürgen (1992) 'Citizenship and National Identity: Some Reflections of the Future of Europe', *Praxis International*, 12(1): 1.

—— (2001) 'Why Europe Needs a Constitution', *New Left Review*, 11: 5.

—— (2003) 'Intolerance and Discrimination', *International Journal of Constitutional Law*, 1(1): 2.

Habermas, Jürgen and Derrida, Jacques (2003) 'February 15, or What Binds Europeans Together: A Plea for a Common Foreign Policy, Beginning in the Core of Europe', *Constellations*, 10(3): 291.

Hadjit, Assia and Moxon-Browne, Edward (2005) 'Foreign Direct Investment in Turkey: The Implications of EU Accession', *Turkish Studies*, 6(3): 321.

Hakyemez, Yusuf Sevki and Akgun, Birol (2002) 'Limitations on the Freedom of Political Parties in Turkey and the Jurisdiction of the European Court of Human Rights', *Mediterranean Politics*, 7(2): 54.

Hannay, David (2006) 'Cyprus, Turkey and the EU: Time for a Sense of Proportion and Compromise', July, Centre for European Reform Policy Brief.

Hannum, Hurst (1991) 'Contemporary Developments in the International Protection of the Rights of Minorities', *Notre Dame Law Review*, 66: 1431.

Hardy, Liam (2008) 'Turkey and the EU: Slowly But Surely', *Middle East Times*, 1 December.

Harvey, Paul (2004) 'Militant Democracy and the European Convention on Human Rights', *European Law Review*, 29(3): 407.

Herschlag, Zvi Yehuda (1988) *The Contemporary Turkish Economy*, London: Routledge.

Hillion, Christophe (2004) 'On Enlargement of the European Union: The Discrepancy Between Membership Obligations and Accession Conditions as Regards the Protection of Minorities', *Fordham International Law Journal*, 27: 715.

—— (ed.) (2004) *EU Enlargement: A Legal Approach: Essays in European Law*, Oxford: Hart Publishing.

Howard, Erica (2010) *The EU Race Directive: Developing the Protection against Racial Discrimination within the EU*, London: Routledge.

Howe, Marvine (2000) *Turkey: A Nation Divided Over Islam's Revival*, Boulder, CO: Westview Press.

Hugg, Patrick R. (2000) 'The Republic of Turkey in Europe: Reconsidering the Luxembourg Exclusion', *Fordham International Law Journal*, 23: 606.

Hughes, James and Sasse, Gwendolyn (2003) 'Monitoring the Monitors: EU Enlargement Conditionality and Minority Protection in the CEECs', *Journal of Ethnopolitics and Minority Issues in Europe*, 1: 1.

Hughes, Kirsty (2004) 'The Political Dynamics of Turkey's Accession to the EU: A European Success Story or the EU's Most Contested Enlargement?', *Swedish Institute for European Policy Studies*, 9.

Huls, Nick, Adams, Maurice and Bomhoff, Jacco (eds) (2009) *The Legitimacy of Highest Courts' Rulings: Judicial Deliberations and Beyond*, Netherlands: TMC Asser Press.

Human Rights Watch (1994) 'Turkey: Forced Displacement of Ethnic Kurds from south-eastern Turkey', A Human Rights Watch Short Report, 6(12).

— (1999) HRW World Report, 'Bulgaria: Human Rights Developments'.

— (1999) HRW World Report, 'Romania: Human Rights Developments'.

— (2004) 'Eradicating Torture in Turkey's Police Stations: Analysis and Recommendations', briefing paper.

Huntington, Samuel P. (1993) 'The Clash of Civilisations', *Foreign Affairs*, 72(3): 22.

— (1997) *The Clash of Civilisations and the Re-making of World Order*, New York: Touchstone.

Hurd, Elizabeth Shakman (2006) 'Negotiating Europe: The Politics of Religion and the Prospects for Turkish Accession', *Review of International Studies*, 32: 401.

Hürriyet (2008) 'Turkey Presses the EU to set a Target Date for Full Membership', 9 May.

Idriss, Mohammad Mazher (2005) '*R (Begum)* v. *Headteacher and Governors of Denbigh High School*: A Case Note', *Judicial Review*, 10: 296.

— (2006) 'The Defeat of Shabina Begum in the House of Lords', *Liverpool Law Review*, 27: 417.

Independent Commission on Turkey (2004) 'Turkey in Europe: More than a Promise?', September.

Inglis, Tom, Mach, Zdzislaw and Mazanek, Rafa (2000) *Religion and Politics: East–West Contrasts from Contemporary Europe*, Dublin: University College Press.

Isik, Ihsan and Uysal, Dogan (2006) 'The Sources of Productivity Growth in Turkish Banks by Ownership: The Initial Responses of Public, Private, and Foreign Banks to Liberalization', *Turkish Studies*, 7(3): 365.

Jackson-Preece, Jennifer (1998) *National Minorities and the European Nation-State System*, Oxford: Oxford University Press.

Janis, Mark W., Kay, Richard S. and Bradley, Anthony W. (2008) *European Human Rights Law: Text and Materials*, 3rd edn, Oxford: Oxford University Press.

Javaid, Makbool (2001) 'EU Race Directive', *International Business Lawyer*, 29: 3.

Joseph, Joseph S. (1997) *Cyprus: Ethnic Conflict and International Politics*, New York: St. Martin's Press.

— (ed.) (2006) *Turkey and the European Union: Internal Dynamics and External Challenges*, New York: Palgrave Macmillan.

Jung, Dietrich (2005) 'Turkey and the Arab World: Historical Narratives and New Political Realities', *Mediterranean Politics*, 10(1): 1.

Jung, Dietrich and Raudvere, Catharina (eds) (2008) *Religion, Politics and Turkey's EU Accession*, New York: Palgrave Macmillan.

Kahraman, Ahmet (2007) *Uprising, Suppression, Retribution: The Kurdish Struggle in Turkey in the Twentieth Century*, London: Parvana.

Kanerek, David A. (2003) 'Turkey and the European Union: The Path to Accession', *Columbia Journal of European Law*, 9: 457.

Karaosmanoglu, Ali (2000) 'The Evolution of the National Security Culture and the Military in Turkey', *Journal of International Affairs*, 54(1): 1999.

Karimova, Nigar and Deverell, Edward (2001) 'Minorities in Turkey', occasional papers no. 19, Swedish Institute of International Affairs.

Kaya, Nurcan and Baldwin, Clive (2004) 'Minorities in Turkey: Submission to the European Union and the Government of Turkey', July, Minority Rights Group International.

Kayalı, Hasan (1997) *Arabs and Young Turks: Ottomanism. Arabism, and Islamism in the Ottoman Empire, 1908–1918*, Berkeley, CA: University of California Press.

Kearney, Michael Gerard (2007) *The Prohibition of Propaganda for War in International Law*, Oxford: Oxford University Press.

Kemal, K. and Winrow, Gareth (1997) *The Kurdish Question and Turkey: An Example of Trans-state Ethnic Conflict*, London: Frank Cass.

Kilpaldi, Pamela (ed.) (2006) *Islam and Tolerance in a Wider Europe*, New York: Open Society Institute.

Kinacioğlu, Müge and Oktay, Emel (2006) 'The Domestic Dynamics of Turkey's Cyprus Policy: Implications for Turkey's Accession to the European Union', *Turkish Studies*, 7(2): 261.

Kinzer, Stephen (1999) 'Europe's Tie to Turkey Takes a Turn for Chillier', *New York Times*, 16 March.

—— (2001) *Crescent and Star: Turkey Between Two Worlds*, New York: Farrar, Strauss and Giroux.

Kittrie, Nicholas N. (2000) *Rebels With a Cause: The Minds and Morality of Political Offenders*, Boulder, CO: Westview Press.

Kocher, Matthew (2002) 'The Decline of PKK and the Viability of a One-State Solution in Turkey', *Journal on Multicultural Studies*, 4(1): 128.

Koğacioğlu, Dicle (2004) 'Progress, Unity, and Democracy: Dissolving Political Parties in Turkey', *Law and Society Review*, 38(3): 433.

Koopmans, Ruud (2007) 'Who Inhabits the European Public Sphere? Winners and Losers, Supporters and Opponents in Europeanised Political Debates', *European Journal of Political Research*, 46: 183.

Kramer, Heinz (2000) *A Changing Turkey: The Challenge to Europe and the United States*, DC: Brookings Institute Press Washington.

Kreyenbroek, Philip G. and Sperl, Stefan (eds) (1992) *The Kurds: A Contemporary Overview*, London: Routledge.

Kurban, Dilek (2003–4) 'Confronting Equality: The Need for Constitutional Protection of Minorities on Turkey's Path to the European Union', *Columbia Human Rights Law Review*, 35: 151.

Kurdish Human Rights Project (2006) 'Suppressing Academic Debate: The Turkish Penal Code', London.

—— (2006) 'Turkey on Trial: The Prosecutions of Orhan Pamuk and Others', London.

—— (2007) 'Reform and Regression: Freedom of the Media in Turkey', London.

Laffan, Brigid (1996) 'The Politics of Identity and Political Order in Europe', *Journal of Common Market Studies*, 34(1): 81.

Lagana, Giulia (2008) 'Roma Face Fear and Loathing in Italy', *Guardian* 24 July.

Lake, Michael (ed.) (2005) *The EU and Turkey: A Glittering Prize or a Millstone?*, London: Federal Trust.

Landau, Jacob M. (ed.) (1984) *Atatürk and the Modernization of Turkey*, Boulder, CO: Westview Press.

Langenfeld, Christine and Mohsen, Sarah (2005) 'Germany: The Teacher Head Scarf Case', *International Journal of Constitutional Law*, 3(1): 86:

Lawyers Committee for Human Rights (1999) 'Obstacles to Reform – Exceptional Courts, Police Impunity and Persecution of Human Rights Defenders in Turkey', Canada.

Lejour, Arjan M, de Mooij, Ruud A. and Capel, Clem H. (2004) 'Assessing the Economic Implications of Turkish Accession to the EU', CPB Netherlands Bureau for Economic Policy Analysis, no. 56.

Letica, Bartol (2004) 'Europe's Second Chance: European Union's Enlargement to Croatia and the Western Balkans', *Fletcher Forum of World Affairs*, 209.

Lewis, Bernard (1975) *The Emergence of Modern Turkey*, 2nd edn, Oxford: Oxford University Press.

— (1988) *The Political Language of Islam*, Chicago, IL: University of Chicago Press.

— (2002) *What Went Wrong?: Western Impact and Middle Eastern Response*, London: Phoenix.

Loewenstein, Karl (1937) 'Militant Democracy and Fundamental Rights', *American Political Science Review*, 31: 418.

Logan, Christina C. (2006–7) 'Liberty or Safety: Implications of the USA Patriot Act and the UK's Anti-Terror Laws on Freedom of Expression and Free Exercise of Religion', *Seton Hall Law Review*, 37: 863.

Lohman, Diederik (2000) 'The International Community Fails to Monitor Chechnya Abuses', *Helsinki Monitor*, 11: 73.

Lugo, Luis (2005) 'Does "Muslim" Turkey Belong in "Christian" Europe?', Pew Forum on Religion and Public Life, National Press Club, Washington, DC, 13 January (event transcript).

Macklem, Patrick (2006) 'Militant Democracy, Legal Pluralism, and the Paradox of Self-Determination', *International Journal of Constitutional Law*, 4(3): 488.

Macmillan, Margaret (2001) *Paris 1919: Six Months That Changed the World*, New York: Random House.

Magnarella, Paul J. (1994) 'The Legal, Political and Cultural Structures of Human Rights Protections and Abuses in Turkey', *Detroit College of Law Journal of International Law and Practice*, 3: 439.

Mancini, G. Federico (1989) 'The Making of a Constitution for Europe', *Common Market Law Review*, 26: 595.

Marquand, David and Nettler, Ronald L. (eds) (2000) *Religion and Democracy*, Oxford: Blackwell Publishers.

Martínez-Torrón, Javier (2005) 'Limitations on Religious Freedom in the Case Law of the European Convention on Human Rights', *Emory International Law Review*, 19: 587.

McCrea, Ronan (2007) 'Limitations on Religion in a Liberal Democratic Polity: Christianity and Islam in the Public Order of the European Union', London School of Economics Law, Society and Economy Working Papers (18).

McDowall, David (1992) *The Kurds: A Nation Denied*, London: Minority Rights Publications.

— (1996) The Destruction of Villages in South-East Turkey: A Report by Medico International and the Kurdish Human Rights Project, London: Kurdish Human Rights Project.

— (2004) *A Modern History of the Kurds*, 3rd edn, London: I.B. Tauris.

McGarry, John and O'Leary, Brendan (2006) 'Consociational Theory, Northern Ireland's Conflict, and Its Agreement, Part I: What Consociationalists Can Learn from Northern Ireland', *Government and Opposition*, 41(1): 43.

McInerney, Siobhán (2002) 'Bases for Action against Race Discrimination in EU Law', *European Law Review*, 72.

McIntosh, Mary E., Abele Mac Iver, Martha, Abele, Daniel G. and Nolle, David B. (1994–5) 'Minority Rights and Majority Rule: Ethnic Tolerance in Romania and Bulgaria', *Social Forces*, 73: 939.

Mead Earle, Edward (1924) 'The New Constitution of Turkey', *Political Science Quarterly*, 40(1): 73.

Meiselas, Susan (1997) *Kurdistan: In the Shadow of History*, New York: Random House.

Menéndez, Agustín José (2005) 'A Christian or a Laïc Europe? Christian Values and European Identity', *Ratio Juris*, 18(2): 179.

Minority Rights Group International (2007) 'A Quest for Equality: Minorities in Turkey', September.

Morris, Chris (2005) *The New Turkey: The Quiet Revolution on the Edge of Europe*, London: Granta Books.

Nachmani, Amikam (2003) *Turkey: Facing a New Millennium. Coping With Intertwined Conflicts*, Manchester and New York: Manchester University Press.

Netherlands Scientific Council for Government Policy (WRR) (2004) *The European Union, Turkey and Islam*, Amsterdam: Amsterdam University Press.

Neuwahl, N. and Rosas, A. (eds) (1995) *The European Union and Human Rights*, The Hague: Kluwer Law International.

Nic Shuibhne, Niamh (2001) 'The European Union and Minority Language Rights', *MOST Journal on Multicultural Societies*, 3(2).

Nicolaïdis, Kalypso (2004) 'Turkey is European ... for Europe's Sake' in *Turkey and the European Union: From Association to Accession?*, Netherlands: Ministry of Foreign Affairs, January.

O'Connell, James (1991) 'The Making of Modern Europe: Strengths, Constraints and Resolutions', University of Bradford, Research Report no. 26, cited in G. Davie (2006) 'Is Europe an Exceptional Case?', *Hedgehog Review* 23.

— (1996) 'The Making of Europe: The Foundations of Unity and the Elements of Belonging' (copy on file with author).

Oğuzlu, H. Tarik 'The EU as an Actor in the Solution of the Cyprus Dispute: The Question of "How"?' (2002) *Journal of Ethnopolitics and Minority Issues in Europe*, 2: 1.

Öktem, Niyazi (2002) 'Religion in Turkey', *Brigham Young University Law Review*, 371.

Olsen, Robert (ed.) (1996) *The Kurdish Nationalist Movement in the 1990s: Its Impact on Turkey and the Middle East*, Kentucky, KY: University Press of Kentucky.

Open Society Institute (2001) *Monitoring the EU Accession Process: Minority Protection*, Hungary, Central European University Press.

Örücü, Esin (2002) 'The Turkish Constitution Revamped?', *European Public Law*, 8(2): 201.

Ovey, Clare and White, Robin C. A. (2006) *The European Convention on Human Rights*, 4th edn, Oxford University Press.

Özbudun, Ergun (1966) *The Role of the Military in Recent Turkish Politics*, Cambridge, MA: Harvard University Center for International Affairs.

Özbudun, Ergun and Gençkaya, Ömer F. (2009) *Democratization and the Politics of Constitution-Making in Turkey*, Budapest: Central European University Press.

Pagden, Anthony (ed.) (2002) *The Idea of Europe: From Antiquity to the European Union*, New York: New York Woodrow Wilson Center Press and Cambridge University Press.

Parker, Jill (2004) 'West Meets East: A Discussion of European Union Enlargement and Human Rights', *Tulsa Journal of Comparative and International Law*, 11: 603.

Parliamentary Assembly of the Council of Europe (2004) 'Council of Europe Parliamentarians Vote to End Monitoring of Turkey', press release, 22 June.

Patton, Marcie, J. (2007) 'AKP Reform Fatigue in Turkey: What Happened to the EU Process?', *Mediterranean Politics*, 12(3): 339.

Pearson, W. Robert (2005) 'Democracy as the Cure for Terrorism: Turkey's Example', *Virginia Journal of International Law*, 45: 1017.

Peers, Steve (1996) 'Living in Sin: Legal Integration Under the EC–Turkey Customs Union', *European Journal of International Law*, 7: 411.

Pelmans, Jacques (2001) 'The Crucial Terms of EU Enlargement – Distinguishing the "Core *Acquis*" from Less Urgent Requirements', *European Journal of Law Reform*, 3: 411.

Pentassuglia, Gaetano (2002) *Minorities in International Law: An Introductory Study*, Strasbourg: Council of Europe Publishing.

Pettifer, James (1998) *The Turkish Labyrinth: Atatürk and the New Islam*, London: Penguin Books.

Pope, Hugh (2005) 'Turkey's Minority Report', *Georgetown Journal of International Affairs*, 6: 95.

Pope, Nicole and Pope, Hugh (2000) *Turkey Unveiled: A History of Modern Turkey*, Woodstock, NY: Overlook Press.

Potz, Richard and Wieshaider, Wolfgang (eds) (2004) *Islam and the European Union*, Leuven, Belgium: Peeters Publishers.

Reed, Howard, A. (1954) 'Revival of Islam in Secular Turkey', *Middle East Journal*, 8(3): 267.

Rehn, Olli (2007) 'Open Debate on Enlargement', European Parliament Foreign Affairs Committee, SPEECH/07/287, Brussels, 7 May.

Reidy, Aisling, Hampson, Françoise and Boyle, Kevin (1997) 'Gross Violations of Human Rights: Invoking the European Convention on Human Rights in the Case of Turkey', *Netherlands Quarterly of Human Rights*, 15(2): 143.

Robins, Philip (1993) 'The Overlord State: Turkish Policy and the Kurdish Issue', *International Affairs*, 69: 657.

Rougement, Denis de (1963) *The Meaning of Europe*, London: Sidgwick & Jackson.

—— (1966) *The Idea of Europe*, London: Macmillan.

Saăba, Isa (2001) 'Central–Local Fiscal Relations in Turkey: A Technical Analysis of Fiscal Equalization', *Turkish Studies*, 2(2): 121.

Saktanber, Ayşe and Çorbacioğlu, Gül (2008) 'Veiling and Headscarf-Skepticism in Turkey', *Social Politics: International Studies in Gender, State and Society*, 15(4): 514.

Salvatore, Armando (2007) 'Authority in Question: Secularity, Republicanism, and "Communitarianism" in the Emerging Euro-Islamic Public Sphere', *Theory, Culture and Society*, 24: 135.

Sandole, Dennis J. D. (2006–7) 'The "Fog of War" on Terrorism: US Policy, Deception, and the Continuing Slide into the Clash of Civilisations', *International Law Students Association Journal of International and Comparative Law*, 13: 149.

Schäuble, Wolfgang (2004) 'Talking Turkey: Is Europe Ready for a Muslim Member?', *Foreign Affairs*, 83: 134.

Schilling, David (2003–4) 'European Islamaphobia and Turkey – *Refah Partisi (the Welfare Party) v Turkey'*, *Loyola Los Angeles International and Comparative Law Review*, 26: 501.

Schimmelfennig, Frank (2008) 'Entrapped Again: The Way to EU Membership Negotiations with Turkey', UCD Dublin European Institute Working Paper 08–8, July.

Schimmelfennig, Frank, Engert, Stephan and Knobbel, Heiko (2003) 'Costs, Commitment and Compliance: The Impact of EU Democratic Conditionality on Latvia, Slovakia and Turkey', *Journal of Common Market Studies*, 41(3): 495.

Shankland, David (2003) *Islam and Society in Turkey*, Cambridge: Eothen Press.

Shaw, Jo, Magnette, Paul, Hoffmann, Lars and Vergés Bausili, Anna (eds) *The Convention on the Future of Europe: Working Towards an EU Constitution*, London: Federal Trust.

Shepherd, Robin (2007) 'Romania, Bulgaria, and the EU's Future', March, *Current History*, 117.

Simon, Thomas, W. (1997) 'Minorities in International Law', *Canadian Journal of Law and Jurisprudence*, 10: 507.

Skach, Cindy (2006) 'Religious Freedom – State Neutrality – Public Order – Role of International Standards in Interpreting and Implementing Constitutionally Guaranteed Rights [decisions]' *American Journal of International Law*, 100: 186.

Smith, Helena (2003) 'Threat to Cyprus Deal as Hardliner Elected', *Guardian*, 17 February .

—— (2003) 'Conciliation Hopes Fade in Tied Turkish Cypriot Elections', *Guardian*, 15 December.

—— (2008) 'Cyprus Elects its First Communist President', *Guardian*, 25 February.

—— (2008) 'Cypriot Leaders Set Date for Reunification Talks', *Guardian*, 26 July.

Smith, Thomas W. (2005) 'Civic Nationalism and Ethnocultural Justice in Turkey', *Human Rights Quarterly*, 27: 436.

Spencer, Michael (1996) *States of Injustice: A Guide to Human Rights and Civil Liberties in the European Union*, London: Pluto Press.

Ssenyonjo, Manisuli (2007) 'The Islamic Veil and Freedom of Religion, the Rights to Education and Work: a Survey of Recent International and National Cases', *Chinese Journal of International Law*, 6(3): 653.

Stahnke, Tad and Blitt, Robert C. (2005) 'The Religion–State Relationship and the Right to Freedom of Religion or Belief: A Comparative Textual Analysis of the Constitutions of Predominantly Muslim Countries', *Georgetown Journal of International Law*, 36: 947.

Stedman, Beirne (1927–8) 'The Republic of Turkey', *Virginia Law Register New Series*, 13: 725.

Steketee, Frank (2001) 'The Framework Convention: A Piece of Art or a Tool for Action?', *International Journal on Minority and Group Rights*, 8: 1.

Stephen, Michael (1997) *The Cyprus Question*, London: British–Northern Cyprus Parliamentary Group.

Stivachtis, Yannis A. (ed.) (2008) *Turkey–European Union Relations: Dilemmas, Opportunities, and Constraints*, Lanham, MD: Lexington Books.

Suvarierol, Semin (2003) 'The Cyprus Obstacle on Turkey's Road to Membership in the European Union', *Turkish Studies*, 4(1): 55.

Tait, Robert (2008) 'Turkey's Governing Party Avoids Being Shut Down for Anti-Secularism', *Guardian*, 31 July.

— (2009) 'Turkey Bans Main Kurdish Party over Alleged Terror Links', *Guardian*, 12 December.

Tapper, Richard (ed.) (1991) *Islam in Modern Turkey: Religion, Politics and Literature in a Secular State*, London and New York: I.B. Tauris & Co. Ltd.

Tarifa, Fatos and Adams, Benjamin (2007) 'Who's the Sick Man of Europe? A Wavering EU Should Let Turkey In', *Mediterranean Quarterly*, 18(1): 52.

Taspinar, Ömer (2007) 'The Old Turks' Revolt: When Radical Secularism Endangers Democracy', *Foreign Affairs*, 86: 114.

Teitel, Ruti (1992–3) 'A Critique of Religion as Politics in the Public Sphere', *Cornell Law Review*, 78: 747.

Thiel, Markus (ed.) (2001) *The 'Militant Democracy' Principle in Modern Democracies*, Surrey, UK: Ashgate.

Thornberry, Patrick (1991) *International Law and the Rights of Minorities*, Oxford: Clarendon Press.

Thornberry, Patrick and Martín Estébanez, Maria Amor (2004) *Minority Rights in Europe*, Strasbourg: Council of Europe Publishing.

Tisdall, Simon (2010) 'Cyprus Leaders Vow to Reunify Island, Says UN Head', *Guardian*, 1 February.

Tocci, Nathalie (2004) *EU Accession Dynamics and Conflict Resolution: Catalysing Peace or Consolidating Partition in Cyprus?*, Surrey, UK: Ashgate.

— (2005) 'Europeanization in Turkey: Trigger or Anchor for Reform?', *South European Society and Politics*, 10(1): 73.

— (2007) *The EU and Conflict Resolution: Promoting Peace in the Backyard*, London: Routledge.

— (ed.) (2008) *Talking Turkey in Europe: Towards a Differentiated Communication Strategy*, Rome: Quaderni IAI.

Todorov, Tzvetan and Bracher, Nathan (2008) 'European Identity', *South Central Review*, 25(3): 3.

Toprak, Binnaz (1981) *Islam and Political Development in Turkey*, Leiden: Brill.

— (2005) 'Islam and Democracy in Turkey', *Turkish Studies*, 6(2): 146.

Traynor, Ian (2006) 'Turkish General Warns Levels of Islamism "Alarming"', *Irish Times*, 27 September.

Troebst, Stefan (1999) 'From Paper to Practice: The Council of Europe's Framework Convention for the Protection of National Minorities', *Helsinki Monitor*, 10: 19.

Tsitselikis, Konstantinos (2004) 'How Far Have EU Policies Affected Minority Issues in Greece and Turkey?', Euroborder Conference Paper, University of Birmingham, 13 November.

Turk, A., Marco (2007) 'Rethinking the Cyprus Problem: Are Frame-breaking Changes Still Possible through Application of Intractable Conflict Intervention Approaches to this "Hurting Stalemate"?', *Loyola Los Angeles International and Comparative Law Review*, 29: 463.

Turkish Daily News (2002) 'Giscard Remarks Cause Uproar in Ankara, and Brussels', 11 November.

— (2005) 'Dink Convicted of Insulting Turkish Identity', 8 October.

— (2008) 'Parliament Approves 301 Amendment, Eyes on Implementation', 1 May.

Turkish National Programme for the Adoption of the *Acquis* (2001) (available at http://ec.europa.eu/enlargement/pdf/turkey/npaa_full_en.pdf).

Turkish Treasury (2007) 'Update on European Union Relations', 18 April (available at www.treasury.gov.tr/iro_files/Newsletter/2007/idi-20070418.pdf).

Uğur, Mehmet and Canefe, Nergis (eds) (2004) *Turkey and European Integration: Accession Prospects and Issues*, New York: Routledge.

Ülgen, Sinan and Zahariadis, Yiannis (2004) 'The Future of Turkish Trade Relations: Deepening vs Widening', Centre for European Policy Studies, EU–Turkey working papers, no. 5, August.

UN Doc. S/RES/186(1964), adopted by the Security Council at its 1102nd meeting, on 4 March.

UN Doc. S/5634 UN Security Council (1964), 'Agreement on the Status of the United Nations Peace-Keeping Force in Cyprus', *International Legal Materials*, 3: 451.

UN Doc. S/RES/353 (1974) United Nations Security Council Resolution 353, adopted by the Security Council at its 1771st meeting, on 20 July.

UN Doc. S/RES/367 (1974), adopted by the Security Council on 12 March 1975.

UN Doc. S/RES/541 (1983) United Nations Security Council Resolution 541, adopted by the Security Council on 18 November.

UN Doc. S/RES/1250 (1999) United Nations Security Council Resolution 1250, adopted by the Security Council on 22 December.

UN Doc. S/2003/398, (2003) 'Report of the Secretary-General on His Mission of Good Offices in Cyprus', 1 April.

UN Doc. S/2004/437, (2004) 'Report of the Secretary-General on His Mission of Good Offices in Cyprus', 28 May.

UN Human Rights Committee CCPR/C/21/Rev.1/Add.4, General Comment No. 22, 30 July 1993.

United Nations General Assembly Resolution 37/253, adopted by the General Assembly on 13 May 1983.

Uslu, Emrullah (2009) 'AKP Prepares a Comprehensive Plan to Address the Kurdish Question', *Eurasia Daily Monitor*, 6(142), 24 July.

Vakulenko, Anastasia (2007) 'Islamic Dress in Human Rights Jurisprudence: A Critique of Current Trends', *Human Rights Law Review*, 7(4): 717.

—— (2007) '"Islamic Headscarves" and the European Convention on Human Rights: An Intersectional Perspective', *Social and Legal Studies*, 16(2): 183.

Voeten, Eric (2008) 'The Impartiality of International Judges: Evidence from the European Court of Human Rights', *American Political Science Review*, 102(4): 417.

Wagstaff, Malcolm (ed.) (1990) *Aspects of Religion in Secular Turkey*, Durham: Centre of Middle Eastern and Islamic Studies.

Wallace, Helen (2002) 'Enlarging the European Union', *Journal of Public Policy*, 9(4): 658.

Weiler, Joseph (1991) 'The Transformation of Europe', *Yale Law Journal*, 100: 2408.

—— (1999) *The Constitution of Europe*, Cambridge: Cambridge University Press.

—— (2003) Un'Europa Cristiana: Un Saggio Esplorativo, Milan: BUR Saggi.

Westering, Jolanda van (2000) 'Conditionality and EU Membership: The Cases of Turkey and Cyprus', *European Foreign Affairs Review*, 5(1): 95.

White, Paul J. (2000) *Primitive Rebels or Revolutionary Modernizers?: The Kurdish National Movement in Turkey*, London: Zed Books Ltd.

Williams, Andrew (2000) 'Enlargement of the Union and Human Rights Conditionality: A Policy of Distinction?', *European Law Review*, 25: 601.

—— (2004) *EU Human Rights Policies: A Study in Irony*, Oxford: Oxford University Press.

Wippman, David (1996) 'International Law and Ethnic Conflict on Cyprus', *Texas International Law Journal*, 31: 141.

Yavuz, M. (2003) *Hakan Islamic Political Identity in Turkey*, Oxford: Oxford University Press.

Yildiz, Kerim (2005) *The Kurds in Turkey: EU Accession and Human Rights*, London: Pluto Press.

Yildiz, Kerim and Muller, Mark (2008) *The European Union and Turkish Accession: Human Rights and the Kurds*, London: Pluto Press.

Yuksel, Edip (1999) 'Cannibal Democracies, Theocratic Secularism: The Turkish Version', *Cardozo Journal of International and Comparative Law*, 7: 423.

Zielonka, Jan (ed.) (2002) *Europe Unbound: Enlarging and Reshaping the Boundaries of the European Union*, London: Routledge.

— (2004) 'Europe Moves Eastward: Challenges of EU Enlargement', *Journal of Democracy*, 15(1): 22.

Zürcher, Erik J. (1997) *Turkey: A Modern History*, New York: Tauris.

Index

For Product Safety Concerns and Information please contact our EU
representative GPSR@taylorandfrancis.com
Taylor & Francis Verlag GmbH, Kaufingerstraße 24, 80331 München, Germany

www.ingramcontent.com/pod-product-compliance
Lightning Source LLC
Chambersburg PA
CBHW072156280326
41926CB00108B/2858